Establishing Academic Freedom

HIGHER EDUCATION AND SOCIETY

Series Editors:

Roger L. Geiger, distinguished professor of Education, Pennsylvania State University

Katherine Reynolds Chaddock, professor of Higher Education Administration, University of South Carolina

This series explores the diverse intellectual dimensions, social themes, cultural contexts, and pressing political issues related to higher education. From the history of higher ed. to heated contemporary debates, topics in this field range from issues in equity, matriculation, class representation, and current educational Federal Acts, to concerns with gender and pedagogy, new media and technology, and the challenges of globalization. In this way, the series aims to highlight theories, historical developments, and contemporary endeavors that prompt critical thought and reflective action in how higher education is conceptualized and practiced in and beyond the United States.

Liberal Education for a Land of Colleges: Yale's "Reports" of 1828
By David B. Potts

Deans of Men and the Shaping of Modern College Culture
By Robert Schwartz

Establishing Academic Freedom: Politics, Principles, and the Development of Core Values
By Timothy Reese Cain

Establishing Academic Freedom

Politics, Principles, and the Development of Core Values

Timothy Reese Cain

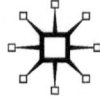

ESTABLISHING ACADEMIC FREEDOM
Copyright © Timothy Reese Cain, 2012.

All rights reserved.

Portions of Chapter 2, used with the permission of *Teachers College Record*, are from: Timothy Reese Cain, "The First Attempts to Unionize the Faculty," *Teachers College Record* 112, no. 3 (2010): 875–913.

First published in 2012 by
PALGRAVE MACMILLAN®
in the United States—a division of St. Martin's Press LLC,
175 Fifth Avenue, New York, NY 10010.

Where this book is distributed in the UK, Europe and the rest of the world, this is by Palgrave Macmillan, a division of Macmillan Publishers Limited, registered in England, company number 785998, of Houndmills, Basingstoke, Hampshire RG21 6XS.

Palgrave Macmillan is the global academic imprint of the above companies and has companies and representatives throughout the world.

Palgrave® and Macmillan® are registered trademarks in the United States, the United Kingdom, Europe and other countries.

ISBN: 978-1-137-00953-1

Library of Congress Cataloging-in-Publication Data

Cain, Timothy Reese.
    Establishing academic freedom : politics, principles, and the development of core values / Timothy Reese Cain.
       p. cm.—(Higher education and society)
       ISBN 978-1-137-00953-1 (hardback)
      1. Academic freedom—United States. 2. College teachers—Tenure—United States 3. Education, Higher—United States. 4. Education, Higher—Aims and objectives—United States. I. Title.

LC72.2.C35 2012
3789.01—dc23   2012010455

A catalogue record of the book is available from the British Library.

Design by Newgen Imaging Systems (P) Ltd., Chennai, India.

First edition: September 2012

For Karen and Simon

Contents

Acknowledgments	ix
Introduction	xi
1 Academic Freedom in Development	1
2 Associating and Academic Freedom	29
3 Treason and the "Farce" of Academic Freedom	51
4 Competition and Collaboration	75
5 Freedom of Teaching in Science	101
6 Education, Protests, and Blacklists	121
7 Toward a Less "Dangerous Occupation"	141
Conclusion	177
Notes	183
Index	229

Acknowledgments

Some of the ideas in this book date to work I began a decade ago while I was a graduate student at the University of Michigan. The support, guidance, suggestions, and critiques offered by Jana Nidiffer, Philo Hutcheson, Jeffrey Mirel, and Maris Vinovskis in those early stages and in the years since have been invaluable.

Steven E. Gump read every word of this book several times, and suggested more than a few. Our conversations about writing, audience, faculty, and tenure helped me consider all in important and different ways.

I have likewise benefited from being part of several groups that have helped me think about academic freedom, faculty work, and the history of higher education. I am thankful for the support I received from friends and colleagues in the University of Illinois College of Education, the Ethnography of the University Initiative, the History of Education Society, and the Illinois Program for Research in the Humanities. HASHE, especially, has played a significant role in my thinking and work. Numerous scholars have provided suggestions and comments on conference papers that led to this work. I greatly appreciate the insights offered by Saran Donahoo, Linda Eisenmann, Marybeth Gasman, Lester Goodchild, David Labaree, Marjorie Murphy, Ellen W. Schrecker, Wayne J. Urban, and Marc A. VanOverbeke in these and related settings. I am likewise appreciative of series editors Katherine Chaddock and Roger L. Geiger, who invited me to submit the proposal for this book and offered useful suggestions for shaping it, as well as Burke Gerstenschlager and Kaylan Connally at Palgrave Macmillan.

The research and writing have been supported by the Illinois Program for Research in the Humanities, the American Federation of Teachers, the Rackham Graduate School at the University of Michigan, the University of Michigan School of Education, and the Franklin and Eleanor Roosevelt Institute. The work was made possible through the assistance of the numerous archivists and librarians across the country who helped me in person and from a distance. AFT archivist Dan Golodner and reference librarian William Lefevre at the Walter P. Reuther Library, Jennifer King at George Washington University's Melvin Gelman Library, and Timothy Pyatt at the Duke University Library were especially helpful. I am thankful, too, to Gary Natriello and *Teachers College Record* for allowing me to reuse several paragraphs of my article: "The First Attempts to Organize the Faculty," *Teachers College Record* 112, no. 3 (2010): 875913.

Finally, and most importantly, I am thankful for the support of my family. Without their love, fries, and steak sauce, this book could not have been written.

Introduction

At their annual meetings in 1941, the American Association of University Professors (AAUP) and the Association of American Colleges (AAC) formally endorsed the 1940 *Statement of Principles on Academic Freedom and Tenure,* the document that has since defined both academic freedom and its procedural protections in American higher education. In doing so, the two organizations—one composed of prominent professors and the other of leaders of liberal arts colleges—agreed that professorial freedoms to teach, research, and retain rights as citizens were vital for the expansion of knowledge, for student learning, and for the common good of society. The rights, though were not without corresponding responsibilities, since faculty members had "special obligations" as members of a scholarly profession. Faculty members, for example, were to avoid the presentation of unrelated controversial material in classes and to forestall having their personal opinions be linked to their institutions. The 1940 *Statement* also provided the basis for modern understandings of faculty tenure and the procedures used to ensure it, justifying them as "indispensable to the success of an institution in fulfilling its obligations to its students and to society."[1] In short, the AAUP–AAC agreement was the fundamental step in establishing the conditions of faculty work for the remainder of the twentieth century. Over two hundred additional organizations have since endorsed the 1940 *Statement,* and numerous colleges and universities use it as the basis for their own institutional policies on academic freedom and tenure.

In the modern era, some of these same issues are being implicitly and explicitly reconsidered. American higher education and its faculty are faced with numerous challenges, including those related to institutional finances, stakeholder power relations, employer flexibility, faculty speech rights, unionization, and the casualization of faculty labor. Though the context and contours of the modern situation are specific to the twenty-first century, many of the larger issues are analogous—and some even identical—to those that were wrestled with in the period from 1915 through 1941. This renegotiation of faculty work is, in other words, a renegotiation of the rights, roles, and responsibilities agreed to by college administrators and professors in the interwar period. The questions at the heart of these historic and ongoing issues include: What rights do faculty members have to speak freely on controversial subjects in public forums? What rights and responsibilities do they have in the classroom? When does criticism of the government during times of war become actionable? What roles do professors—and instructors—have in institutional governance? What are the most effective responses to perceived threats to faculty freedoms? Does a tenure system provide appropriate protections and help attract qualified candidates to the profession or hamstring institutions and preclude their ability to work efficiently? What are the roles and rights of untenured academic laborers, and who speaks for them? Does unionization protect faculty rights and offset power imbalances, or does it diminish professional authority and status? What public and private influences are appropriate in higher education? The suggested answers to these and related questions provided by the 1940 *Statement* were the specific result of several years of intermittent negotiations between committees representing the two national organizations. Viewed more broadly, however, they were the product of 25 years of interactions, relations, and conflict between and among the AAUP, the AAC, and other interested associations, including the American Civil Liberties Union (ACLU) and the American Federation of Teachers (AFT).

Although the ideas embedded in the 1940 *Statement* helped to define the modern professoriate, only a quarter of a century earlier, its endorsement could hardly have been foretold. When the then-new AAUP released its *General Declaration of Principles of Academic Freedom and Academic Tenure* in 1915, the claims for professional status and academic freedom were far from secure. The *New York Times* panned academic freedom as the right of a faculty member to "make a fool of himself and his college by vealy, intemperate, sensational prattle."[2] Two years later, the AAC offered a similar, though less colorfully worded, assessment of the AAUP claims. Yet, by agreeing to the 1940 *Statement,* the two organizations codified notions of academic freedom, established a standard tenure system, and conditionally agreed to the contours of faculty work, rights, and responsibilities. They thus helped bring order to the ideas swirling around academic freedom, but, at the same time, that order placed bounds on appropriate professorial behavior. The period in between saw wartime threats to academic freedom from both inside and outside the professoriate and two waves of anti-Communism that threatened the livelihoods of a sector of the professoriate. Fundamentalist groups attacked the teaching of evolution in public and private colleges and schools. Less sensational—though just as devastating to the individuals involved—were the ongoing battles over whether and how faculty could comment on the governance and leadership of their institutions.

The organizations that were integral to these debates and developments arose at roughly the same time amid a larger trend in associating both in higher education and more broadly. It was, as Millikin University president George E. Fellows claimed at the AAC's first meeting, "an age of organization."[3] These organizations were founded, though, with different purposes and for different constituencies. The AAUP's origins can be traced to academic freedom battles and increasing professionalization at the turn of the century. Beginning in 1913, Johns Hopkins University philosophy professor Arthur O. Lovejoy led a group of elite faculty from leading universities to consider forming what would, two years later, become the AAUP. From the start, AAUP leaders including Lovejoy asserted a professional purpose and sought to provide established faculty with opportunities for input that existing disciplinary associations were inherently unable to do. In January 1915, the same month that the AAUP formally organized, the presidents of denominational and liberal arts colleges founded the AAC for separate reasons: their specific concerns related to the shifting views of higher education and the increasing power of research institutions and state colleges. Academic freedom was a concern from the AAUP's founding—indeed, leaders were bothered by how much it seemed to dominate both the association's activities and the public perception of them—but held little interest for the new AAC. When it later weighed in, the AAC staked a claim for institutional academic freedom, rather than professorial rights. Just as important as these two eventual partners was the constellation of additional associations and organizations that viewed academic freedom as both a legitimate end to pursue and a means of organizational development, especially the ACLU and AFT. The National Civil Liberties Bureau was founded out of the antiwar movement in 1917 and then reorganized as the ACLU three years later. The ACLU viewed the issue from a freespeech and legal perspective; it did not interest itself in tenure issues. Though narrower in this respect, the ACLU was the group most interested in the liberty of students and speakers on college campuses, highly contested issues throughout the era. The

AFT, which was often aligned with the ACLU, was itself formed in 1916 when a group of existing teachers unions joined together with a national charter from the American Federation of Labor (AFL). Two years later, it expanded to college campuses, challenged notions of professionalism, and attracted younger faculty ineligible for membership in the AAUP. The union struggled throughout the 1920s but reemerged on college campuses at the end of the decade and, by the late 1930s, was a vocal advocate for leftist faculty and a rival to the AAUP. Indeed, the differences between the AFT and the AAUP were at times stark, prohibited a unified front, and generated a great deal of animosity. They also shaped the understandings of faculty rights and responsibilities that emerged from the era.

Analyzing faculty experiences and organizational interaction reveals several overlapping and longstanding issues that are central to academic freedom, its establishment, and its defense. Principal among these issues is the struggle over whether organizations should serve preventative or protective roles; in Ellen Schrecker's terms, this struggle concerned whether they should defend "principles instead of people."[4] Early in their histories, no organizations identified the defense of specific aggrieved teachers and professors as a primary purpose. Rather, organizations sought to use individual cases to establish codes, educate the profession and populace, and prevent future similar situations. The AFT and AAUP each faced internal calls for more aggressive action designed to defend individuals. The former embraced them, while the latter remained wary of threatening its professional standing. A related issue is the continuing tension between swift action and judicious investigation. Critics inside and outside the AAUP recognized the limitations of the association's emphasis on prudently investigating alleged violations. While crucial to the AAUP's collaborative and respectable approach, the delays pushed other groups into acting on behalf of academic freedom and created rifts within and among organizations. Still, immediate protest was not necessarily a more appropriate reaction to faculty dismissals. Quick action, when unjustified, raised questions about organizations' judgments and threatened to undermine their efforts. More significantly, the AAUP argued that the AFT's rush to publicize cases and protest dismissals in the late 1930s was harmful not only to larger principles but also to individual professors.

A significant concern related to these considerations was whether faculty should unionize or continue to pursue professional status, two approaches that some believed to be contradictory. The AAUP identified itself as similar to the American Medical Association (founded in

1847) and American Bar Association (1878) from its outset, although the different nature of academic employment posed continuing challenges. AAUP leaders asserted their expertise and autonomy from institutional control, arguing that only faculty had the specialized knowledge needed to determine professorial competence and fitness for continued employment. Defining academic freedom and tenure policies addressed important issues of self-regulation and control over the conditions of employment. To the leaders of the AAUP, although not always to its members, claims for professional status and faculty autonomy precluded both the employer/employee model and the emphasis on economic self-interest that they believed faculty unionization would imply. Still, some educators inside and outside the AAUP were drawn to union approaches, and the AFT organized teachers and professors around social, educational, and work issues. At the same time, factionalism within the union, ongoing struggles with the AFL, and debates between those who emphasized bread-and-butter issues and those interested in societal change demonstrate that even the AFT was unsure of appropriate stances for unionized educators. Ultimately, these larger concerns over unionization and professionalization intertwined with organizational politics to influence approaches to academic freedom.

* * *

This book examines the development of academic freedom and its procedural protections during this era of organization and codification. In doing so, it addresses both historiographical and historical concerns. Two classic works, one nearly sixty years old and one now over twenty-five years old, help to define and frame modern understandings of the history of academic freedom. Richard Hofstadter and Walter P. Metzger's *The Development of Academic Freedom in the United States,* written as two distinct parts amid the turmoil of the 1950s, is much broader in scope than its title suggested and has served as a defining early history of American higher education. Though Hofstadter's interpretation of nineteenth-century colleges has been questioned by the waves of revisions that have since re-shaped the historiography of education, the work as a whole retains a central role in our understanding of the early experience of and debates over academic freedom. Metzger's contribution on academic freedom in the post–Civil War era details the conflicts over economic and religious issues and highlights the growing self-consciousness of the professoriate in the era. It ends, though, with the founding of the AAUP and the struggles over loyalty in wartime.[5] Ellen W. Schrecker's *No Ivory Tower: McCarthyism and the Universities* offers a striking indictment of anti-Communist activities inside and outside institutions of higher education after World War II. Her work demonstrates the depth of the difficulties, their personal effects on faculty, and the failure of faculty to uphold espoused values in the 1940s and 1950s.[6] Many of the other important books in the field join Hofstadter and Metzger's in exploring the early development of professionalism culminating at the turn of the century or shortly thereafter; others, similar to Schrecker's, focus on the political attacks on allegedly Communist professors in the late 1940s and 1950s.[7] This book sits squarely in between.

Others have engaged with smaller parts of this whole—Shrecker's background chapters on Communism and anti-Communism in the 1930s, for example, remain the best treatment of leftist faculty in that decade—but no book has yet examined the combination of organizational and experiential issues over the more than two-and-a-half decades in which the modern conditions of the professoriate were defined. At the fiftieth anniversary of the 1940 *Statement*, Metzger provided an important history of the document, highlighting the political processes that were involved. More recently, Matthew W. Finkin and Robert C. Post have discussed the essential components of academic freedom and pointed to their origins. Additional studies have examined other specific cases, institutions, or threats, including, most notably, Carol S. Gruber's discussion of academic freedom in her history of American higher education during World War I. This book builds on, extends, and, at times, counters these and related works. In doing so, it considers Sheila Slaughter's 1980 critique of the AAUP and her suggestion that other organizations offered more robust protections. Certainly, there were multiple and competing definitions and numerous organizational avenues for establishing and protecting academic freedom. In the face of persecution, resistance, and organizational infighting, all of them were limited, problematic, and politically charged. Ultimately, though, they moved academic freedom and tenure forward.[8]

This book is organized largely, though not entirely, chronologically. Chapter 1 provides the background and context of academic freedom in development. It examines the increasing notion of professorial freedoms in the 1800s and highlights the cases involving economists and social scientists that helped unite disciplinary groups at the end of the century. It counters the idea that the first decade of the twentieth century was one of few struggles over academic freedom, as the experiences of John Spencer Bassett, Enoch Banks, and others demonstrate.

The resolutions of these cases spoke to both the growing commitment to academic freedom and the continuing limits on heterodox educators. Chapter 2 centers on the founding of the AAUP, the association's immediate immersion in academic freedom investigations, the release of the 1915 *Declaration,* and the reactions to the document, including those of the newly established AAC. Chapter 3 documents the violations of faculty freedoms before, during, and immediately after World War I. It demonstrates the complicity of faculty in the purges, points to the AAUP's equivocation in the midst of the war, and identifies the impetus for civil liberties–based approaches. Chapter 4 addresses both the increasing organizational activity around academic freedom and the realization that even expanded efforts fell short of achieving desired ends. The 1925 *Conference Statement on Academic Freedom and Tenure* was a significant step toward addressing the challenges but was one that remained ambiguous.

Chapter 5 examines the growing fundamentalists' attacks on the teaching of evolution in both public and private educational institutions. Organizations such as the World Christian Fundamentals Association pushed for legislative interventions, while opponents—both organized and not—raised an alarm and countered them. The ACLU was particularly active, pursuing tests cases in Tennessee and Arkansas, before finally suspending its efforts in 1931. Chapter 6 returns to broader issues, including the reemergence of the AFT, the ACLU's reworking of its principles on academic freedom, and the AAUP's controversial decision to censure institutions. The AAUP was confident that academic freedom and tenure were becoming embedded in American higher education but, in 1931, again found itself overwhelmed with cases. Chapter 7 demonstrates the widespread but conflicted interest in the topic. The Progressive Education Association (PEA) attempted to unite organizations to pursue academic freedom across educational levels, including by trying to embarrass the National Education Association into supporting educators' rights. The new National Advisory Committee on Academic Freedom, the outgrowth of this work, was a failure by almost any measure, and the PEA itself was forced to suspend its efforts amid allegations that its emphasis on quick action had damaged both the organization's creditability and the causes for which it was working. It then details the influential battles at the end of the 1930s and beginning of the 1940s. For a brief period, the left wing of the AFT undertook dramatic protests of alleged violations, but both the union and the ACLU struggled with how best to handle members who were in the Communist Party; each eventually acted against them. Ultimately, heightened concerns over Communism, increased agitation by the AFT, and both inter- and intraorganizational conflicts interacted to set the stage for—and influence the terms of—the 1940 *Statement* and America's subsequent understandings of academic freedom and tenure.

1

ACADEMIC FREEDOM IN DEVELOPMENT

In delivering his 1916 annual report, American Association of University Professors (AAUP) president and Northwestern University Law School dean John H. Wigmore noted of academic freedom: "This is a world-old theme.... [It] is not a problem to be solved in a year or in ten years by this Association or by any other."[1] Wigmore knew well that the AAUP's recent claim for academic freedom, though an important step, was part of a much longer struggle that had played itself out in the battles over sectarian control of colleges, debates about slavery and abolition, divides over economics and politics, and disagreements about disinterested research and political advocacy. The founding of Wigmore's association and the concurrent beginnings of other educational and voluntary associations marked a new and vital era in the understandings and experience of faculty work, but the longer history of conflict over faculty rights and responsibilities set the stage for these modern conditions while highlighting their contested nature. With no unifying themes and few published statements on issues that would later be thought of as involving academic freedom—itself a term that did not appear until the late nineteenth century—much of this early development can be understood in terms of key and illustrative cases that cumulatively affected nascent ideas of academic freedom but also reveal complex understandings and perspectives.[2] Moreover, these cases expose the competing notions of academic freedom and demonstrate that its development was one of fits and starts, competing viewpoints, and few, if any, uncomplicated actors.

DEEP HISTORY OF ACADEMIC FREEDOM

More than half a century ago, historian Richard Hofstadter opened his landmark *Academic Freedom in the Age of the College* with the comment: "Academic freedom is a modern term for an ancient idea."[3] While the direct linkages may be tenuous and the history is discontinuous, controversies that would now be understood to involve scholars' freedoms to teach and inquire existed long before formalized higher education; Hofstadter and others point as far back as conflicts involving Plato and Socrates as evidence of the enduring nature of these controversies. They have further been identified in the earliest Western universities, with AAUP president Ralph F. Fuchs attributing the ideal of academic freedom partly to the "idea of autonomy for communities of scholars, which arose in the universities of Europe."[4] Indeed, professors in the Middle Ages held unique positions that provided them with more autonomy than others in their societies. The issues that were off-limits, especially those that challenged church orthodoxy, were rarely contested by the communities of scholars themselves. In the context of their worldviews, there were few restrictions on intellectual pursuits in areas that many would reasonably consider.[5] Still, no modern version of academic freedom existed then, in the following centuries in Europe, or in early American colleges. Violations in the United States date to the early days of Harvard College, when its first president, Henry Dunster, forfeited his position to avoid having to recant his opposition to infant baptism.[6] A trend toward liberalism at the handful of colonial colleges was interrupted at times, most famously with the domineering control of Thomas Clap, president of Yale College from 1740 to 1766. Although the Enlightenment fostered increased attention to intellectual freedom, significant restrictions remained in American institutions of higher education.[7]

Hofstadter termed the period from 1800 to 1840 "The Great Retrogression" and argued that colleges in the era were rife with sectarian disputes. Faculty members were liable to be fired at the whims of their presidents or, significantly, their trustees.[8] Historians have since revised Hofstadter's depiction of troubled and troubling institutions that retreated from any innovation or experimentation by emphasizing their place in, relevance to, and coherence with American society in the early nineteenth century.[9] Still, his concerns about professorial freedoms and stagnation in some areas more broadly remain. Even notable early efforts for change faced challenges, including those of Thomas Jefferson, who intended his new University of Virginia, founded in 1819, to be built upon "the illimitable freedom of the human mind." He explained, "For here we are not afraid to follow truth wherever it may lead, nor to tolerate any error so long as reason is left free to combat it."[10] Yet Jefferson himself, though intent on forestalling sectarian rivalries and impositions, took a different tack on partisan political matters. Faculty were offered the then-unusual liberty to choose their own teaching materials in all areas except law; Jefferson retained that privilege for himself to ensure that students would be protected from Federalist writings. Just as significantly, before the institution even opened, it suffered its first sectarian assault on faculty in response to Jefferson's selection of Thomas Cooper as the institution's first professor. Cooper, a materialist, Deist, and anticleric, roused the ire of Presbyterians and others who found him unfit for the position. As pressure mounted and the university was beset by other difficulties, Cooper tendered his resignation before ever beginning his work.[11] Unsuccessful in his efforts to protect Cooper, Jefferson regretfully concluded, "I do sincerely lament that untoward circumstances have brought on us the irreparable loss of this professor, whom I have looked to as the corner-stone of our edifice."[12]

Cooper's resignation was facilitated by his receipt of an offer of a professorship at South Carolina College (later the College of South Carolina and now University of South Carolina); within a year, he was named president of the college. Cooper's wide-ranging intellect, controversial ideas, and outspoken criticism of Calvinism and of Presbyterian clergy soon caused him difficulties. These escalated in the early 1830s due to Cooper's increasingly provocative writings on materialism and in support of states' rights to nullify federal laws that they believed to be unconstitutional. Amid increasing turmoil and campaigns for his ouster, state legislators alleged a range of religious transgressions and sought his removal. Cooper denied some of the charges against him but claimed freedom of religion and a nascent form of academic freedom. He argued that faculty members' very roles and responsibilities required their freedom to teach without limitations or suppression. Cooper withstood the immediate storm—the trustees vindicated him and he maintained his position—but could not withstand the toll that it took on the college. He resigned in 1834.[13] Importantly, Cooper was not uncomplicated, and neither was his battle for academic freedom. Historian Michael Sugrue argued that Cooper's self-styling as a "defender of individual freedom" was more often "a posture than a principle." He was a provocateur who filled the faculty with "a group of cronies" and fostered a highly politicized campus.[14] Though Cooper argued for freedom from restrictions on airing political views in the classroom, his concern was only about *his* views and not about those of his opponents. Still, considering the extremity of some of his views, his lengthy tenure can be read as evidence of freedom, as well as that of restrictions.[15]

In the absence of an analogue to modern tenure, job security was tenuous; but public battles such as Cooper's were somewhat rare. As in the medieval European universities, restrictions on freedom were widely in place but were infrequently felt by those otherwise eligible for faculty positions, a small category that excluded women and nonwhites. Generally, faculty were unlikely to pursue positions at institutions with which they had theological disagreements and were unlikely to expect to maintain their positions when they disagreed with an institution's well-known views. Indeed, it was more likely that college presidents such as Cooper would find themselves challenged than would faculty. It is not that robust freedom existed but that the lack of freedom was generally accepted and expected, especially in the small colleges that emphasized, rather than challenged, the teaching of accepted knowledge.[16]

Abolition

Discussions of restrictions in antebellum colleges frequently focus on sectarianism and colleges' denominational ties—at times encumbrances. They emphasize the conflict that appeared over the religious orthodoxy but, in doing so, can obscure the effects of debates over slavery and abolition on American colleges. In addition to the more pressing restrictions of freedom that were at the heart of a slaveholding society, between 1833 and 1863 at least 15 colleges dismissed students, faculty members, or presidents in conflicts involving slavery and related issues.[17] Though most of these restrictions were placed on abolitionists, presidents of Bowdoin, Dartmouth, and Franklin Colleges were forced from their positions for pro-slavery statements or for defending the South's right to secession. Judge Edward Greely Loring lost his lectureship at Harvard due to his 1854 upholding of the Fugitive Slave Act. In the middle of the nineteenth century, there were increasing allowances for speaking against slavery in Northern institutions and increasing restrictions on any expression that could be interpreted as questioning it in the South. As historian Clemont Eaton argued, in the "1850's a powerful movement developed to sterilize Southern colleges from antislavery ideas," and "a definite effort was made to establish colleges that would be free from the radical teachings of the North."[18] While noting that restrictions also existed in the North, Eaton concluded: "With student opinion so hostile to independent thought, and with trustees and newspapers solidly lined up against freedom of expression, it is no wonder that academic freedom was a frail reed in the Old South."[19] For those in control of Southern institutions, freedom from Northern dominance was desired, not freedom to pursue ideas.

The ordeal of Benjamin Sherwood Hedrick, a chemistry professor at the University of North Carolina, demonstrates the regional and racial politics involved. Hedrick was a registered Democrat but was rumored to support Republican free-soiler John C. Frémont in the 1856 presidential election.[20] In September of that year, William W. Holden published an editorial in his Raleigh newspaper, the *North Carolina Standard*, calling for "all schools and seminaries of learning [to] be scrutinized; and if black Republicans be found in them, let them be driven out."[21] Holden clearly aimed to remove Hedrick from his position and generated a groundswell of support by many means, including printing an alumnus' letter to the editor demanding a purging of "poisonous" faculty, as they presided over impressionable students.[22] Hedrick tried to ameliorate the situation by responding with a letter of his own. Linking his ideas to those of George Washington, Thomas Jefferson, and other "Great Southern statesmen," Hedrick argued that he was not advocating the end of slavery but was against expanding it to areas where it was not already entrenched.[23] Amid growing furor, including students burning Hedrick in effigy and trustees denouncing the professor, president David L. Swain called on the university's faculty to consider Hedrick's letter, specifically arguing that "cautious forbearance" had been the norm among faculty so as to ensure both "internal harmony" and the reputation of the university.[24] The faculty responded by resolving against Hedrick's public statements of political opinions. In doing so, though, they undercut their own argument for neutrality by simultaneously declaring that no faculty members shared his opinions on the topic.

Shortly thereafter, the executive committee of the Board of Trustees declared that Hedrick's letter had ended the professor's usefulness, since through it he had become "an agitator in the exciting politics of the day."[25] Swain protested to the secretary-treasurer of the board, former North Carolina governor Charles Manly, that the committee lacked the legal authority to remove Hedrick; such power, he argued, was provided only to the full board.[26] Manly agreed to delay any action until the full board met but noted, "If he does not resign the Board will take him up next winter and cut his head 'clean off'; but so as not to suffer the blood of martyrdom for opinion's sake to decorate and adorn his garments."[27] Ten days later, as pressure mounted and threats of a student riot emerged, the executive committee knowingly overstepped its authority and dismissed Hedrick. When Hedrick appeared at a public event in the western part of the state later that week, he was pursued by a mob, hanged and burned in effigy, and threatened with tarring and feathering. With the assistance of several prominent citizens, the situation was calmed when he agreed to leave the town before sunrise. By the end of the week, barely a month after the first editorial had appeared in the *Standard*, Hedrick fled the state, not to return until after the Civil War.[28]

Hedrick's difficulties attracted more attention than others' in the era—New York newspapers, for example, offered them as evidence of the volatility of the South—but were not unique, and a pair of commentators later called them "illustrative of the typical Southern conditions."[29] Hedrick's case indeed highlights key themes in the history of academic freedom, including the importance of what would later be known as extramural speech. Hedrick's expression of political views in a public forum spurred the controversy and led his detractors to claim he was unfit to teach impressionable students. Hedrick's troubles also demonstrate the importance of public opinions in determining the outcomes of these early cases. Institutions relied on the public for their support; housing a professor whose views were in opposition to stakeholders threatened needed resources.[30] Even if trustees had wanted to keep Hedrick, they would have found it difficult to do so. President Swain's repeated emphasis on Hedrick's public expression of a political opinion points both to the real concern about neutrality on controverted issues and to the political nature of decision making in academic freedom cases. In the midst of the struggle, Swain and Manly agreed any dismissal needed to be justified by the public nature of Hedrick's partisanship, rather than its content, so as not to benefit Frémont's campaign.[31] Hedrick's wife, Mary Ellen Hedrick, believed, in fact, that his letter to the editor was merely used as cover; the public outcry generated by the original editorials caused the firing.[32] The faculty's denunciation of Hedrick emphasizes faculty roles in enforcing conformity for the perceived greater good of the institution. Even Hedrick's friends on the faculty supported his dismissal, with only one instructor, Henry Harrisse, protesting.[33] Professor Charles Phillips, in correspondence with Hedrick's college roommate W. C. Kerr, wrote that their mutual friend's difficulties were his own doing: "When we wish to work for people to that people's good, we are bound to consider their characteristics and not arouse their prejudices unnecessarily, else they won't let us work for them."[34] Hedrick had ignored this imperative and thereby threatened the institution's ability to attract students and public support. Finally, the letters and resolutions condemning Hedrick pointed to the pronounced regional divides and argued that Hedrick was "subversive" and a "traitor," themes that would be repeated in different contexts in later years.

EVOLUTION AFTER THE CIVIL WAR

Colleges could not escape from the rupture of American life caused by the Civil War. Most Southern institutions suspended operations by 1865, and many in the North suffered losses of students and faculty. American higher education experienced great change in the years after the conflict, inspired in part by the shock waves of Darwinism and furthered by both the opportunistic passage of the Morrill Act and the importation of the German academic tradition. In the standard histories of higher education, it was only with these great changes—including the end of sectarian control, the growth of research, the beginning of graduate education, and, in Veysey's terms, the "emergence of the American university"—that higher education began to achieve its current form. It was in these changing institutions that new conceptions of academic freedom emerged. The evolving understanding of truth as discovered, rather than ordained, played an important part of this new development.[35]

Darwinism influenced the creation of modern academic freedom and was simultaneously implicated in individual violations. Academic scientists were among the first to accept the theories of Darwin and related evolutionists, though many others in society did not share their views. Darwinism was viewed as a threat to orthodoxy and raised questions about who was competent to speak on issues involving science and religion. It caused further epistemological shifts in a new generation of scholars, aided the growth of science, and promoted the importance of the human environment, each of which helped usher in a new era in higher education. Controversies over the teaching of evolution and attempts to integrate aspects of the theory into interpretations of the Old Testament led to dismissals at a number of institutions in the late 1800s, although the extent of the restriction is unknowable. While many have conceded that the restrictions relating to evolution were greater in the South than in the North, some freedom and some restrictions existed in both regions. Moreover, the dismissals of faculty and public controversies relating to religious orthodoxy (including but beyond those involving evolution) were more frequent in Northern institutions than in Southern institutions, evidencing a range of opinions, a willingness to test the limits of restrictions in certain contexts, and uncertainty as to the extent of freedom allowed.[36]

Alexander Winchell's 1878 dismissal from Vanderbilt University and Columbia Theological Seminary's firing of James Woodrow ten years later demonstrate both the complexity of the circumstances and the differing perceptions of faculty speech. They also point to the inadequacy of viewing these simply as recent episodes in the centuries-old "struggle between science and dogmatic theology," as former Cornell University president Andrew Dickson White did in his 1896 *History of the Warfare of Science with Theology in Christendom*.[37] In 1875, after many years of teaching at the University of Michigan and a brief stint as the first chancellor of Syracuse University, Winchell, a known, if conservative, evolutionist, was hired by Vanderbilt University to lecture on geology a few months each spring. Recently endowed by Cornelius Vanderbilt, the institution remained under the control of the Methodist Church and the direct influence of Methodist bishop Holland Nimmons McTyeire, who chaired its board. Winchell was well regarded at Vanderbilt, though his views on evolution quickly became a concern. His 1878 publication of "Adamites and Pre-Adamites," a pamphlet that argued that some human ancestors—specifically of the "black race"—existed before the biblical Adam, brought the issues to a head and led the board to invite Winchell to deliver a commencement address on the topic of evolution. An hour before Winchell was to speak, McTyeire visited him and asked him either to resign or repudiate his beliefs in the address. Offended by the meeting, Winchell refused to comply, leading the board to eliminate his position without comment. Winchell publicly challenged the board's action, generated a great deal of publicity, and garnered support in the press. The case was purported to demonstrate the ongoing challenges to academics at Southern institutions and was famously included in White's screed, which praised the University of Michigan for rehiring Winchell and demonstrating its commitment to freedom.[38]

White likewise condemned the treatment of James Woodrow, an uncle of Woodrow Wilson who only hesitantly committed to Darwinism in response to Columbia Theological Seminary's Board of Directors' request that he respond to circulating rumors. In a public speech before the directors and alumni, Woodrow argued that the biblical Adam was physically descended from other animals but that his soul was the creation of God. He asserted that his views were not in contradiction to scripture and that his understanding of evolution only strengthened his faith. Though the board decided to retain Woodrow, the four synods overseeing the seminary all held hearings and all eventually passed resolutions against the teaching of evolution, as did other Presbyterian synods in the Southeast. In turn, the seminary's board then reversed itself, requested Woodrow's resignation, and, when his resignation was not forthcoming, dismissed him. Woodrow appealed to the synods, two of which upheld the dismissal and two of which did not. The board allowed Woodrow to remain but repeatedly requested his resignation while church courts continued to hold trials on his continuation, often with fellow faculty member John L. Girardeau as the key witness against him. Eventually, in 1888, the case was resolved when the General Assembly of the Southern Presbyterian Church voted against Woodrow's final appeal, thereby removing him from his position at the seminary.[39]

The Winchell and Woodrow cases point to potential difficulties facing faculty, yet neither provides the entire picture nor justifies the assumption that either the academy or the South was trenchantly opposed to evolution. Woodrow himself remained in South Carolina, teaching at the College of South Carolina and, in 1891, becoming its president. While restrictions certainly existed, as both Winchell and Woodrow discovered, there remained opportunities at other institutions. Versions of theistic evolution were taught across the South, often with little controversy, and great variation in what was deemed allowable existed both between and within institutions.[40] Their experiences further point to the complexity of the cases both in substance and in process. A combination of internal and external pressures could be placed on an institution as it weighed maintaining a faculty member with discordant views. The cases show a new willingness of faculty to make public the reasons behind their dismissals and aggressively fight for their positions. Of course, as in other areas, focusing on the known violations or examples of free expression is necessarily problematic. Far more difficult to ascertain—yet equally important—are the restrictions in hiring, the decisions to self-censor in fear of retaliation, the unanimity of opinion within the academy on ideas contested elsewhere, and the quiet dismissals or nonrenewals that can frequently go unnoticed.[41] While there may have been few "heresy trials" in the late nineteenth century, voices could still be muted.

Woodrow's and Winchell's cases further demonstrate that faculty protests of their dismissals did not necessarily translate to a broad support for what would today be termed academic freedom; no such understanding yet existed. The very faculty decrying one dismissal could be implicated in another. In fact, early in his career, Winchell was the faculty member most involved with the University of Michigan's dismissal of President Henry Tappan. He secretly originated a resolution censuring the institution for moral delinquency that was passed by the state's Methodist Conference, roused opposition to Tappan in newspapers and church publications, and otherwise plotted for his removal. Their disagreements were largely personal and centered on Winchell's belief that Tappan was too liberal and inappropriately nonsectarian.[42] More strikingly, in 1891 Woodrow did nothing to support William J. Alexander, a professor of philosophy who was dismissed because he was a Unitarian. Indeed, one of Woodrow's biggest supporters in his academic freedom battles accepted Alexander's former position at the College of South Carolina.[43] At the same time, an overemphasis on Darwinism can obscure other threats to scholars' livelihoods, involving other religious disagreements, extramural activities, and, of course, broader discrimination in a hierarchic society.[44] On the same day that Winchell was dismissed from Vanderbilt, the board also removed two other faculty members, one of whom was deemed unfit for reportedly drinking alcohol.[45] Certainly, modern notions of the full rights of citizenship for educators were as yet unknown. Although American higher education was changing, these were institutions of their time and their society, complete with respective perspectives and institutionalized restrictions.[46]

Broader Questions of Religious Orthodoxy

The controversies at Vanderbilt and Columbia Theological Seminary are the most well known of these cases but they were not the only ones to implicate Darwinism or broader concerns about religious orthodoxy. Robert L. Adams identified 14 controversies involving heterodoxy at Protestant seminaries between 1879 and 1900. Eight of these ended in dismissals and one in resignation.[47] Even the new, secular universities struggled with the public reactions to religious heterodoxy in the era.[48] In August 1876, just months after opening, Johns Hopkins University was stung by the public reactions to leading Darwinist Thomas Huxley's invited public speech. Five years later, the wounds were fresh enough that the institution declined to hire a chair of philosophy rather than hire one who was viewed as heterodox.[49] Cornell University faced public criticism for its open nonsectarian stance and its lack of religiosity from its founding. The 1874 appointment of Felix Adler as professor of Hebrew and Oriental literature was well received in some circles and pointed to a rare willingness to appoint a Jewish scholar. But when he claimed, for example, that Christianity shared precepts with other religions, his lectures were also condemned. President White, despite his avowal of freedom from religious restraints, quietly refused to reappoint him. This was a retreat from stated ideals but, at the same time, helped establish another principle at Cornell. Adler's appointment had been funded through a private gift; when the donor protested the dismissal, the institution declared that it would no longer allow funders to name the holders of endowed chairs.[50]

From 1879 to 1881, Yale College president Noah Porter and professor William Graham Sumner tussled over Sumner's right to assign Herbert Spencer's *Study of Sociology,* which Porter believed was dangerous to immature students.[51] Amid much publicity, Sumner refused to grant Porter's assertion that a college president had the authority to veto any course text. In a letter sent to each member of the Yale Corporation and of the faculty, he outlined an early argument for the importance of process:

> I have had no controversy on the question whether the President has a veto on textbooks. I do not admit that he has it, and I do not know of any college officer who admits it, but I have not raised that question. It is plain that if a professor is indiscreet, silly, negligent, incompetent, immoral, or otherwise unfit for his position, he ought to be disciplined, and it is plain that the President is the proper agent for bringing him to discipline.... To use an improper textbook would simply be a case under this general principle. But it is plain also that the President can himself impose no sanctions whatever. He is only a reporting officer for that purpose. It is also plain that the Corporation cannot impose sanctions on the report of the President. They could not sustain him in a position of pure prerogative and sustain his authority at the expense of the rights of a professor.[52]

After describing that the controversy had made the book's continued use untenable, Sumner declared, "I have made no concession.... I consider that it involves the rights and interests which no honest teacher ever ought to concede."[53] Sumner indicated his intent to leave the institution, but, with public interest waning and faculty supporters urging him to reconsider, he opted to remain. Little was settled and neither side conceded, but the controversy passed.[54] A less dramatic variation of this conflict over texts emerged at Johns Hopkins in 1885, when the Episcopal bishop of Maryland complained that a book professor Herbert Baxter Adams assigned to his undergraduates, Edward Clodd's *Childhood of Religions,* was unfair to Christianity and, hence, unsuitable. President Daniel Coit Gilman, without reading the work, appealed to Adams and called on him to remove the book from his course. Gilman acknowledged that he did not know if the complaint was correct, but the fact that a person "of high education & standing" had issued it was enough to warrant its removal. Adams bowed to the wishes of the bishop and the president.[55]

Controversies over extramural statements and writings continued, as well, especially at institutions with religious affiliations. In 1902 at the Methodist-sponsored Northwestern University, Charles W. Pearson, a faculty member in English of 30 years' standing, angered the Methodist press and local citizens when he published "Open Inspiration versus a Closed Canon and Bible" in a local newspaper. In the piece, Pearson challenged the Methodist Church and argued that "modern preaching lacks truth and power because so many churches cling to an utterly untenable tradition that the Bible is an infallible book. This dogma is their besetting sin.... It is the palpable lie that gives the ring of insincerity to all their moral exhortations."[56] Pearson was compelled to submit his resignation and noted that the institution's trustees, too, would have been forced out had they not accepted it.[57] These and other cases demonstrated continued tensions around religious views, personal beliefs, and the public pressures placed on individuals and institutions.

ECONOMICS AND THE BEGINNINGS OF THE MODERN ERA

The academic acceptance of Darwinism was joined by the influence of German higher education in setting the stage for modern conceptions of academic freedom. In the second half of the nineteenth century, thousands of American scholars traveled to Germany for advanced study, where they were exposed to a new sense of graduate education and gained a reverence for the German ideas of academic freedom, if in an altered form. In Germany, academic freedom consisted of *Lehrfreiheit,* the freedom of inquiry and teaching, and *Lernfreiheit,* the freedom of learning. *Lehrfreiheit* was vital to the university model and the search for truth, especially in science, where only highly educated specialists were deemed adequate judges of expert knowledge. Institutions were arms of the state but were run with little interference, little bureaucracy, and no lay boards. Professors lectured to mature students—who themselves were free to make curricular choices with few restrictions—with few bounds on their topics or approaches. This freedom did not, however, extend outside the university to include political speech or political activity.[58] These concepts neither easily nor directly translated to the American system: in the 1920s, former Western Reserve University president Charles F. Thwing could still argue that "the contrast between the freedom of scholarship in Germany and the limitations of scholarship in the presumed new world of freedom, is impressive."[59] Still, returning scholars brought with them the conviction that *Lehrfreiheit* was crucial for university education. Combined with an appreciation of freedom of speech and grafted onto a diverse American educational system replete with lay boards and young students, the German understanding of *Lehrfreiheit* provided an impetus for the development of academic freedom in the United States. Issues of professionalism, the influence of big business, and further challenges to restraints on freedom would help consolidate these ideas in ways that both pushed boundaries beyond the German ideas and offered greater limitations. While American faculty increasingly made claims for free speech outside of academic settings, they simultaneously acceded to restrictions in their internal activities and soon articulated a belief in neutrality over persuasion in teaching.[60]

Though elements of later challenges to and claims for academic freedom were already evident, the beginning of the modern era of American academic freedom is often dated to the last 15 years of the nineteenth century, the period in which the term became adopted and accepted.[61] At first the term was used in reference to student choice and the elective system, as in Princeton classicist Andrew Fleming West's 1885 article "What Is Academic Freedom?" Near the turn of the century, however, University of Chicago sociologist Albion Small wrote specifically and entirely about professors in his article "Academic Freedom." Small's singular focus is evidence of a new ethos wherein issues of faculty freedoms took precedence and the distinctions between the German conceptions of *Lehrfreiheit* and *Lernfreiheit* became entrenched in American higher education.[62] Small's article was a commissioned response to a report asserting "there is not a single institution of learning in this country in which the teaching of economics or sociology is not muzzled by the influence of *wealth*... or *partizan* [sic] *politics*." Small denied that assertion and argued the opposite. He was aware of no institution in which faculty were "muzzled" by external bodies. Any restrictions were self-imposed by the responsible and professional professoriate.[63] The actual state of freedom, however, lay somewhere in between. The increased and significant attention to professorial academic freedom in the last two decades of the twentieth century was related to the limits imposed by intrusive trustees and, at times, presidents. It also implicated faculty members' willingness to push the sometimes nebulous boundaries between professional and unprofessional, between acceptable and forbidden. The late 1880s were also the beginning of an era in which controversies over academic freedom spread from theology and biology to the social sciences. Economics proved to be an especially controversial subject, with faculty members sanctioned and dismissed for their public stances on socialism, immigration, the currency, and other issues that had financial implications for trustees. While they were largely hidden at the time, the difficulties of economist Henry Carter Adams began this new era.[64]

Adams was the first recipient of a PhD from Johns Hopkins University and, like many of his peers, was educated in Germany and intrigued by ideas of academic freedom that had not yet been adopted in the embryonic American universities. Upon returning to the United States, he taught briefly at Johns Hopkins and then obtained two half-time appointments, one at Cornell University and one at the University of Michigan. Both positions were tenuous. Trustees at the institutions disapproved of Adams's support for free trade and his increasing interest in using his economic scholarship to benefit the working classes. Each time he sought permanency at one of the institutions, he faced questions about his economic beliefs, including those involving property rights and socialism. These issues came to a head when, in April 1886, Adams provided the Sibley College Lecture at Cornell University. In the talk, he blamed industrialists for inciting panic over anarchism; spoke favorably about the controversial Knights of Labor, who were then striking against the rail systems owned by Jay Gould; and linked the labor movement to a natural extension of American rights. While stopping short of advocating socialism, Adams's public support of the Knights of Labor offended industrialist interests—including Henry Sage, a lumber magnate and the powerful chairman of Cornell's Board of Trustees. Sage pressured Cornell president Charles Kendall Adams to terminate the offending professor effective at the end of his two-year contract and made it impossible for the president to pursue a permanent appointment for him. The professor, who had long found the split appointment unsatisfactory, refused the possibility of an extension and was forced to turn to Michigan for a full-time position.[65]

In March 1887, University of Michigan president James Burrill Angell asked Henry Carter Adams to clarify his stands before the University of Michigan would consider providing full-time appointment. Adams was not surprised by the request but considered it inappropriate. He responded:

> If you make a man's opinions the basis of his election to a professorship, you do, whether you intend to or not, place bonds upon the free

movement of his intellect. It seems to me that a Board has two things to hold in view. First, is a man a scholar? Can he teach in a scholarly manner? Is he fair to all parties in the controverted questions which come before him? Second, is he intellectually honest? If these two questions are answered in the affirmative, his influence on young men cannot be detrimental.[66]

Angell replied by noting that while he believed in academic freedom, "the German idea of *Lehrfreiheit* cannot be fully accepted in this country when colleges depend on friendly public sentiment for their support."[67] Despite his aversion to the questioning, Adams carefully disavowed his controversial remarks in his correspondence with Angell. He further claimed that he had seen the inconsistencies in his statements and pledged not to repeat his mistakes.[68] As a result of his contrition, his rejection of socialism, and his abandonment of union causes, Adams was rewarded with a full-time position at Michigan, where he remained until his retirement in 1921. For the rest of his lengthy career, he not only maintained his promise to avoid controversy and reshaped his economic thought to be more acceptable, but also refused to support colleagues who were dismissed for expressing the opinions that he once espoused.[69]

While Adams kept the details around his leaving Cornell quiet, other cases received attention in both academic and popular circles. In 1893, University of Wisconsin economist Richard T. Ely's alleged association with unionists and advocacy of strikes led to a trial before the institution's governing board. Ely's lawyer defended him against the specific charges rather than on an ideal of academic freedom; and Ely admitted that if the charges were true, he would not be worthy of holding the position. Ely was acquitted of the charges and retained his employment, as the board famously declared, "We believe the great State University of Wisconsin should ever encourage that continual and fearless sifting and winnowing by which alone the truth can be found."[70] Although Ely's retention and the board's statement of support are often viewed as a victory for academic freedom, both Ely's defense strategy and the continued threats at Wisconsin indicate that the issue was hardly settled.

In the ensuing years, other alleged violations also received considerable attention. In 1895, University of Chicago president William Rainey Harper, elsewhere an advocate of academic freedom, reprimanded Ely's student Edward W. Bemis for his public condemnation of the railroad industry and warned him against making public statements on contested social and economic issues. When Harper pushed

Bemis out of his faculty position, Bemis publicly contended that his political stance had caused the dismissal. Some colleagues privately supported him, but others lined up behind Harper's tenuous justification of the removal on the basis of incompetence. In 1897, economist and Brown University president Elisha Benjamin Andrews resigned under pressure from trustees over his support of free silver. Both university presidents and leading economists supported Andrews's right to state his scholarly opinion on current economic issues, even if some drew a line separating expression from advocacy. Just as significantly, Columbia University economist and future AAUP leader Edwin R. A. Seligman urged the American Economic Association (AEA) to protest the forced resignation. Concerns over the authority of the organization's leadership to act on behalf of the entire body, the potential that outspoken action could divide rather than unify the profession, and the likely ineffectiveness of such a protest led the economists to act independently rather than as official spokesmen for the AEA. Leading social scientists joined Seligman in signing a petition on behalf of freedom of speech and intellectual freedom, which helped persuade the Brown Corporation to request that Andrews withdraw his resignation. While not the formal organizational action for which Seligman had hoped, the growing recognition that professional associations had a legitimate interest in academic freedom was an important step toward establishing faculty rights.[71]

J. Allen Smith's career demonstrates that the divisions over currency were deep and could affect faculty careers in multiple ways. In 1897, his appointment at Marietta College was not renewed in a controversy that implicated his advocacy of free silver, as well as his support of William Jennings Bryan's 1896 presidential campaign. Smith turned down an offered position at the University of Missouri, as it was to be created by dismissing a faculty member who advocated for the gold standard on the currency issue. His next offer came from Kansas State Agricultural College (now Kansas State University), which was in need of instructors, as the newly elected Populists had recently dismissed the entire faculty. Most were rehired but the new president, Thomas Elmer Will, sought Populists for positions in economics and history. Instead, though, Smith accepted a position at the University of Washington and enjoyed a much longer career than he almost certainly would have had in Kansas. When Republicans returned to power in 1899, Will and two of his recent Populist hires, Bemis and Frank Parsons, were dismissed.[72]

Perhaps the most notorious case of the era was that of Edward A. Ross, an outspoken Stanford University professor who had long clashed with cofounder and trustee Jane Lathrop Stanford. In 1900, following Ross's criticism of the railroad industry and his offensive depiction of immigrant labor, Stanford president David Starr Jordan dismissed him at Jane Stanford's request. In response, esteemed historian George Howard condemned the dismissal as an abrogation of academic freedom in front of his class. Jordan then forced Howard to resign, further dividing the faculty. While many remained loyal to Jordan, a total of seven faculty members resigned in protest, including Arthur O. Lovejoy, who would go on to be the driving force behind the AAUP, and Frank A. Fetter, who would serve on its Committee A on Academic Freedom and Tenure. It was neither the first nor the last controversy at the institution, but Ross's national stature and decision to publicize his dismissal caused a sensation. Details of the Ross case were relayed across the nation, and, following Ross's attendance at the national meeting of the AEA, the members present launched an investigation into the firing. Although not an official action of the association, the AEA's unofficial investigation was the first of the kind. The resulting report carried no weight—and Ross was not reinstated—but AEA leaders later would be instrumental in founding the AAUP. Importantly, as Mary O. Furner showed, Ross benefited from his place within the larger field. Others could be dismissed with little notice or controversy, including Harry Huntington Powers, an obscure Stanford professor dismissed at Jane Stanford's request in 1898 following his comments on religion and criticism of the gold standard.[73]

Race and Regionalism at the Turn of the Century

At the turn of the twentieth century, racial animosities continued to provoke confrontations and impose burdens on college faculty. Between 1902 and 1911, four faculty at Southern institutions—Emory College classicist Andrew Sledd, Trinity College historian John Spencer Bassett, Randolph-Macon College historian William E. Dodd, and University of Florida historian Enoch Marvin Banks—were involved in public showdowns against powerful interests intent on preventing changes to the hierarchical racial and class structure of the South. These challenges implicated regional divides, as faculty who published in Northern journals or questioned Southern practices were accused of treason, and demonstrated that institutions needed to tread carefully when responding to public outcries. Acquiescing to demands that a professor be dismissed proved risky and could generate a damaging backlash. Taken together, these cases also illuminate the significant relationships among different actors. These controversies were not happening in isolation: presidents conferred with presidents and faculty conferred with faculty. In an era of increased professional cohesion, these linkages were important to developing ideas of academic freedom.

Andrew Sledd's difficulties were specifically tied to his publication of a July 1902 article in the *Atlantic Monthly* but also implicated larger institutional and state politics, as well as his alienation of key institutional stakeholders through his efforts to reform Emory College and Southern education.[74] The article, spurred in part by Sledd's own witnessing of the mobs intent on lynching African Americans and the specific horrors of the 1899 lynching of Sam Hose, began with the argument that blacks' "inferiority is radical and inherent, a physiological and racial inequality that may, indeed, be modified by environment but cannot be erased without the indefinite continuance of favorable surroundings and the lapse of indefinite time."[75] Still, Sledd contended that blacks retained "inalienable rights" and should not lose them because of race. His harshest critiques were directed at the dehumanization of lynching, the fallacies of Southern defense for the practice, and the gruesome bloodlust that it entailed. Several weeks after the article's publication, Rebecca Latimer Felton, a leading figure in Georgia political circles, brought attention to the article and condemned its author.[76] In a letter published in the *Atlanta Constitution* on August 3, Felton alleged that the article was "slander," "defamation," and "rot" that Sledd had "vomited." She accused Sledd of self-hate, implied he was syphilitic, and warned that he should leave the South for his own safety.[77]

Felton, who approved of lynching as a way to protect white women's virtue, was offended by the article's publication in a Boston venue and its condemnation of certain aspects of Southern society. Moreover, she was involved in a long-running feud with Sledd's father-in-law, Bishop Warren Akin Candler, an Emory College trustee and a former president who viewed Felton's letter as an attack on him. New college president James E. Dickey at first claimed that Sledd wrote the article as a private citizen, not in his role as a faculty member, and that the article was therefore not of concern. Amid growing pressure from trustees and the general public, and increasingly concerned about Sledd's effect on potential donors, he quickly changed his stance. On August 7, the same day that Sledd was burned in effigy in nearby Covington, Georgia, Dickey privately called on Sledd to resign. Sledd initially declined but, after considering the effect of the controversy on both the college and his family, agreed to leave in exchange for a partial year's salary. The resignation was formally accepted on August 14, 11 days after Felton's letter appeared in the *Constitution*. Evidence indicates that neither the trustees nor President Dickey had yet read Sledd's article, but, then, the article itself was not nearly as important as the reaction to it.[78]

Sledd's resignation did not immediately quell the controversy, as many Northern and a few Southern publications condemned Emory's decision as both a specific evil and evidence of a larger problem. The college's reputation and finances suffered as a result.[79] Among those who were highly critical of Emory was John C. Kilgo, the 41-year-old president of Trinity College in Durham, North Carolina. Kilgo, who had a reputation as a passionate speaker willing to undertake controversial stands, was a close friend of Candler's. When Candler asked for Kilgo's assistance in securing Sledd a new position, Kilgo agreed, noting, "I will never desert a brave man." He continued by lamenting Sledd's decision to resign rather than fight and by offering a rousing critique of the restrictions of freedom in Southern society and higher education. Noting that state institutions were already under the control of powerful forces, Kilgo warned that attacks then focused on denominational institutions, with disastrous results: "Now old Emory...falls down before this set, and surrenders forever the old College into their hands. It is enough to make the Angels weep. Trinity stands alone now in this conflict, and the struggle deepens."[80]

The struggle deepened further for Kilgo when John Spencer Bassett, perhaps the most renowned member of Trinity's faculty and the founding editor of the *South Atlantic Quarterly*, published an article in 1903 calling for increased racial understanding. In "Stirring Up the Fires of Race Antipathy," Bassett called Booker T. Washington "a great and good man, a Christian statesman, and take him all in all the greatest man, save General Lee, born in the South in a hundred years."[81] The article retained some of the racism of its time, but the very mentioning of Washington alongside Lee—along with the larger critiques of Southern society and of recent sensationalistic newspaper coverage of Washington having dined in with whites while visiting North Carolina—was sure to cause controversy. Indeed, Bassett added the line about Lee specifically to garner attention to his argument. Led by Josephus Daniels, editor of the *Raleigh News and Observer*, North Carolina newspapers roundly attacked Bassett and Trinity, eventually culminating in a lengthy board hearing to determine Bassett's future.[82]

As with Sledd's and other cases, issues larger than just the specific catalyst were involved. The line-drawing and antagonisms in the Bassett Affair were informed by entrenched political divides between Democrats and Republicans, concerns over the influence that the wealthy Duke family held over Trinity, populist antitrust sentiments aimed at the Duke family's control of the American Tobacco Company, rivalries within the Methodist Church, and divisions over the appropriate roles for and support of state and church colleges. Kilgo's polarizing presence both set the stage for the difficulties and suggested that the outcome might be different from that of some other recent cases. And, as elsewhere, the individuals involved were complicated. Daniels had railed against violations of academic freedom when Andrews was forced to resign his presidency at Brown University but he viewed the Bassett Affair as a political struggle that did not involve academic freedom, as it dealt with a settled question at the heart of Southern society. Bassett, writing in 1897 in Kilgo's *Christian Educator,* himself equivocated on academic freedom, suggesting that skepticism was a legitimate cause for dismissal.[83] Kilgo, too, saw somewhat similar restrictions. His early writings presupposed the necessity of a larger Christian understanding of truth; elsewhere, though, he repeatedly called for the full pursuit of knowledge.[84]

The drama played out over six weeks in autumn 1903, with increasing attacks on Bassett and the college stoked by Daniels's coverage in the *News and Observer.* Kilgo tried to defuse the situation by interviewing Bassett and circulating the resulting statements, which were conciliatory but stopped short of retracting the offending article. By mid-November, Bassett indicated his willingness to resign if such an offer were requested by the board; but he did not resign outright, thus putting the onus of action on the board. Efforts to condemn Bassett at the state's Methodist conferences were forestalled by Kilgo's friends, including Candler. Supporters of Bassett (including Dodd) and of the college, wealthy benefactors, and alumni studying at Northern universities rallied behind Bassett and implored the decision-makers to retain him. Key stakeholders viewed the case as an opportunity not only to defend a principle but also to convince Benjamin Duke that defending the college could quell claims made against his family's influence at Trinity while also differentiating it from benefactors' actions at Stanford, Chicago, and elsewhere. On campus, students pledged support for Bassett's rights (though not the article's content), and faculty expressed admiration for their colleague. Each member of the faculty who could be contacted provided Kilgo a letter of resignation to be used if Bassett's was requested. Kilgo prepared his own resignation letter, as well. Still, as a December 1 board meeting approached, most observers felt that Bassett would be removed from his position, including Bassett himself.[85]

The trustees met into the early morning hours, beginning with Kilgo's hour-long defense of Bassett and attack on Daniels. Next, a faculty resolution disclaimed agreement with Bassett's article but declared that the situation was not about a single individual but about a larger principle rooted in rights of citizenship and affecting all of higher education: "The principle of academic freedom, as we understand it, merely requires that while the public hold him to his duty as it holds other men, it shall not invade his rights, which are not less than other men's. To persecute him for his opinion's sake, to drive him into exile, to deprive him of the means of livelihood,—these are invasions of his rights.... It is far better to tolerate opinions which seem to be wrong than to punish the expression of opinions because they are contrary to those generally accepted."[86] The faculty noted that other colleges that failed to preserve academic freedom were "disgraced in the eyes of the academic world" and claimed that upholding principles outweighed any potential loss in students, revenue, or local support generated by retaining Bassett.

Over the next few hours, eleven trustees spoke, including US Senator Furnifold M. Simmons, who considered the struggle his "last fight for white supremacy,"[87] before a committee of trustees recommended the adoption of a short statement prepared in advance by dean William Preston Few and his friend, author William Garrett Brown. The statement, which was adopted by a vote of 18–7, largely with the backing of business leaders and over the opposition of members of the clergy, disassociated the college from Bassett's article and pointedly noted that Bassett himself did not believe in racial equality.[88] While expressing "regret" over the article, it offered early evidence of recognition of different spheres of speech and individual, rather than institutional, responsibility for the content of faculty statements. The trustees then offered an affirmative claim for liberty and bemoaned its recent violation at other institutions, warning that infringements on academic freedom caused "high-minded men to look with suspicion upon this noble profession." They continued, "The search for truth should be unhampered and in an atmosphere that is free. Liberty may sometimes lead to folly; yet it is better that some should be tolerated than that all should think and speak under the deadening influence of repression."[89]

The decision and resolution were widely praised—students rang the chapel bells and held a victory bonfire when the decision was announced shortly before 3 a.m. In an ironic twist, several burned an effigy of Daniels, leading his allies to condemn it as an attack on the freedom of the press. Where Emory had suffered for accepting Sledd's resignation, Trinity flourished and grew in stature. Though Daniels remained chagrin, national newspapers and faculty hailed the decision as an impressive defense of academic freedom, especially for a Southern institution.[90] When President Theodore Roosevelt visited the campus two years later, he praised the institution as a bastion of freedom: "You stand for all those things for which the scholar must stand if he is to render real and lasting service to the state. You stand for academic freedom, for the right of private judgment, for the duty, more incumbent upon the scholar than upon any other man, to tell the truth as he sees it, to claim for himself and give to others the largest liberty in seeking after the truth."[91] Despite these claims, larger societal pressure remained and took a toll on Bassett. In 1906, he left Trinity for Smith College, where he believed he could undertake and publish his scholarship with fewer pressures and in "a more peaceful atmosphere."[92]

William E. Dodd's struggles at Virginia's Randolph-Macon College lasted longer than Bassett's at Trinity but were somewhat less sensational. A historian born in North Carolina and trained at the University of Leipzig, Dodd almost lost his position several times for his views on Southern society and its willful misrepresentations of the Civil War. In a 1902 article in the *Nation*, he critiqued Confederate honorary societies over their distortion of history, especially through their successful efforts to ban school textbooks that did not conform to pro-Confederacy interpretations of slavery and the war. The school was urged to dismiss Dodd but resisted. Drawing on Trinity's affirmation of Bassett, it again resisted calls for Dodd's removal in 1904 after Dodd criticized Southern education and educators in a speech that Bassett published in the *South Atlantic Quarterly*.[93] These pressures on Dodd never truly receded but again came to the fore in April 1907 when his letter to the editor of the *Nation*, appearing under the heading "Freedom of Speech in the South," critiqued aspects of Southern society, especially the hold that that wealthy had and the restrictions on speech that they implemented in the schools and elsewhere. He pointed to the growth of economic trusts and argued that their influence now restricted freedom, including at Trinity, whose faculty had never criticized the Duke family.[94] Dodd urged Southern scholars to work together and take up the cause of freedom, but he, himself, soon withdrew. He was able to withstand the specific attempts to dismiss him, but, in 1907, he followed Bassett's lead north by accepting a position at the University of Chicago. Though his work for academic freedom remained—he continued his efforts to counter pro-Confederacy textbooks and was one of the founders of the AAUP—he was unwilling to withstand the constant pressures at Randolph-Macon.[95]

Enoch Banks was not nearly as fortunate. Hired by Sledd, who served as the first president of the University of Florida from 1904 to 1909, Banks was a young professor of history and economics when the New York–based *Independent* published his article "A Semi-Centennial View of Secession" in February 1911.[96] The article claimed that the South had been out of touch with the changed economic environment of the mid-nineteenth century, that slavery was "an anachronism," and that Lincoln was legally incorrect to invade the South but was acting for a higher purpose that was appropriate for its time.[97] Though recognizing that his article was unlikely to cause a wholesale change of opinion, Banks wrote that it "may serve the purpose of showing that conditions are changing, and that the South is becoming more tolerant of a free discussion of its past and present policies."[98] Banks's expectations for free discussion and belief that an honest appraisal was possible were unmet. The public reaction was swift and forceful, led by Confederate societies and fostered by local newspapers. The board delayed a decision on Banks's future when it met in early March, hoping that the furor would subside. Banks, though, was shaken by the controversy and offered his resignation on March 9. Albert A. Murphree, who had by then succeeded Sledd as president, worried that accepting the resignation would stain the institution and violate its core principles. Still, at its April 1 meeting, he joined the board in bowing to the external pressures.[99] In one of several pieces condemning the situation to appear in the ensuing issues of the *Independent*, Sledd wrote of his correspondence with Banks and the immediate foreboding that Banks's article had caused. He described academic freedom as "vague, a sort of academic myth concocted by impractical and visionary men and failures" and wrote that "freedom of teaching in the university had to be weighed against possible loss of appropriations and patronage, and political office for the members of the State Board of Education."[100] Though the scales had tipped differently at Trinity and Randolph-Macon, Banks and academic freedom lost at Florida.

Banks's predicament demonstrates the continuing hold of patriotic societies and continued regional divides that limited speech and caused some, like Bassett and Dodd, to pursue their careers elsewhere.

Yet, there were also signs of change. Though greater emphasis in the historiography of academic freedom has been placed on the professionalization of faculty in economics, it is clear that other faculty were networking and undertaking similar processes. As Kilgo and Candler's relationship shows, it was not just the faculty who were connected and interacting around academic freedom. These cases also demonstrate the importance of faculty strategies in the ultimate outcomes of the cases; resigning reduced pressure on institutions, while Bassett's offering to resign only if it was requested kept the burden of action on the board. This could prove crucial, as momentum for increased freedom was building. Institutions such as Emory suffered for their actions, while Trinity benefited from upholding freedom. Additionally, while these four cases all involved speech issues, political maneuverings unrelated to the specific issues were implicated. Personal grievances and connections could be instrumental in both the pursuit of faculty and their defense.

These cases were, of course, set amid larger social, political, and educational struggles of the time, struggles in which some of the key participants were engaged. Dodd's aforementioned 1907 article took aim at the General Education Board (GEB), founded by John D. Rockefeller in 1903, and its subsidiary, the Southern Education Board (SEB), headed by Robert Ogden. With vast resources that dwarfed individual school endowments, the GEB offered the potential to restructure Southern higher education. Yet Dodd noted the unwillingness of GEB members to criticize Rockefeller and found it indicative of a repression that could affect Southern institutions. Bassett lamented Ogden's leadership and his lack of understanding of the South's needs.[101] Candler, in his self-published 1909 "Dangerous Donations and Degrading Doles," lambasted the GEB and SEB as attempts to overwhelm and either control or destroy Southern denominational colleges as part of a larger "scheme" to change Southerners' "political thinking, religious beliefs, and social organization."[102] He warned that the money would make trustees subservient and claimed, "Our colleges must be something more than the caged birds of the 'General Education Board,' fed by its hand and made to sing at its bidding."[103] The GEB's funding for African American institutions was tied to an industrial approach to education; accepting the needed money also meant accepting external restrictions on curricular and institutional matters. The roles and intents of Northern philanthropists was contested territory, but the restrictions imposed are clear.[104] Of course, issues of race and racism did not affect only Southern institutions, as widespread discrimination occurred across the nation.

Until 1941, no black faculty member held a regular appointment at a white institution.[105]

Growing Faculty Consensus; Continuing Concerns

As these cases were being fought and debated, literature germane to academic freedom continued and multiplied both in relation to specific events and in definitional efforts. In 1900, Elmer E. Brown provided a historical analysis of the development of academic freedom from the Middle Ages through the nineteenth century. He saw the emerging public universities as fostering increased freedom paired with responsibility, but he warned that partisan politics could also lead to restrictions. In 1901, two years after his dismissal from Kansas State, Will declared that the "educational trusts" were stifling freedom while proclaiming to uphold it.[106] The following year, John Dewey argued that the lack of codified methods in the social sciences caused difficulty for university professors. Due to the relevance of these faculty members' work and their likelihood of addressing sensitive issues, Dewey argued that they should be allowed leeway in their research. While concerned about financial pressures and overspecialization, Dewey, a key figure in the subsequent founding of the AAUP as well as in the American Federation of Teacher's efforts to unionize college faculty, foresaw increased academic freedom in universities preserved by joint action of the academic community, though he remained uncertain if it would take hold in denominational colleges.[107]

University presidents likewise offered opinions about the concept. In *College Administration,* Western Reserve University's Charles Thwing wrote about academic freedom from several viewpoints, including those of trustees and the general public. He linked the perspectives of presidents and professors, indicating an understanding that threats came largely from outside the institutions. While arguing for the principle of academic freedom, he also noted the importance of comportment, writing, "academic freedom is more often a question of good breeding than it is of liberty. Every college professor is to be absolutely free to hold and to express whatever opinion he chooses, so long as he maintains the character of a noble man and the manners of a gentleman."[108] Harvard's Charles W. Eliot echoed the importance of "courtesy and honor." He discussed both external and internal threats, including those posed by other faculty members, a topic that would long be ignored by historians. Columbia's Nicholas

Murray Butler similarly lauded academic freedom while emphasizing the responsibility of scholars not to offend "common morality" lest they "outlive their usefulness."[109] These influential presidents were promoting the ideal of academic freedom while at the same time making the case for limiting that freedom in the name of propriety. West, by then dean of Princeton University's graduate school, was more direct. At the 1906 meeting of the Association of American Universities, the new organization uniting a handful of elite universities, West claimed that many faculty members were not worthy of freedom, declaring, "there has been a great deal of folly talked about the freedom of faculties and of individual professors. Would that the fact a man is a professor were sufficient proof that he is also a man of sense. Sometimes it is not even proof that he is a scholar."[110] The tensions between rights and responsibilities, between freedoms and restrictions, would be integral to the development of academic freedom and the codification of policies as they played out over the ensuing decades. Significantly, it was not just administrators who were conflicted, but faculty members and educational organizations, as well.

While this period just after the turn of the century did see important writings on academic freedom, it is often considered one with few significant cases. Laurence Veysey, for example, noted a "long lull during which few new incidents arose" following the Ross case.[111] Both Veysey and Karen Christine Nelson argued that this lull might have been due to wider, if temporary, acceptance of Progressive ideas. Edward Silva and Sheila Slaughter added that the lack of sensational cases was also due to a combination of faculty members' demonstrated willingness to fight for academic freedom and established social scientists exchanging their more controversial activism to serve as respected experts.[112] Evidence indicates, though, that the lack of cases might be overstated. As the resignations of Banks and Sledd, plus the trials of Bassett and Dodd, show, threats involving race and regionalism remained. Moreover, less publicized cases existed, including that of Arthur Calhoun, a faculty member forced out of Florida State College for Women in 1911 when local newspapers blamed him for students' commencement speeches that appeared to evince socialism. Calhoun's removal received little attention outside the local newspapers. At the time, even he did not realize the issues of academic freedom involved.[113]

Perhaps more telling is the case of William Bohn, a rhetoric instructor at the University of Michigan who was accused of being a "revolutionist" who advocated social reorganization.[114] Alumni and concerned citizens called for his immediate dismissal, many noting that taxpayers should not be required to support a man who advocated such ideas, leading to an institutional investigation.[115] Private correspondence among institutional leaders demonstrates that they were concerned about Bohn's politics and the backlash they caused, but they were careful to avoid being accused of dismissing someone for his political expression. When professor Charles H. Cooley wrote to university president Harry Burns Hutchins expressing his concern, it was not over whether his colleague would be dismissed but how the dismissal would appear to the public. He trusted Hutchins's judgment but asked not to act in a way that link a dismissal to Bohn's socialism. Hutchins responded the following day by disclaiming "sudden or ill-advised action" but concluding that Bohn would not remain at the institution for much longer.[116] The Board of Regents joined Hutchins in hiding the truth about Bohn's forced resignation, publicly declaring that they upheld freedom of speech and that the resignation had not been forced.[117] This duplicity foreshadowed future controversies in which administrators denied that faculty dismissals were due to heterodox speech, even though their internal communications document the opposite. Bohn's case was different from the impending struggles in one important way, however: Bohn was dismissed because of the fear that his socialist speech would offend taxpayers and donors. In the ensuing years, with the outbreak of war in Europe, such speech would be troublesome, not just because it offended moneyed interests, but because it was thought to be treasonous.

Conclusion

American colleges and universities underwent tremendous changes over the course of the nineteenth and early twentieth centuries. The scope and scale of higher education grew dramatically as the nation expanded, public and private dollars infused the system, and institutions took on new roles and purposes. Advances in science, the cross-Atlantic travel of aspiring American scholars, and an increasing emphasis on discovering, rather than discovered, knowledge combined to affect attitudes about the appropriate roles and rights of faculty, especially at the century's turn. The conflicts over religion, race, economics, and other issues evidenced both ongoing restrictions and new willingness to test already expanding limits. Likewise, they implicated and furthered the professionalization of college faculty and their increasingly national and disciplinary, rather than local and institutional, focuses. The apparent, though misleading, tranquility in the early twentieth century would be broken by a handful of celebrated cases, including the 1913 forced resignation of John Moffat Mecklin from Lafayette College, the 1913 dismissal of Willard C. Fisher from Wesleyan University, and the dismissal of Scott Nearing from the University of Pennsylvania in 1915. These cases and others like them combined with additional factors to provide the stimulus for concerted organizational efforts to protect academic freedom and led to the founding of the AAUP. Certainly, as Wigmore noted, the problems of academic freedom and tenure were long standing and were far from being solved. Yet in the years leading up to 1915, progress had been made, and academic freedom had become a contested and contestable element of American higher education. Though differences between and within faculty, administrators, and trustees continued to exist—and faculty espousing heterodox opinions faced visible and hidden dangers—faculty professionalization had expanded the opportunities for dissent. In ensuing years, these new freedoms would become both further established and harshly challenged.

2

Associating and Academic Freedom

Informed by his own trials and in direct response to Enoch Banks's forced resignation from the University of Florida, Andrew Sledd warned in 1911 that academic freedom was a "vague...academic myth."[1] Fewer than five years later, it would be something much more: it would be a central element in efforts for and debates around faculty professionalization. The key events in this shift were the founding of the American Association of University Professors (AAUP), its creation of Committee A on Academic Freedom and Tenure, and its issuance of the 1915 *Declaration of Principles of Academic Freedom and Academic Tenure*. The establishment of the AAUP offered new opportunities for defining and protecting educators' rights and signaled a new era in the long history of academic freedom, though an era in which academic freedom would remain highly contested. Importantly, this new association of professors, at times termed a "union" to the consternation of its leaders, was not alone. The proximal founding of the Association of American Colleges (AAC), American Federation of Teachers (AFT), and American Civil Liberties Union (ACLU) provided additional opportunities for those interested in educational liberty to advocate competing visions of the principle. Over the next 25 years, their collaborations and competition changed American higher education and defined both the very idea of academic freedom and the policies that could be used to protect it. The organizations and their interactions created the conditions of the modern professoriate. At first, though, they largely worked separately and rarely acknowledged each other, except occasionally to criticize one another or to differentiate themselves. Moreover, the approaches that they took and the claims that they made emphasized the stratification that existed not only among American colleges but also within their faculties.

Prelude

The 1915 founding of the AAUP was neither a hasty response to recent threats nor the result of a widespread grassroots movement of college educators. Rather, Arthur O. Lovejoy led a group of elite university professors to organize the national association along the lines of disciplinary groups that had been founded in preceding decades, including the American Economic Association (AEA; founded in 1885), American Political Science Association (APSA; founded in 1903), and American Sociological Society (ASS—now American Sociological Association; founded in 1905). In many ways, the founding of the AAUP was a response to the recent changes that the American academic profession had experienced, including increased notions of professionalism, changes related to bureaucracy and academic governance, and desires for reform related to Progressive impulses.[2] Indeed, in his address at the association's first meeting in January 1915, AAUP president John Dewey noted, "We are in a period of intense and rapid growth of higher education.... Within almost a single generation our higher education has undergone a transformation amounting to a revolution."[3] He argued that, although American higher education had made great strides through local and institutional action, much more could be done through the cooperative action of reform-minded faculty.

Lovejoy's interest in founding an overarching association to unite the professoriate across disciplinary boundaries dated to his experiences at Stanford University at the turn of the century. When Edward A. Ross was dismissed from the institution at the direction of benefactor Jane Lathrop Stanford in 1900, Lovejoy was one of a handful of faculty to resign in protest. At the time, he believed that a single unifying organization could overcome the limitations of the new disciplinary societies and allow for interventions into both alleged violations of academic freedom and broader issues of educational policy. Yet, Lovejoy recognized that status was crucial in the academic profession and waited until 1913—by which time he was established at the elite Johns Hopkins University—to undertake the project.[4] Although faculty had noticed fewer violations of academic freedom in the intervening years, concern over the perceived declining status of faculty had blossomed and shown itself in the increasingly confrontational writings of college and university professors.[5]

Thorstein Veblen's lengthy *The Higher Learning in America: A Memorandum on the Conduct of Universities by Business Men* is perhaps the most famous of these attacks on centralization, bureaucratization, and business principles in higher education. Veblen called for the elimination of college executives and governing boards as the only possible solution for the troubles plaguing universities, noting, "It is of...the essence of this scheme of academic control that the captain of erudition should freely exercise the power of academic life and death over the members of his staff, to reward the good and faithful servant and to abase the recalcitrant."[6] To Veblen, the very existence of governing boards was problematic; that they were dominated by business leaders was "ingeniously foolish" and did "not promise well for the future of science and scholarship."[7] Others, including Joseph Jastrow, J. E. Creighton, James P. Munroe, and Stewart Patton similarly decried administrative overreaching, while John Jay Chapman and H. W. Boynton were among those who denounced the reticence of faculty to stand up for themselves and their colleagues.[8] In 1913, novelist and occasional faculty member George Cram Cook called on faculty to unionize in response to these conditions, noting that it was the only action "capable of taking 'professor' out of the category of the ridiculous."[9] His argument, however, was more radical than many academics were willing to heed, including University of Colorado dean F. B. R. Hellems. Hellems's scathing critique of Cook's argument included a claim for the existence of considerable freedom and the contention that "so far from feeling themselves 'somewhat ridiculous,' they are too nobly and generously proud to fight over pennies, or contend about the trappings of place and power."[10]

Columbia University psychologist James McKeen Cattell likewise condemned modern business practices in education and the influence of autocratic leaders. In his 1913 *University Control,* he presented his plans for institutional reorganization along with solicited responses to his ideas. He wrote that a college president's "despotism is only tempered by resignation" and termed presidential control of appointments and salaries the "most sinister side of our present system of university administration."[11] He further contended that either high salaries or tenure—something that was as yet rare and informal—was needed to attract the ablest men to the profession and suggested that faculty should organize a national association to attend to their shared educational and professional concerns.[12] Cattell's ideas were not, though, new: He had been arguing along the same lines since at least 1902, including to colleagues at Johns Hopkins University, where he had taught prior to moving to Columbia University. Cattell's early discussions at Johns Hopkins, along with the successful short-term administration of the institution by a committee of faculty and trustees in the wake of president Ira Remsen's resignation in 1912, contributed to the call to start the AAUP.[13]

Cattell's and others' arguments were instrumental in setting the stage for the founding of the new professors' association, but more immediate circumstances also contributed. In January 1913, Willard C. Fisher was dismissed from Wesleyan University when newspaper reports indicated that he had negatively commented on church attendance.[14] Even more notorious was the June 1913 forced resignation of Lafayette College professor John M. Mecklin due to his liberal religious teachings. Mecklin appealed to the American Philosophical Association and the American Psychological Association for assistance, claiming that the pragmatist texts he taught were used at other Presbyterian institutions.[15] The two organizations—headed by Lovejoy and Princeton University psychologist Howard Crosby Warren, also to become an influential AAUP leader—formed a joint committee to investigate. This seven-member committee requested information on Mecklin's departure from Lafayette president Ethelbert Dudley Warfield, claiming that ascertaining the quality and extent of freedom at the institution was necessary for members of their associations. Warfield, though, viewed the investigations as illegitimate and refused to cooperate. In its final report, the committee described the unacceptable conditions at Lafayette, concluding that continued appointment required assenting to Warfield's doctrinal beliefs. It declared a bifurcation of American institutions, some allowing freedom but other serving as "instruments of...propaganda," thereby setting the stage for future AAUP understandings of restrictions at proprietary institutions. The committee simultaneously asserted its right to investigate issues of academic freedom, an idea that was far from established. Warfield resigned under pressure shortly after the report was released, though the influence of the report in his disassociation is unclear. Although the investigation was an important step—Warren called it the "first active step" toward securing professorial freedoms in a 1914 *Atlantic Monthly* article[16]—Mecklin was never allowed to return to his position, and the episode attested to the faculty's precarious position and lack of authority in such matters.[17]

While the American Philosophical and American Psychological Associations were adopting the report on Mecklin's dismissal at their annual meetings at the end of 1913, three other professional associations, the AEA, APSA, and ASS, were agreeing to form a joint committee "to examine and report upon the present situation in American educational institutions as to liberty of thought, freedom of speech and security of tenure for teachers."[18] This nine-member committee, which was led by Edwin Seligman and included Princeton University economist Frank A. Fetter, Harvard University law professor Roscoe Pound, Wisconsin's Richard T. Ely, and Indiana University economist Ulysses G. Weatherly—all of whom would be central to the AAUP's early efforts—looked into Fisher's dismissal from Wesleyan but quickly shifted its focus to the larger issues of academic freedom and tenure. Released in December 1913, the committee's "Preliminary Report of the Joint Committee on Academic Freedom and Academic Tenure" argued that academic freedom was important not just for faculty but for the general public, the creation of knowledge, and the education of students. Still, the report was tentative and cautious. Rather than asserting rights, it raised questions as to appropriate limits to professorial freedoms, including asking whether public sentiment should confine professors' speech and whether the concept should apply only to scholarly activities or more broadly. It asked whether a single standard should apply across all institutional types and whether the extent of freedom in teaching should be contingent on the age of students being taught. The report suggested that faculty should retain the rights of citizenship and be able to speak freely outside of the classroom as both specialists and nonspecialists, key elements of what, in modern times, is known as extramural freedom.[19] Although the report was not a bold claim for academic freedom, it provided a vital basis for the ensuing work of the AAUP's forthcoming Committee on Academic Freedom and Academic Tenure, which would include seven of the nine members of the joint committee among its fifteen members.

The AAUP

The combination of the return of highly publicized dismissals and growing concerns over both bureaucratization and decline in status provided momentum for efforts to form what would become the AAUP. In March 1913, the majority of the full professors at Johns Hopkins proposed to colleagues at nine leading research institutions that they consider organizing a new association that could supplement existing disciplinary associations by attending to policy issues that affected the professoriate as a whole.[20] The new association would be designed "to promote a more general and methodical discussion of the educational problems of the university; to create means for the authoritative expression of the public opinion of the profession; and to make possible collective action, on occasions when such action seems called for."²¹ Professors at each of the nine institutions responded favorably, and, in November 1913, eighteen representatives from eight institutions met in Baltimore and agreed to draft a constitution and form a committee to consider eligibility for membership and related issues.²² Over the next year, Dewey led the intentionally multidisciplinary Committee on Organization as it contemplated the basic functions of the organization, the issues that the association would address, and the requirements and nature of membership in the association. The committee debated who should be allowed to enter the group, whether members should be selected as individuals or based on their institution affiliations, and whether administrators should be invited. In April 1914, a subcommittee recommended refining the purpose statement to emphasize "bringing about more effective cooperation amongst the members of the profession in the discharge of their special responsibilities as custodians of the interests of higher education and research in America"—and to conclude by noting "and in general to maintain and advance the ideals and standards of the profession."²³ A November meeting resulted in the invitation of a small group of renowned professors at recognized research institutions who were engaged primarily in academic work to attend the first formal meeting of a "National Association of University Professors" on January 1 and 2, 1915, in New York City.²⁴ The emphasis on membership requirements throughout was indicative of the new association's concern for status and its desire to establish itself as an elite, respected society of professionals.²⁵

The invitation to the New York meeting was also accompanied by a short document outlining the purposes of the new organization. This first official statement of intent built on the original call and incorporated the changes made at the April meeting. The document likened the group to the American Medical Association (established in 1847) and the American Bar Association (1878), expressly emphasized its professional nature, and noted a range of issues with which it could engage. Included among them were considerations of university and departmental organization; concerns over teaching and its relationships with research; and issues of graduate education, faculty governance, and tenure. Though the new group was not formed exclusively around issues of academic freedom, it would, from the start, be deeply involved with them. And as its proclaimed desire to pursue "the impartial determination of the facts" in academic freedom cases demonstrated, it would not imprudently rally around all professors who claimed they were aggrieved.²⁶

The reluctance of members of the AAUP to explicitly forefront academic freedom is noteworthy in light of the importance of academic freedom in the development of the organization. In his 1914 *Atlantic Monthly* article, Warren clearly linked the new organization with professionalization and academic freedom. He wrote of the eminent status of the men involved and of the restrained nature of their work, specifically denying that the group would be a "grievous society or a trade union of the economic type," as the organizers were "too well balanced," scholarly, and idealistic.[27] Instead, he claimed that the primary purpose would be the elevation of the "standards of the teaching profession, by promoting self-respect, initiative, and responsibility." To this end, Warren believed the AAUP would actually make a greater impact by focusing on relations between professors and students, professors and professors, and professors and the external world rather than by emphasizing professors' interactions with their governing boards.[28] Still, his discussion of the new association for professors was framed in terms of academic freedom. Academic freedom was a vital issue for the new group and would remain so, even as some downplayed its predominance and sought to establish the organization's reputation in other venues.

Dewey broached this issue of academic freedom in his address at the opening of the new association. Following a discussion of structural changes in American higher education and the need for a representative body of professors to consider educational issues, he denied that the organization was formed specifically for the purpose of defending academic freedom, as had been reported in the press. He argued that while violations of academic freedom were detrimental to professional status, they were relatively rare, and the existing associations were already handling such cases. He continued: "I am confident that the topic can not be more than an incident of the activities of the association in developing professional standards, standards which will be quite as scrupulous regarding obligations imposed by freedom as jealous for the freedom itself."[29] Despite this demurring, the AAUP acted on a proposal by Seligman and approved the absorption of the AEA, APSA, and ASS joint committee into its own new Committee on Academic Freedom and Academic Tenure—later to become known as Committee A—with the express intent to define principles with which professors and administrators could agree. The committee could not remain intact, however, as the AAUP's newly imposed eligibility standards, which required that members be established professors of ten years' standing, eliminated two of the joint committee's members, Herbert Croly and Frederick N. Judson.[30]

Early Investigations

Dewey's suggestion that the AAUP would spend little time on academic freedom quickly proved erroneous, as investigations into alleged violations soon assumed a prominent place in the association's work. In April 1915, before the absorption of the joint committee could be completed, Lovejoy fortuitously read an editorial describing the resignation of 17 members of the University of Utah faculty in response to the dismissal of other faculty. Lovejoy later recounted that, in response to the editorial's contention that the AAUP would surely investigate, he "thought 'it is up to us.'"[31] In fact, Lovejoy decided it was up to *him* and immediately appealed to John Dewey to fund an investigative trip to Utah. Dewey acceded to the request, and Lovejoy interrupted his vacation and left for Salt Lake City the following day.[32]

Lovejoy's Utah investigation set the tone for future AAUP inquiries and helped spur the association to take further action. He was intent on an investigation that would befit a professional organization and wrote to University of Utah president J. T. Kingsbury that amid allegations of institutional or administrative impropriety "the facts should be carefully determined in a judicial spirit by some committee wholly detached from any local or personal controversy, and in some degree representative of the profession at large."[33] Kingsbury agreed to participate in the investigation, and Lovejoy spent four days in Utah interviewing current and former faculty, administrators, and trustees. Lovejoy's final 80-page report, which was endorsed by the Committee on Academic Freedom and Academic Tenure, detailed President Kingsbury's willingness to suppress freedom and displace faculty members to appease powerful interests, including the state officials and religious leaders. However, the removals specifically under investigation were apparently brought about by personal animosity and perceived disrespect for authority, including faculty members' statements that had been uttered in private conversations. Lovejoy, and through him the committee, concluded that the dismissal of faculty members for their private speech or in the interest of squelching criticism was intolerable.[34]

In the ensuing months, Lovejoy attempted to share the burden of investigatory work with other committee members but himself undertook additional investigations at the Universities of Colorado, Montana, and Pennsylvania. Colorado law professor James Brewster asked for assistance after his appointment was not renewed following the 1914–15 academic year. The AAUP pursued the case in part due to the suspicion that it might be able to find that Brewster's academic freedom had *not* been violated. To Seligman, such a finding could help establish the investigations as legitimate and fair. Lovejoy traveled to Colorado and did, in fact, find that the president had not severed Brewster's connection to the institution due to the professor's political speech. Significantly, however, the final report argued that Brewster was aggrieved in that he had not been given proper notification that his contract would not be renewed. The AAUP argued that professors deserved at least three months' notice, foreshadowing its emphasis on appropriate dismissal procedures. The association also took seriously Brewster's contention that his desire to testify before a legislative hearing had contributed to his removal; it argued that the right to contribute to the public good through legislative testimony must be protected. Here, too, the AAUP staked claims to professorial freedoms in and out of the classroom, as well as procedural protections for accused faculty.[35]

Lovejoy's work on the cases at Montana and Pennsylvania was similarly important. He gathered the information used by the subcommittee and reported that the dismissals of three professors and the president of the University of Montana were based on their public speech about the expansion of the institution, both for and against. The committee rejected a desire for "harmony" as an appropriate cause for dismissal, as it had in the Utah case. The subcommittee investigating Scott Nearing's dismissal from the University of Pennsylvania criticized the institution not only for dismissing the professor due to his political speech but also for refusing to participate in the investigation. It further argued that disregarding faculty recommendations for continued appointment, as had been the situation in Nearing's case, was acceptable only in extremely rare circumstances. Together, these early reports helped establish the contours of investigative processes, helped set the foundation upon which the right to academic freedom would be argued, and demonstrated that academic freedom was separate from but intertwined with larger concerns involving the terms of faculty employment.[36]

The AAUP's one investigation during its first year in which Lovejoy was not intimately involved is also instructive. Two years after Willard C. Fisher was forced to resign from Wesleyan University, Seligman inquired into the situation on behalf of both the AAUP and the AEA. Fisher alleged that the forced resignation was caused by long-standing animosity between him and president William Shanklin, as well as inflammatory newspaper reports about Fisher's speech concerning religious observance. Seligman's report noted the lack of clear evidence in the case but declared that academic freedom included speech outside of one's specific discipline and articulated the need for due process for professors. Due to the length of time since the resignation and uncertainties about the evidence, however, the Committee on Academic Freedom and Academic Tenure failed to endorse the report but published a brief statement instead.[37] The issues involved in these cases were important, but so too were the tempered approach and judicious nature of the reports—reports that were befitting of an organization seeking to establish and maintain a professional reputation.

These five cases were not the only ones that were brought to the committee's attention during this first year of activity. Numerous other professors appealed to the new organization for assistance in controversies that extended beyond issues of academic freedom, with cases being presented at the rate of one per week in late summer. Each investigation was time-consuming and expensive, leading the committee to decline many requests for intervention. As the year progressed, the committee created parameters for choosing its investigations, leaving aside those in which administrators rather than professors were aggrieved and those it deemed less significant due of the low status of the institution or small number of individuals involved. This unexpected influx of cases and resulting need to delimit the committee's activities also led the committee to return to its initial task of outlining a policy statement on academic freedom.[38]

A Magna Carta?

Neither the AAUP nor its Committee on Academic Freedom and Academic Tenure were founded to investigate alleged violations of academic freedom, but the work quickly consumed the latter and become synonymous with the former. When the association met in December 1915, Dewey offered his reassurance that the circumstances were unusual and that the "investigations of particular cases were literally thrust upon us." Not investigating "would have been cowardly; it would have tended to destroy all confidence in the Association as anything more than a talking body."[39] Seligman's committee, which had been charged with extending the work of the joint committee and reporting on the problems of academic freedom, then presented the "General Report of the Committee on Academic Freedom and Academic Tenure," commonly referred to as the 1915 *Declaration of Principles on Academic Freedom and Academic Tenure*. The document, which was initially drafted by Seligman but then substantially revised by Lovejoy, consisted of two main parts: a statement of principles and a set of "Practical Proposals" designed to help achieve them. The former outlined three main aspects of academic freedom as "freedom of inquiry and research; freedom of teaching within the university or college; and freedom of extra-mural utterance and action," and the latter called for tenure and for due process before faculty dismissals. Together, they established the terms on which ensuing AAUP efforts would be based.[40]

The 1915 *Declaration* staked its claim for academic freedom on the special relationship between higher education and society. That relationship—and higher education's concomitant responsibility to create, preserve, and transmit knowledge—required that trustees and legislatures refrain from interfering with professors' scholarly activities or otherwise limiting their freedoms. Proprietary institutions and those that otherwise saw their purpose as inculcating preordained doctrines were duty-bound to admit that they were of a different type and not part of that same special relationship. For the majority of institutions serving the public good, though, the document argued that only by preserving academic freedom could universities attract the most desirable men to the profession, sustain the public's trust in scholarly expertise, offer disinterested criticism, and further the development of knowledgeable public servants. It argued that freedoms to research were widely protected but that those involving classroom teaching and extramural speech faced greater danger. Though noting threats posed by intrusive trustees and legislative bodies, it warned that public opinion more broadly presented the gravest danger. For institutions of higher education to fulfill their responsibilities, they must be an "inviolable refuge" from the "tyranny of public opinion." Academic freedom was thus needed for societal, not individual or institutional, benefit.[41] It was, likewise, accompanied by corresponding responsibilities befitting professional scholars. Faculty were responsible for expressing a variety of opinions when discussing controversial topics in the classroom and, when dealing with young students, needed to be particularly careful. Responsibilities extended outside the classroom, as well, with professors' rights to address controversial issues, including those outside their specialties, tempered by their being "under a peculiar obligation to avoid hasty or unverified or exaggerated statements, and to refrain from intemperate or sensational modes of expression."[42] Although able to participate in political activities, professors should also remain above political intrigue or partisan party concerns. Importantly, it was the profession alone that should determine if its members were failing to meet these responsibilities.

The comparatively brief "Practical Proposals" called for faculty committees to advise presidents or boards on faculty reappointments. They argued for permanent tenure for associate and full professors after ten years of service, a minimum of three months' notice prior to nonrenewal of a contract when tenure was not an issue, and a full year's notice for those who had achieved a rank higher than instructor. They further called on institutions to clearly define grounds for dismissal and identify any doctrinal requirements placed on faculty. Finally, the report argued that teachers should not be dismissed or demoted without written charges and fair hearings before bodies chosen by and including members of the faculty.[43] With these proposals, the new AAUP linked the protection of academic freedom to tenure rights and due process, but at the same time acknowledged that only established faculty at the highest levels—not instructors or assistants—would qualify for the full protections of tenure.

The 1915 *Declaration* was endorsed by the AAUP at its second meeting, with one participant calling it a "magna carta for our profession for a long time to come."[44] Though widely supported within the association, the document nonetheless caused a few concerns. John H. Wigmore complained that some of his suggestions were not included in the final draft and that the statement was flawed because it did not specifically delineate the limits of free speech. He believed the statement needed to go further in its defense of professors' freedoms and needed to enunciate professors' explicit right to disagree with trustees and alumni.[45] He would build on these points a year later when, as AAUP president, he critiqued the emphasis on procedures over content: "They formulate rules for the giving of a hearing to the professor, and for employing other measures of fair and cautious procedure, before action upon the issue of dismissal; but they do not formulate any definition of the kind of defect or conduct which is to form just ground for dismissal."[46] Another professor complained that the document went too far in claiming special privileges for faculty that went beyond the rights of ordinary citizens and that it implied that professors could not be removed for cause. Dewey disagreed, noting that the document did not claim that professors were irremovable but that it only made legitimate claims based on the needs of the profession. While he endorsed the report, Dewey himself did not entirely agree with it, believing it might inappropriately restrict trustees. The meeting's attendees considered spending another year debating the document, but Seligman was able to convince the body to allow for the more expeditious route of circulating the document for comments. He argued that it was a useful starting point and could be amended as situations required. Seligman's committee was charged with finalizing the document and completing its investigative reports in preparation for its replacement by a new, permanent committee to be known as Committee A.[47]

The 1915 *Declaration* was met with a mixed response when it was published shortly after the meeting. The United States Commissioner of Education funded the distribution of the report to three thousand college and university presidents and trustees, and the Bureau of Education endorsed the efforts of the AAUP.[48] The *Nation* lauded the document, as did other liberal publications, with at least one echoing the sentiment that it was a "scholar's magna carta."[49] Others were not as flattering. The *New York Times* notably lambasted academic freedom as "the inalienable right of every college instructor to make a fool of himself and his college by vealy, intemperate, sensational prattle about every subject under heaven, to his classes and to the public, and still keep on the payroll or be reft therefrom only by elaborate process."[50] A little more than a year after its official founding, the AAUP had made its historic claim for faculty freedoms, a claim that remained highly contested.

THE AAC

Though many remained silent about the 1915 *Declaration,* an organization that was forming alongside the AAUP took the professors' association seriously. At the encouragement of the Council of Church Boards of Education, which itself was formed in 1911 partly to promote liberal arts colleges, a group of presidents from denominational colleges discussed their shared interests at the 1914 National Education Association (NEA) meeting. These initial conversations led to the January 1915 establishment of the AAC, an organization composed of senior officers of liberal arts colleges and intent on advancing their interests.[51] At the founding meeting, Whitman College president Stephen B. L. Penrose argued that the small colleges had unique missions and that the new organization could foster self-consciousness among them.[52] Richard Watson Cooper, president of Upper Iowa University, noted that the NEA was too influential in educational circles and that its efforts to reform American education worked to the detriment of small colleges.[53] Earlham College president Robert L. Kelly, who would be a longtime leader of the

AAC, argued that the new body was intended to form "social solidarity" of private institutions and to develop a national educational consciousness.[54] The transformations in higher education that Dewey addressed while opening the AAUP were felt by more than just the professoriate, and the once-dominant denominational and liberal arts colleges feared being trampled by them.

Despite the specific references to other educational associations, neither the new AAUP nor academic freedom appeared in the proceedings of this first meeting. The following year, the situation was quite different, as the AAC met in the immediate wake of the 1915 *Declaration*. The discussions are particularly noteworthy in that they were neither dismissive of the AAUP's efforts nor uniformly opposed to its provisions. Instead, three distinct opinions on the topic were presented as part of the discussion on academic freedom and tenure. Ohio Wesleyan University president Herbert Welch initiated the conversation by arguing that college presidents were uniquely positioned to consider academic freedom, as they had both ties to faculty and responsibilities to trustees. He contended that the existing amount of academic freedom was actually impressive and argued that maintaining incompetent professors was more problematic than the few violations of academic freedom that occurred. Welch also argued for limitations in some areas, especially for denominational institutions. Calling claims for the necessity of the limitless search for truth "misleading," he argued: "We stand not only for the search for truth but for the belief that some truth has really been discovered and put beyond reasonable controversy."[55] Moreover, as teaching was a public profession, educators had special responsibilities that placed limits on their pursuits. Welch also specifically addressed the new AAUP, including its claim for academic freedom. Terming the AAUP's report on the firings at Utah "very interesting, somewhat amusing, and sometimes irritating," he noted that in it, the AAUP had recognized that extreme and exaggerated criticism of a university's administration could justifiably lead to dismissal.[56] More significantly, he focused on the limitations on freedoms outlined in the 1915 *Declaration* and argued that the AAUP had opened the door for further limitations. In sum, he called the document "admirably balanced."[57] He then proposed a series of procedures that were in many ways similar to those offered by the AAUP. Welch suggested faculty involvement in hiring and dismissal decisions, removal of faculty only with cause, and due notice for dismissals. He argued that without fair hearings before faculty and trustees prior to dismissals, the AAUP would continue to investigate, a practice that he believed held the potential for bias. Still, Welch believed that ultimate authority in all institutional matters must remain in the hands of trustees and that faculty were only advisory.

The AAUP's Weatherly was on hand to respond. After providing some background to the AAUP efforts, he emphasized that the AAUP recognized restrictions in teaching "conditioned by the nature of the students taught, by the nature of the subjects, by the nature of the social relationships involved in the institution and what might be called the social staging of the institution." He continued that professorial rights were "conditioned by the restriction of good sense, good judgment and the social environment in which the teaching takes place."[58] Weatherly also agreed with Welch that external utterances were more problematic than classroom teachings or research and admitted that the AAUP was not itself settled on how to handle political activities of faculty. Indicative of the similarities between Welch's ideas and those offered by the AAUP, Weatherly mistakenly believed that Welch's proposals were, in fact, the AAUP's recommendations. He did, however, stress that the AAUP was adamant about the need for faculty to control teaching and research functions of colleges or universities. Trustees and presidents were rightfully involved in academic appointments but thereafter should remain absent from academic affairs.[59]

The third speaker, Amherst College president Alexander Meiklejohn, dissented from both Welch and Weatherly, arguing for a much more expansive idea of academic freedom than either previous speaker had suggested. He disputed the appropriateness of the limitations on instruction that Welch had outlined and argued that it was unethical for institutions to proclaim freedom in teaching when students were actually "being led by the nose to some fixed and determined conclusion."[60] While his disagreement with Welch was evident, Meiklejohn saved most of his criticism for the 1915 *Declaration,* which he claimed did "not treat its task seriously enough."[61] Meiklejohn disapproved of the idea that academic freedom was one that pitted presidents and trustees against professors and argued that the AAUP considered how presidents and trustees violated professors' freedoms but disregarded the freedoms of presidents or colleges. The AAUP failed to challenge the basic assumptions of college funding relationships, in essence requiring that presidents prostrate themselves to donors but refusing to insist that faculty do the same.[62] Meiklejohn further argued that if the principles were insufficient, the corresponding proposals on reappointment and dismissals were useless in the face of the real threat: freedom was more restricted by hiring decisions than through dismissals. Meiklejohn also pointed to the structure of the AAUP, criticizing as emblematic of larger problems within the professoriate the fact that only established professors of ten years' standing with national reputations were eligible for membership. Rather than creating true freedom or even a democracy, he argued, the AAUP was forming an oligarchy in which powerful professors could determine the fates of their peers.

At the same meeting, the AAC created its own Committee on Academic Freedom and Tenure of Office, chaired by Kelly and including Meiklejohn, among others. When it reported to the 1917 convention, conciliatory statements were notably absent. The report specifically challenged the AAUP, noting that the professors' association did not represent all college teachers and was flawed in its exclusion of college presidents from membership. The committee separated academic freedom from tenure, argued that violations of academic freedom were not as large a problem as the AAUP averred, and claimed that faculty unfitness was more to blame for recent controversies than were executive or governing board abuses. When executives did interfere with freedoms, the committee maintained that it was almost always in an honest attempt to help an institution rather than an effort to inhibit productive faculty members. The report offered a plea for securing executive authority by limiting faculty input into administration and limiting faculty access to governing boards. Most strikingly, the committee argued that it would be better to unjustly dismiss a few faculty members who had grievances with an institution than to change institutional leadership frequently. With the publication of this report, the AAC argued for institutional, not professorial, academic freedom. Although professors should be able to pursue their interests, the AAC proclaimed that institutions were free to dismiss them if those interests contradicted larger institutional goals.[63] This was, of course, a claim that the AAUP would counter.

Defense, Tenure, and Procedural Protections

Meiklejohn's denunciation of the AAUP as a professorial oligarchy highlighted a tension within the association that would be intertwined with the association's pursuit of academic freedom. From the initial 1913 call to organize, the leaders of the association were concerned that their new organization would appear to be a union and thus diminish both the professional nature and status of faculty work. Correspondence demonstrates profound concern on the part of prospective members, and the founders went to great lengths to assure them and the larger population of the conservative nature of the association.[64] While Cattell's rhetoric helped set the stage for the new organization, he refrained from taking a leading role in the organizational efforts specifically out of fear of alienating more moderate professors.[65] Others who had argued for radical changes and organizing along union models were notably absent from the association's planning efforts. Even the joint committee, which merged with the AAUP's committee in 1915, specifically dismissed union tactics.[66] Opposing sentiments, such as those expressed by the University of Michigan's Alexander Ziwet, who withdrew from the planning efforts for fear that it threatened "to become a self-constituted aristocracy of older men," were rare.[67] Yet the potential appearance of unionism was a main concern of AAUP leaders, as even Dewey assured members of the AAUP's conservative nature. In his initial address to the AAUP, he proclaimed his admiration for unions and acknowledged the relevance of economic considerations to education but argued: "The fear that a 'trade unionism' of spirit will be cultivated is ungrounded.... I have never heard any one suggest such a danger for the American Bar Association or the American Medical Association. Pray, are the aims of college teachers less elevated?"[68] Dewey's successors similarly denounced allusions to the association as a professors' union, including Frank Thilly, who argued in 1917 that the AAUP's growth could be attributed to its convincing potential members that it would refrain from union tactics.[69]

Dewey and Thilly both noted that economic issues might cause some to link the AAUP to unionism, but it was the central role of academic freedom investigations that gave greatest urgency to the concerns. In public statements, letters to the editors of newspapers, and internal documents, AAUP leaders repeatedly disclaimed any linkages to organized labor and denied that the association was designed to serve individual interests or protect its membership.[70] In 1918, AAUP president J. M. Coulter dedicated an open letter to the membership to the issue, noting that the association's work for academic freedom and tenure had led to the impression that it was "sort of a labor union seeking to protect itself from the tyranny of its employers." He countered that "academic efficiency is our excuse for existence" and that academic freedom and tenure were merely one important part of achieving that larger goal—though one that had garnered inappropriate attention.[71] Although the AAUP maintained its work for academic freedom in subsequent years, its activities were indeed influenced by concerns over public perception. As with the investigation of the University of Colorado, these concerns also led the organization to choose some cases specifically to emphasize its conservative nature and willingness to support presidents and trustees.

Despite the AAUP's concern about appearing to place too great an emphasis on academic freedom and protection, Committee A played a central role in the association, although one that was increasingly difficult to fulfill. One problem was the trouble in finding members willing to serve as chairmen of either Committee A or its investigative subcommittees. Each investigation was a burdensome task that had to be handled with a good deal of care.[72] In 1916 and 1917, more than 30 cases of alleged infringement of academic freedom were appealed to the association, overwhelming the small and informal committee and highlighting the need for an established procedure in selecting which cases to investigate.[73] As had become clear the previous summer, the AAUP could not investigate all cases but instead focused only on those it deemed most important because of the individuals involved, the early evidence that the cases involved academic freedom, and the publicity that they had received.[74] When these guidelines were published the following year, a fourth consideration, whether a specialist disciplinary association could be called on to handle the case, was added. Committee A chairman Allyn Abbot Young, an economist at Cornell University, described the decisions as related to establishing principles rather than assisting individuals. Denying the ability to investigate each case, he wrote, "Our work will have a more effective influence if we concern ourselves primarily with the establishment of proper standards and only secondarily with the question of remedying individual cases of injustice."[75] Neither a defense organization nor a protective association, the AAUP was instead a professional group working to establish its core values and principles.

These early reports of Committee A are further important in their explicit recognition that tenure was crucial to the protection of academic freedom. In 1916, Committee A faced a number of cases that concerned alleged violations of tenure but lacked corresponding concerns regarding academic freedom, leaving the committee unsure as to how or whether to proceed with these cases.[76] The following year, after a reiteration of the emphasis on future principles rather than past dismissals, the majority of Committee A's annual report addressed tenure considerations. According to the report, less than one-third of all cases presented to the committee involved academic freedom, but all implicated the security of tenure. Committee A argued that only tenure could ensure academic freedom, and only fair, judicious, and appropriate procedures for dismissal could safeguard tenure. This plea included a case for justice for individual professors but hinged on a broader argument analogous to that made by Cattell in *University Control*, as well as in the 1915 *Declaration*. Businesses could rightly emphasize competition due to the potentially lucrative nature of employment with them, but higher education offered no such financial benefits. In order to attract the most able and skilled people to the profession in the absence of such incentives, the security of tenure was needed. If continued employment relied on pleasing capricious administrators and trustees, the quality of teaching and research would diminish, and society would suffer. After specifically refuting the attacks on tenure made by Cattell's antagonist, Columbia University president Nicholas Murray Butler, the report admitted some potential costs of tenure but acknowledged that proper procedure could be used to remove grossly inefficient professors. Moreover, while tenure would support and improve the work of the most skillful and productive scholars, the lack of tenure would not necessarily remove the lazy and incompetent. High standards should be achieved through appropriate appointments, not ease of dismissal.[77] The report offered the AAUP's most pronounced defense and clearest articulation of tenure to date and pointed to the prominence that the issue would take in the AAUP's future work.[78]

The American Federation of Teachers

At the same time that elite faculty members were organizing the AAUP, K–12 teachers were forming a different national organization that would, over time, grow to challenge the association of professors. Concerned with legislation that forbade teacher unionization and with the administrative control and conservativeness of the NEA, unaffiliated teachers unions from Chicago and Gary, Indiana, founded the American Federation of Teachers in April 1916. They were joined by locals from New York City, Washington, DC, and elsewhere under the umbrella of the American Federation of Labor as the first national teachers union. Though not able to bargain collectively, the founders believed that they could provide teachers with greater input into educational decisions, work for tenure legislation, and otherwise improve the conditions of both teachers and students through their affiliation with organized labor.[79] Although the AFT eventually played a significant role in the development of professorial academic freedom, this role would not have been foreseen at its outset. From its initial meeting, the AFT was dominated by high school teachers despite the important role that elementary school teacher Margaret

Haley of the Chicago Teachers Federation had played in its founding. Charles Stillman of the Chicago Federation of Men Teachers was elected as the union's first president, a position he held until 1923. Along with other male high school teachers, Stillman led the union down a more conservative path than might have been pursued under different leadership.[80] In these first few years, college teachers were largely absent from the national scene, and higher education issues were largely ignored, although many locals did include college members. It was not until 1918 that the AFT changed its constitution and, as part of a larger effort to expand its potential membership base, allowed locals to be formed on college campuses. Later that year the first explicitly college local was founded at Howard University in response to what one member termed the faculty's "degradation."[81]

Although the new AFT national did not work on behalf of professorial academic freedom in these early years, union locals did recognize the issue as important and related to their own members' situations even before the affiliation of the separate locals. In September 1915, the Chicago Federation of Men Teachers' *Federation Bulletin* included an article on the threats to academic freedom. The article blamed the dismissals at the Universities of Pennsylvania, Colorado, and Utah on "an unmistakable, country-wide attempt by the 'interests' to gain control of the educational system of the nation" and linked them to ongoing controversies in Chicago schools. It continued: "The university men have recognized this danger, and have organized the American Association of University Professors along approximately union lines."[82] Though the AAUP would have protested the characterization, the Federation of Men Teachers was attempting to establish its credibility and recruit new members to its cause through such allusions. The union was not yet, however, joining the fray at the college or university level.

In December 1916, at its second convention, the AFT adopted a resolution that shared some of the language of the *Federation Bulletin* article and condemned the dismissals of teachers and professors for expressing their opinions on controverted social and economic issues.[83] Calling on the public to protest such actions, the resolution argued that the dismissals diminished educators' abilities to complete their work and discouraged potential teachers from entering the field. While the AFT recognized the importance of educational liberty, this resolution was the only specific mention of academic freedom or college issues at this important early meeting, and the convention platform points to the predominance of other issues in the union's work. Out of 27 planks, only a few points touched on issues relevant to academic freedom. The union advocated for tenure laws and condemned political influences on promotions.[84] The convention delegates further pushed for more liberal use of school facilities for social and civic purposes, an issue that became important as schools and universities attempted to prevent leftist groups from publicly meeting. Still, other union matters dominated until the difficulties of World War I led the AFT into its first battles over academic freedom. These difficulties—and the organizational responses to them—are the focus of the next chapter.

Conclusion

The founding of the AAUP in 1915 was a crucial development in the creation of the modern concepts of academic freedom and tenure, as well as the modern professoriate. In the preceding decades, the rise of disciplinary associations had provided new outlets for faculty to engage, but the very nature of these associations had precluded a unified faculty voice on educational and administrative issues. The AAUP offered an attempt to ameliorate this divide, albeit in a limited way. Its emphasis on established faculty, including its initial exclusion of those with fewer than ten years' experience, provided only one segment of the educational workforce with input into its deliberations and policy-making efforts. Fundamentally concerned about the freedoms, privileges, and responsibilities of the professoriate, the AAUP was also committed to establishing the professional nature of faculty employment. As such, the 1915 *Declaration* was both bold and restrained. It elaborated on the joint committee's calls for both freedom and responsibility, while allowing for restrictions at proprietary and narrowly sectarian institutions. Further, it argued for the freedom of teaching, research, and extramural speech, but with the caveats that they needed to be undertaken with the temperament of a scholar. The combination of numerous requests for investigation and the desire to demonstrate the professional nature of the AAUP led Committee A to emphasize principles and policies rather than attempt to assist all educators who claimed aggrievement. The committee's processes and the claims that they faced demonstrated the importance of tenure, both in relation to academic freedom and as a key feature of professorial authority. But, as the tumult of the war years showed, even the AAUP struggled with how best to treat faculty, institutional, and societal interests.

At the same time, from these earliest associations, we can begin to see what would eventually grow into different approaches to and beliefs about academic freedom. From its start, the AAUP emphasized responsibility and staked claims for the professional nature of scholarly work. The AAC, by 1917, was arguing for an institutional approach and asserting colleges', not faculties', rights to determine the perspectives offered and the opinions espoused. The AFT, though not yet active in higher education, foretold a different approach, one that could reach out to the disenfranchised educational professionals—though one that brought with it concerns about status. Over the ensuing years, the relationships among these and a small group of related organizations would determine the future of faculty working conditions, rights, and responsibilities in the United States.

3

TREASON AND THE "FARCE" OF ACADEMIC FREEDOM

While American faculty members were organizing around academic freedom and asserting the professional nature of professorial work, far greater struggles were taking place in Europe. Beginning in July 1914, first Europe and then much of the world was at war, with the United States finally eschewing its formal neutrality in April 1917. Higher education was just one of the many sectors of American society that experienced new demands and pressures in the build up to participation in World War I. With American entry, higher education was further reshaped as faculty and students abandoned their institutions to join the war cause as soldiers, administrators, or advisers. Colleges, some threatened with closure due to the loss of students, joined the effort themselves; with federal support, more than five hundred institutions formed Student Army Training Corps (SATC) branches, argued "It's patriotic to go to college," and turned their campuses into military training grounds. Amid these larger international struggles and the massive national war effort, American college faculty faced new challenges to their still contested claims for academic freedom—challenges that originated from both inside and outside the professoriate.[1]

The pressures of war and the ensuing First Red Scare raised fundamental issues of rights and responsibilities in wartime and beyond. Through struggles over conscription, sedition laws, mob violence, and competing claims over loyalty, some people grappled with what it meant to be a loyal American and with what rights were inscribed in the US Constitution. For others, there was no grappling: only 100 percent Americanism would suffice. Modern understandings of civil liberties evolved, in part, from the reactions to their severe curtailment during these years. Key to these efforts was the new National Civil Liberties Bureau (NCLB), founded in 1917. The NCLB, which grew out of the antiwar movement, recognized the war hysteria to be a broad threat to individual liberties, as well as a specific threat to academic freedom. Other organizations, including the American Association of University Professors (AAUP), were not as sanguine. Just over two years removed from declaring that universities needed to be an "inviolable refuge" from the "tyranny of public opinion," the association reconsidered its stance and conceded the tenuous nature of freedom in wartime.[2] Indeed, both larger principles and individual rights were fundamentally challenged, though often with little recognition of what was at stake. Typical of the reaction to concerns over academic freedom was Princeton University president John Grier Hibben's declaration, "When any member of a college faction throws about himself the cloak of academic freedom to utter treason, then academic freedom is a farce."[3] Of course, conceptions of treason were wide-ranging and resulted in harsh restrictions, vituperative attacks, and the premature end of faculty careers.

From Neutrality to Intervention

When long-standing feuds, imperialistic policies, and encumbering alliances combined with the assassination of Austrian Archduke Franz Ferdinand to launch what became World War I, American society was divided. Recognizing the split opinion and the threat that war posed to his domestic agenda, US president Woodrow Wilson, a former president of Princeton University, outlined a policy of strict and thorough neutrality. Although the country was increasingly linked with England and France because of munitions and lending arrangements, as well as the loss of American lives due to Germany's 1915 sinking of the passenger ship *Lusitania,* opinions were far from unanimous. Organizations such as the American Union Against Militarism (AUAM) urged the government to stay out of the war but others, including the National Security League (NSL), pushed preparedness and intervention on the Allied side. Moreover, large German populations in the Midwest supported Germany's cause, and many Irish-Americans argued against England and her allies. Wilson achieved reelection in 1916 under the slogan "He Kept Us Out of the War," but, amid growing public sentiment for intervention, the United States formally entered the conflict on April 6, 1917.

By the time America declared war on Germany, most of higher education had committed to the cause. Initially, though, institutions and faculty evinced a range of opinions on the war—and on the appropriate response. Many viewed German universities as the most elite in the world; American universities were, in part, based on elements of German institutions. Academic freedom itself grew partly from Germanic origins.[4] In the late nineteenth and early twentieth centuries, thousands of American students studied at German universities, and American college faculties often included scholars born or educated in Germany, resulting in frequent institutional affiliations with Germany.[5] Yet this affinity also set the stage for a backlash against Germany, including due to perceptions that the German professoriate abdicated objectivity in its service to the state. Perhaps most unsettling was the document addressed "To the Civilized World" and signed by 93 leading German scholars and professors. The document, which was written in September 1914 and circulated in pamphlet form, claimed that Germany was not at fault in the war, denied the widely known (and accurate) reports of German activities in Belgium, and made other dubious claims.[6] It offended American audiences, as did other German propaganda efforts, and contributed to a dramatic shift in opinion.[7] Essayist John Jay Chapman wrote of the "feebleness of German intellect" and that "a boorish self-assertion pervades the document."[8] William Roscoe Thayer, a member of the Harvard Board of Overseers, declared that the manifesto showed "the complete subservience of the German university professors to the Kaiser and his Ring." He continued: "The Government cracked the whip, and the Ninety-three fell into line, clicked their heels together, saluted, and repeated their formulas."[9] In a letter to the editors of the *Nation*, Arthur O. Lovejoy termed the document a "scandalous episode" and argued that it signaled the ultimate failure of German intellectuals to perform their "proper function—the function of detached criticism, of cool consideration, of insisting that facts, and all relevant facts be known and faced."[10] Both in published writing and in his private correspondence, Lovejoy suggested that the German scholars' betrayal of professional ideals could serve as a warning to the American professoriate; it was a warning that went unheeded.[11]

It was soon clear that American faculties and institutional leaders overwhelmingly, though not exclusively, blamed Germany for the war. Newspapers reported that Germans' attempts to attract American intellectuals to their cause had failed. A German-American participant in the efforts pointed to American college presidents' unwillingness to "do or sanction anything which might annoy the pork and oil barons who give them occasional donations" as a prime cause.[12] Yet while the institutions and many on their faculties were so sympathetic to the Allied cause that they would later be accused of leading the country into the war, neutrality was the official policy on most campuses in the early years of the conflict. This neutrality was enforced through restrictions on faculty speech, including in 1914 when University of Wisconsin president Charles Van Hise cautioned faculty against speaking about the war on campus or in public forums; a trustee responded by warning that it was the first step toward limiting academic freedom.[13] At Cornell University, a professor was censured for violating the university's neutrality stance when his letter containing anti-German slurs was made public.[14] Widespread restrictions were in place at the University of Michigan, where the governing board limited political speech in key campus venues and prohibited foreign nationals from addressing students. William Henry Hobbs, an AAUP founder who would himself attempt to restrict liberties through his work with the NSL, routinely complained that his pro-intervention speech was muzzled by campus censors. More dramatically, when 14 Michigan professors signed a petition urging US entry in April 1916, national newspapers reported that the institution was planning on disciplining them, and the AAUP inquired into the controversy. President Harry Burns Hutchins assured the AAUP that no such action was being considered. At the same time, he repeatedly warned a pro-German instructor to refrain from public comments on the war, ultimately removing him from extension service when complaints about his war speech continued.[15]

As the American public and the American professoriate rallied behind the Allied cause, initial efforts for neutrality gave way on many campuses. Though dissent remained, calls for preparedness were often succeeded by calls for intervention. By early 1917, campus-based demands for US participation were widespread, and anti-intervention efforts were further marginalized. In March, an estimated one hundred students at the University of Illinois hanged isolationist Wisconsin senator Robert M. La Follette in effigy; the student newspaper supported the action and the administration declined comment.[16] At Illinois and across the nation, many faculty and entire institutions pledged their support for Wilson's increasing move toward intervention, including his decision to arm merchant ships. At the end of March, for example, the presidents and deans of the nine largest women's colleges in the nation sent a joint resolution to Washington declaring their and their faculties' belief that "war is fundamentally wrong" but that "in a world crisis such as this, it may become our highest duty to defend by force the principles upon which Christian civilization is founded."[17] As did many others, they offered their full services to the nation.

Of the minority of academics who had not embraced the American war cause by the beginning of April 1917, a few stand out. Most prominent was Stanford University chancellor David Starr Jordan, who had stepped down from the institution's presidency to devote more time to his pacifist activities. In late March 1917, he travelled to the East Coast to work with the Emergency Peace Foundation and planned lectures in many college towns, including several under the auspices of the AUAM.[18] He was mostly met with opposition from both inside and outside of academe. Princeton's Hibben refused two students' request to allow Jordan to speak on campus, a decision that one instructor called "a violation of the most sacred trust of the university."[19] Jordan spoke at a local church instead. Columbia University allowed him to speak in order to avoid cancelling a pacifist's lecture for the second time in less than a month. At Harvard University, his talk proceeded uninterrupted, but its student organizers were assaulted by a group of classmates.[20] Yale University's president was reluctant to let him speak but relented under pressure that a prohibition would violate the institution's principles.[21] Most dramatically, Jordan's talk in Baltimore ended in a riot when an estimated four thousand people stormed the academy where it was being held. Though some details were later rebutted, the Associated Press reported, "Just as Dr. Jordan was beginning his plea for peace, the crowd of anti-pacifists, composed of business men, professors of schools and colleges in the city and students from the same, made a sally through the cordon of police and rushed the aisles of the theatre to the stage, where they demanded that the meeting cease."[22]

The difficulties involving pro-Germanism at Harvard were longer lasting but eventually resulted in a strong statement in support of professorial rights. In October 1914, a former Harvard student named Clarence Wiener wired the university and threatened to withdraw a planned $10 million bequest if outspoken psychologist Hugo Münsterberg was not dismissed from the faculty. Münsterberg, a German citizen who had recently been accused of being a German agent, offered to resign in exchange for immediate payment of half of the money to the institution. The institution's president, A. Lawrence Lowell, intervened, refused Münsterberg's resignation, and reproached him for embarrassing the institution. Both knew that even had Harvard been willing to sell its faculty's freedom, Wiener would not have been able to purchase it; despite his offer, he had little money to his name. Two years later, Münsterberg was again at the center of controversy, and calls for his removal were again widespread, this time as a result of a speech he gave in Hoboken that he claimed was widely misinterpreted. The Boston chapter of the American Rights League, led by Harvard Overseer Thayer and Harvard professor Robert C. Cabot, was among the groups that petitioned the institution to dismiss him.[23]

Lowell again resisted these calls and eventually used his annual report at the end of 1917 to argue against succumbing to the war hysteria. In a famous defense of academic freedom, Lowell argued that teachers must have full autonomy to teach within their fields of knowledge and to undertake and publish research in scholarly forums. His emphasis, though, was on extramural speech and the rights of citizenship. Lowell argued that restricting professors' speech would impose burdens unmatched by those facing other professionals and "tend seriously to discourage some of the best men from taking up the scholar's life. It is not a question of academic freedom, but of personal liberty from constraint, yet it touches the dignity of the academic career." He continued: "If a university or college censors what its professors may say, if it restrains them from uttering something that it does not approve, it thereby assumes responsibility for that which it permits them to say. This is logical and inevitable, but it is a responsibility which an institution of learning would be very unwise in assuming.... If the university is right in restraining its professors, it has a duty to do so, and it is responsible for whatever it permits. There is no middle ground."[24] Lowell thus made strong claims for the professional nature of faculty work, for the importance of institutional neutrality, and for protections from public pressures. In doing so, he advanced ideas that the AAUP had espoused in 1915 but with which it struggled during the war.

Even in 1917, Lowell's defense was rightly hailed as an important statement on academic freedom, but Harvard did not escape the war pressures unscathed. In 1914, the institution withdrew a lectureship offered to University of Berlin faculty member Kuno Meyer over his support for Ireland, alleging propaganda that violated the institution's neutrality. The following year, when Meyer objected to a pro-German publication, though, Lowell proclaimed that freedom of speech and academic freedom precluded his limiting students or faculty from expressing their views.[25] Münsterberg was protected from dismissal but was so ostracized by his fellow faculty members that he stopped attending faculty meetings and periodically withdrew more deeply. He faced threats to his life and believed that three out of every four Harvard faculty members actively sought his removal. Official neutrality on his opinions was accompanied by unofficial and pervasive scorn.[26] Münsterberg died before American entry into the war—he collapsed while giving a lecture at Radcliffe College in December 1916—but Harvard's other renowned and acknowledged Germanophile, professor and museum director Kuno Francke, felt the wrath of anti-German sentiment. Despite Lowell's appeal to stay, Francke resigned from his position in April 1917. He was officially welcome to stay, but the pressure that the Harvard community placed on him was too great to bear.[27]

War Workers

Though momentum for war had been building and preparations were already underway, the United States' April 1917 entry into the war fundamentally changed higher education. Male students left campuses in droves. Faculty increased their war work, either through official government service or participation in other related activities, including the propaganda efforts of the Committee on Public Information and the National Board for Historical Service. Colleges and universities were entirely disrupted, with one, Olivet College, closing for several years due to war-related strains.[28] Other institutions remained open but shifted their efforts and revised their curricula. By fall 1918 more than five hundred campuses had been turned over to the SATC. Faculty members were at the forefront of these shifts, pushing their institutions into action, generating materials to promote the war cause, and requesting leaves for further engagement. The dedication and contributions were such that a professor could, in a 1919 *Atlantic Monthly* article, question both the potential long-term effects of the war on higher education and whether professors would be able to readjust to their faculty positions after its conclusion. He humorously lamented:

> It is a pity that, before being discharged, the Association of University Professors cannot march down Fifth Avenue in full battle-array, headed by its own band, protected by its own airplanes soaring overhead, and by its own artillery and tanks. There should be floats bearing the trophies, the death-dealing gases and explosives, the life-saving surgical and medicinal devices, the new offensive and defensive engines of war, which have sprung from the professor's inventive brain.... To make such a pageant complete, the college presidents should line the curb to applaud the returning heroes.[29]

This overwhelming support for the war and the rapid shifting of institutional foci quickly affected academic freedom on campuses across the nation. Threats to faculty began almost immediately, as institutional presidents declared their intent to rid their campuses and the country of anyone whose loyalty was—or, at times, merely could be—questioned. Dismissals soon followed. Faculty members who had previously advocated neutrality or who supported Germany and its allies were immediately under suspicion of disloyalty, as were German nationals and German-Americans. They were pursued on and off campus by fellow faculty, institutional leaders, concerned alumni, and members of the general public. The war hysteria provided both the impetus to dismiss offending professors and the justification to remove professors who were otherwise deemed expendable.[30]

At times, entire colleges came under attack for their alleged ties to and support of Germany. Among these was Bethel College, a Mennonite institution that was founded and supported by the German-American community in North Newton, Kansas. As public pressure across the state forced German-language primary and secondary schools to close, Bethel was scrutinized for its ties to German culture; for its private academy, which was believed to keep students from the "American" public schools; and for Mennonites' faith-based opposition to war and militarism. Local vandalism and threats of violence caused students to seek shelter in the institution's administration building. The college's German-language church services were suspended for the duration of the war, and, in direct response to requests from the Loyalty League, the institution ended all German classes. College president John W. Kliewer and the faculty did so explicitly to maintain and provide robust evidence of their loyalty rather than for educational reasons.[31]

More frequent, though, were the attacks on individual faculty members. The extent of the purges will necessarily remain unknown, as the cases are complicated by the duplicity, rationalizations, and misdirection of those involved. At some institutions, faculty who were thought to be disloyal were dismissed under other pretenses, as was Simon Patten, an antiwar professor at the University of Pennsylvania who was quietly eliminated for having reached the age of retirement.[32] At others, disloyalty was the excuse used to remove otherwise objectionable personnel. The University of Maine's William E. Walz was a popular dean of the law school who frequently clashed with president Robert J. Aley and board chairman William H. Looney. In addition to struggling over standards and even the location of the law school, they were at odds because Walz would not grant Looney a law degree without sitting for coursework. Walz managed to maintain his position until January 1918, when Looney seized on Walz's well-known regard for Germany—Kaiser Wilhelm was an honorary member of the law school—and launched an investigation into his fitness for his position. On March 9, following a six-hour meeting, Walz was told to resign. When he refused, he was dismissed.[33] Certainly, the animosity toward Germany was real; Maine was one of many universities that eliminated German language instruction. More important in this case, though, were the battles for control of the law school that would continue in ensuing years.[34]

Controversies at Columbia University—which were fueled by long-standing disputes involving James McKeen Cattell, divides within the faculty, and broader concerns about academic freedom at the institution—had greater national repercussions. Cattell, though respected as a scholar, was also a polarizing figure known for his bluntness and lack of social graces. He frequently clashed with Columbia president Nicholas Murray Butler and was almost dismissed several times in the 1910s. In early 1917, his precarious tenure was made even more so when his harsh critiques of Butler became public. Leading faculty members, including AAUP leaders Dewey and Seligman, publicly rebuked Cattell, criticizing both his language and his stance. At the time, Seligman chaired and Dewey was a member of the institution's Committee of Nine, a group of deans and faculty members whom the University Council had appointed to work with the trustees to ensure protection of faculty interests. The Committee of Nine responded to the renewed threats to Cattell by intervening on his behalf, eventually convincing Cattell to sign an apology that would allow him to maintain his position while also making a claim for academic freedom. The seeming breakthrough was quickly erased by the publication of Cattell's apology, which Cattell viewed as a violation of trust. It set off a series of recriminations and accusations, including Cattell's discountenance of the committee because it was appointed rather than elected by the faculty. That summer, with two members absent, the Committee of Nine voted unanimously that Cattell was no longer fit to serve at the institution due to his personal transgressions and attitude.[35]

The case took a new and crucial turn when, in August 1917, Cattell sent a personal letter to members of the US Congress soliciting relief for conscientious objectors to the war. The letter included the university as part of his return address, thereby violating Butler's moratorium on free speech during the war. When three congressmen shared the letter with Butler, the institution had its justification to act. On October 1, the Board of Trustees dismissed both Cattell and Henry Wadsworth Longfellow Dana, an assistant professor who had been active in pacifist causes. As Carol Gruber demonstrated, the dismissals were both opportunistic acts to remove troublesome faculty members and responses to the tumult of wartime. Moreover, these were not just administrative actions. The Committee of Nine, with its faculty representatives, met in September and urged the removal of the two educators, although without referencing loyalty concerns. Others, though, objected, including Dewey, who withdrew from the committee rather than support the decision. More significantly, distinguished historian Charles A. Beard resigned a week after the dismissals, citing the autocratic control of reactionary trustees and the institution's repressive atmosphere. There was no unified protest, however, as there was neither uniform opinion nor a mechanism for collective action.[36]

The Maine and Columbia dismissals involved numerous issues and existing grudges, but other cases were more narrowly focused on claims of disloyalty. In November 1917, Franklin and Marshall College formed a committee to investigate the loyalty of long-standing professor Richard Conrad Scheidt, who had argued on behalf of his native Germany prior to US entry. In late January, when a teacher from Wellesley College's Dana Hall preparatory school claimed that Scheidt had uttered a pro-German statement, Scheidt resigned under pressure. Although the teacher soon admitted that she was mistaken and that Scheidt was innocent of her charge, Scheidt never returned to his position.[37] Some cases seem comical, except for their effects on the aggrieved and the hatred that they revealed. Wisconsin's Ernst Feise, a citizen of Germany, lost his position due to comments about a formerly pro-German colleague who had turned conspicuously patriotic: Feise suggested the colleague apply a liberty loan button to the seat of his pants so that his loyalty was apparent, even when his back was turned.[38] Other incidents were more vicious. In Ashland, Wisconsin, Northland College hired E. A. Schimler, a German-born American citizen, as a French and German language instructor in February 1918. Over the next two months, the institution's president twice investigated rumors of Schimler's disloyalty but found no evidence to support the claims. On March 31, members of the vigilante group the Knights of Liberty abducted Schimler; drove him to the outskirts of town; stole his possessions; and stripped, tarred, feathered, and abandoned him. Two days later, the college declared that Schimler was innocent of any wrongdoing but dismissed him anyway. The existence of rumors and the negative publicity that the attack had generated had ended his usefulness to the institution. Later that week, Northland's faculty publicly condemned the violence, and a public hearing on the matter confirmed that Schimler had been loyal in his campus activities. Still, his career at Northland was over, and vigilantism continued in the area.[39]

These cases and events were most frequent in the Midwest but occurred in every region of the nation and across institutional types as both internal and external actors persecuted those whose loyalty they questioned. At the University of Illinois, federal and university officials investigated a small group of progressive faculty in 1918; all were exonerated, but only one remained at the university several years later.[40] The University of Nebraska publicly investigated sixteen faculty members, dismissing three and reprimanding two.[41] University of Oregon professor Allen Eaton was forced to resign when the local business community learned that he had attended a People's Council of Democracy and Peace meeting while travelling through Chicago.[42] The University of California required students to pledge their loyalty before receiving diplomas and gave president Benjamin Ide Wheeler the "power summarily to dismiss any faculty, or employee, who voices disloyal views." At least three faculty were removed from the institution.[43] Variations of these dismissals and forced resignations took place at the Universities of Akron, Minnesota, Texas, Vermont, and Virginia; at Indiana, Ohio State, and Tulane Universities; and at Hawaii College. Occasionally, suspect faculty survived the investigations, such as at Haverford College and Hebrew Union College. At others, faculty were forced to leave for the duration of the war but allowed to return after its conclusion, including at Cornell University and Oberlin College. Elsewhere, against the professors' wishes, these temporary leaves became permanent, including at Wellesley College and the University of Michigan. And, of course, faculty were not the only campus employees forced out due to their views or alleged views on the war; the presidents of Marietta College, Martin Luther College, and Northern Arizona Normal School were among those to resign or be dismissed.[44] Certainly, many who kept their positions were silenced or otherwise impeded, as faculty across the nation were warned that only conspicuous patriotism would be accepted.

World War I concluded in November 1918, but struggles over academic freedom continued. As the country entered the First Red Scare, colleges and universities expanded their persecution of those deemed un-American to include professors suspected of harboring socialist beliefs or supporting the recent Bolshevik revolution in Russia. The situation at the University of Michigan, though extreme, demonstrates the complexity of these cases and their continuation after the fighting had ceased. During the war, AAUP founder and

NSL leader Hobbs led faculty in their attacks on their colleagues, allegations of subversion, and campaigns for dismissals. Hobbs and other professors provided the institution's trustees with evidence that was used to remove faculty whom they viewed as insufficiently loyal. Powerful alumni supported these efforts but were only partly satisfied when the university expelled suspect professors without remarking on their alleged disloyalty. As the war raged, President Hutchins broadened his attacks, first dismissing a law professor for his socialist statements and then warning of the threats posed by the growth of Communism and socialism caused by the war disruption. After the war, the attacks on both allegedly pro-German and socialist faculty persisted. In 1919, the university dismissed Edward Allen for both lingering concerns about his loyalties during the war and his continuing critique of the government. It simultaneously removed Otto Marckwardt, with engineering dean Mortimer Cooley noting that Marckwardt's socialism was his sole offense. The following year, Hutchins used his commencement address to claim that socialism had assumed Germany's place as the most dangerous enemy facing the country.[45] Of course, Michigan was not alone in these concerns over socialism and Communism, as dismissals from the University of Texas, Vanderbilt University, Rice Institute, and elsewhere demonstrate.[46] Speech was suppressed on campuses, allegedly Bolshevik tracts were removed from libraries, leftist faculty were persecuted, and fear of "un-American" elements remained. Just as, according to Gruber, "the theme of absolute good versus absolute evil was retained by simply putting the Bolshevik in place of the Hun" in the war aims courses of the era, a similar substitution threatened faculty in the years after the war.[47]

The Professors in Battle Array

These challenges placed immediate pressures on the AAUP and other organizations concerned with academic freedom and civil liberties. The AAUP's inquiry into the possibility that Michigan faculty members would be disciplined for petitioning for American entry occurred only four months after the 1915 *Declaration of Principles of Academic Freedom and Academic Tenure* was presented.[48] The association's leaders were concerned about potential threats, and Lovejoy hoped that the AAUP could forestall a wholesale retreat from scholarly norms such as had occurred in Germany. The actions against professors deemed to be insufficiently loyal after the United States' declaration of war pushed the AAUP to become much more engaged with the issue. With knowledge of at least six war-related dismissals by fall 1917 and in direct response to Cattell's situation at Columbia, Committee A on Academic Freedom and Tenure recognized both the need to respond and the dangers inherent in doing so.[49]

Correspondence among members of Committee A demonstrate the desire to uphold principles of academic freedom while also ensuring that their new organization be viewed as sufficiently patriotic. In October 1917, Lovejoy suggested that a subcommittee of conspicuously patriotic men be formed to draft a statement of principles in relation to the war, arguing that rights that existed during peace were no longer in place. These newly redefined principles could then be used as the basis for addressing wartime cases. Failure to act could diminish the progress that the AAUP had made, but acting without reasoned guidelines could prove just as dangerous. Committee A chairman Allyn Abbott Young agreed with the need to delimit academic freedom but argued that the subcommittee should produce a revised statement applicable during times of peace as well as war. He argued that legitimate limits to academic freedom should be acknowledged: professors should have the right to discuss public policy and point out benefits and flaws to different approaches but not be allowed to advocate illegal activities or interfere with federal policies. At the same time, he warned that the subcommittee should not succumb to war pressures by relenting on the insistence of the right to criticize public policies, as long as such criticism was made with the restraint suggested in the 1915 *Declaration*. Some within the association likewise recognized the precariousness of the AAUP's position. A resolute stance in favor of freedom of expression risked the appearance of disloyalty; ignoring dismissals would diminish academic freedom and due process. Either could cost the AAUP members. The situation was even more challenging, as the most famous case, that involving Cattell, was complicated by both loyalty and personality issues, raising questions over how the AAUP would be able to tease out the reasons for his dismissal without alienating large segments of its audience.[50] Others did not see reason to equivocate. The University of Michigan's Hobbs urged that a subcommittee issue a statement removing any impediments that might limit the ability of universities to dismiss disloyal faculty. George LeFevre of the University of Missouri argued that anyone whose speech embarrassed the government while at war was disloyal and that the AAUP would be significantly damaged if it claimed otherwise. While acknowledging the need for caution, the University of Wisconsin's Richard T. Ely called for the dismissal of faculty who harmed American war efforts through their speech and noted that in Germany, they would likely be "shot."[51]

Formally organized in October 1917, the Committee on Academic Freedom in Wartime was composed by Lovejoy, Young, and Princeton University professor Edward Capps after other suitably patriotic members willing to take on the task were not found.[52] The committee's final report, submitted December 24, 1917, repeatedly declared the loyalty of the writers and of the vast majority of the professoriate. Adhering to Lovejoy's rather than Young's approach, it began by noting that the 1915 *Declaration* addressed academic freedom in a time of peace, but war required different obligations: war-related restrictions on liberty should not only be expected but were also legitimate. Yet recent dismissals pointed to the contested understandings of what constituted disloyalty. The committee assumed the task of delineating what actions were inappropriate for professors to take, specifically arguing that university administrators should report alleged disloyalty to government officials but could also dismiss faculty members prior to action by the government. The committee identified four different justifiable reasons for removing a faculty member due to war-related attitudes and actions.[53] These included being convicted of violating a law related to the execution of the war; propagandizing against the war, including through statements that might lead others to resist conscription; and specifically encouraging others to refrain from voluntarily supporting the war effort through the purchase of war bonds and similar activities.[54]

The final ground dealt specifically with the members of faculties in American colleges and universities who were of German or Austro-Hungarian birth. These educators were presumed to be pro-German, and the committee recognized that it would be nearly impossible for them to drastically change their feelings toward their native countries due to American entry into the war. Their responsibility, then, was to "abstain from any act tending to promote the military advantage of the enemy or hamper the efforts of the United States; to take care not to give, by their utterances or associations, reasonable ground for the belief that they contemplate such acts or are conspiring with other disloyal persons; to refrain from public discussion of the war; and, in their private intercourse with neighbors, colleagues and students, to avoid all hostile or offensive expressions concerning the United States or its government."[55] While asking that some consideration be given to German faculty members, the report agreed that even private conversations could be grounds for dismissal, a stance exactly opposite that which the AAUP had taken two years earlier in the report on conditions at the University of Utah. More drastic restrictions were considered, including whether indifference or avoidance of conversations about the war were fireable offenses, but the committee ultimately emphasized actions rather than beliefs.[56]

The report was accepted and endorsed first by Committee A and then by the larger AAUP on December 29, 1917, with only two recorded dissensions. In a letter to Lovejoy, University of Kansas historian Frank Heywood Hodder, a member of Committee A, argued that the report had gone too far and that the AAUP should limit the acceptable grounds of dismissal to encouraging criminal activities, "abusive and scurrilous attacks" on the government, and speech that was damaging to military operations.[57] At the annual meeting, only University of Chicago classicist Elmer Truesdell Merrill opposed immediate adoption of the report, instead offering a resolution that would have printed the report and urged scholars to live up to the standards outlined in it, but would have refrained from approving dismissals without government action. Merrill was concerned that the statement would threaten academic freedom after the war and questioned whether those who were accused of disloyalty were necessarily guilty. Merrill's alternate motion evoked such a negative reaction that it helped ensure the passage of the initial report with only Merrill voting against it.[58]

The editors of the *Nation* took the AAUP to task for its new statement, claiming that it proceeded from a "false principle to conclusions fraught with almost unlimited possibilities for mischief."[59] They declared that universities, especially, must avoid imposing any restrictions not otherwise imposed by the government and that the explicit allowance for institutional intervention prior to government action was a grave error. In his published response to the editorial, Lovejoy not only repeated the committee's claims but also extended them. He argued that the AAUP had never linked academic freedom to avoiding criminal activity during peace, so there was no reason to do so during war. He noted that the AAUP never argued that academic freedom was violated when a professors was dismissed "for grave moral delinquencies, or for violations of professional ethics, or for gross and habitual discourtesy. It has, in short, never adopted the principle which appears to be the major premise of the *Nation*'s reasoning—the principle of complete academic anarchism."[60] Further indicating the conservative nature of the association and adumbrating the coming struggles of the First Red Scare, Lovejoy also claimed that pursuing the *Nation*'s plan of neutrality would foster a Bolshevik revolution in the United States. The only point on which the *Nation* and Lovejoy agreed was that professors accused of disloyalty should be given fair trials by their peers.

Although the AAUP's retreat from a staunch defense of academic freedom with its "Report on Academic Freedom in Wartime" is notable, evidence indicates that individual members were even more intimately involved with the attack on freedom. Influential members Lovejoy and Ely were among those involved in the NSL; and after the AAUP's Committee on Patriotic Service encouraged AAUP members to volunteer for the group's propaganda efforts, the two organizations were briefly formally affiliated.[61] In the summer of 1917, the NSL called on trustees at all American colleges and universities to investigate the loyalty of all faculty members, regardless of whether there were any grounds for suspicion.[62] Hobbs, both as an NSL leader and on his own, led attacks on faculty freedoms that resulted in multiple dismissals.[63] When, in the days after the war began, an Iowa newspaper printed an Indiana University faculty member's comments that German atrocities were overstated and the institution's president launched an investigation, the professor found little backing from the AAUP's most prominent member on campus: Ulysses G. Weatherly was among those who advised him to resign, noting that his "usefulness" had come to an end due to his statements.[64] In doing so, Weatherly resorted to a claim routinely challenged by the AAUP. The AAUP neither simply failed to defend academic freedom under the pressures of war nor retreated in the face of the war hysteria. Some of its members were among those who attacked the freedoms and livelihoods of their fellow professors. As such, the Committee on Academic Freedom in Wartime's suggestion that faculty could offer fair and judicial hearings for allegedly disloyal professors was dubious.

Antimilitarism and Civil Liberties

As the founders of the AAUP sought to reform higher education and improve the status of the professoriate, others organized along very different lines. In 1914, reformers Lillian Wald and Paul U. Kellogg formed the AUAM to prevent the United States from entering the war. At first, the AUAM demonstrated no interest in either academic freedom or in the larger issue of civil liberties. Rather, it was an avowedly pacifist association that used its ties to President Wilson's administration to lobby on behalf of an isolationist policy. It changed only with its failure to meet its stated purpose. Following the United States' entry into the war, AUAM executive secretary Crystal Eastman and her colleague Roger Baldwin quickly moved to oppose military conscription, defend conscientious objectors, and protect civil liberties amid the growing war hysteria. Their vocal opposition to wartime government policies was countered by Wald and Kellogg, who believed that the organization could be most effective by lobbying behind the scenes to end the war rather than by openly opposing the government or shifting attention away from a sole emphasis on peace. This disagreement led first to the creation of three separate subcommittees (on civil liberties, wartime labor conditions, and peace) and, ultimately, to Eastman and Baldwin's October 1917 creation of the independent NCLB.[65]

War-related concerns dominated the NCLB's early work, although the organization was conflicted over how best to achieve its desired ends. Eastman preferred provoking confrontations to attract attention to civil liberties issues, but others were fearful of repercussions during the war hysteria. Shortly after its founding, the NCLB announced its intentions to help pacifists and conscientious objectors but specifically noted that it would do so through legal and cooperative, rather than obstructionist, means. Despite these intentions, increasing government repression, including of the Industrial Workers of the World, led to the NCLB's more aggressive action and Baldwin's personal refusal to submit to the draft.[66] The NCLB broadened its defense of civil liberties in these early years, first under the leadership of Baldwin and then of Albert DeSilver during Baldwin's yearlong imprisonment for refusing conscription. Although the group's fight began with the threat of war, its fears were only exacerbated with the end of the war, restrictive Supreme Court rulings, the Department of Justice's raids on radical organizations, and the First Red Scare. The NCLB leadership decided to reorganize and expand to meet what it perceived to be increased demands for the protection of civil liberties, eventually resulting in the January 1920 establishment of the American Civil Liberties Union.

Focused elsewhere, the NCLB approached the topic of academic freedom as it related to World War I from a different perspective than did the AAUP. The aforementioned case of Michigan's Edward Allen is instructive. Allen appealed to the NCLB when his dean threatened his termination in the summer of 1919 for alleged disloyalty during the recently concluded war. In the aftermath of its "Report of the Committee on Academic Freedom in Wartime," with Hobbs as a key voice on campus, and with the explicit intent to focus on policies rather than individual grievances, the AAUP offered Allen little support. Years later, Allen—who remained an AAUP member, though one concerned about the association's treatment of younger faculty—would argue that the 1918 report had required propagandizing for the war, rather than protecting faculty from public opinion, and should be disavowed.[67] The NCLB was more sympathetic to his situation. In anticipation of upcoming meetings with institutional officers about his pending dismissal, Allen wrote to the NCLB asking for advice, simultaneously making his first contribution to an organization that he would serve for the rest of his life. Allen outlined the six arguments he intended to use in his defense and asked the NCLB to evaluate them. Four of Allen's arguments involved general issues of civil liberties in wartime, and a fifth argued that threatened dismissals amounted to "coercion."[68] The sixth took up the issues specifically related to academic freedom. Allen offered, "Any doctrinal requirements of teachers:—whether on political, economic, or religious matters, whether in war or in peace,—will inevitably increase the percentage of cowards and hypocrites among the faculty, and probably do more harm to the quality of the university's educational service to the State than the presence of heretics on Campus."[69] In his response on behalf of the NCLB, DeSilver agreed with Allen's argument, noting that teaching would become "sterile and stagnant" in the absence of academic freedom.[70]

In addition to offering Allen advice, the organization inquired into Schimler's tarring and feathering in Wisconsin, wrote letters protesting the New York Training School for Teachers' dismissal of Frances Isabel Davenport for her failure to sign a loyalty pledge, and pursued other similar cases.[71] In all, the NCLB identified potential violations of faculty freedoms at 20 institutions between 1917 and 1919. In 1920, the organization itself was touched by a threat to academic freedom relating to the still lingering Red Scare. Zechariah Chafee Jr. was a young law professor at Harvard University and a key early member of the organization when his articles in the *Harvard Law Review* critiquing the 1917 Espionage Act and its enforcement outraged members of the Justice Department. Chafee was investigated by federal officials, who then shared their findings with Harvard Overseer Austen Fox, who tried to use them to remove Chafee as unfit to teach. Fox's allegations against Chafee resulted in the "Trial at the Harvard Club," during which Chafee was accused of improprieties in his writings and forced to answer to the 14-member Committee to Visit the Law School. Chafee survived the trial and maintained his position, partly due to President Lowell's support.[72] The NCLB, though eager to help, was not yet in the position to provide much beyond giving advice to Chafee and other aggrieved professors. In rare instances, the organization asked a cooperating attorney to intervene on an educator's behalf, but, limited by its small staff and precarious finances, it most often wrote letters, appealed to others for help, and attempted to generate publicity.[73]

Henry Linville and the AFT

Barely more than a year old when the United States entered the war, the AFT was similarly limited on the national level and largely operated as a group of distinct but affiliated locals. And even with the 1918 changes in the organization's constitution that broadened membership eligibility and allowed for the creation of locals on college campuses, the union consisted primarily of schoolteachers in the late 1910s. The union's early efforts on behalf of academic freedom were thus mostly taken at the local level and almost exclusively involved high school teachers. The most notable of these efforts took place in New York City, where the Board of Education instituted a loyalty oath requirement for public schoolteachers. Arguing that it was unfair to make teachers pledge their allegiance when other city workers were not required to do so, New York Teachers Union (Local 5; formally the Teachers Union of the City of New York) president Henry Linville attacked the political motives of those who supported the requirement. Over one hundred teachers, many of them union members, signed Linville's petition protesting the oath on principle, while also declaring their loyalty and patriotism.[74] In fall 1917, lingering hostilities over the loyalty oath and student protests over a plan to extend the length of the school day led to investigations into the loyalty of teachers at DeWitt Clinton High School. Three Local 5 members—Thomas A. Mufson, A. Henry Schneer, and Samuel D. Schmalhausen—were suspended for allegedly disloyal statements, and six others were transferred to different schools. The union rallied to Mufson's, Schneer's, and Schmalhausen's defense, with Linville and Abraham Lefkowitz heading the efforts and others, including Dewey and Beard, lending their support.[75] These endeavors began with mass rallies and a publicity campaign in support of the teachers. After their official dismissal, the union appealed the decision and waged an 18-month court effort for their reinstatement, accruing significant debt as a result.[76] The teachers were never reinstated, but the union's efforts demonstrated that it would pursue academic freedom in a fundamentally different way than the professionally oriented and policy-focused AAUP.

The issues involved in the dismissals from DeWitt Clinton High School were complex and involved both allegations of disloyalty and concerns over the teachers' involvement in the student protest.

Linville was particularly incensed by associate superintendent John L. Tildsley's misdirection in alleging disloyalty but discharging the teachers for "conduct unbecoming a teacher." While highly nationalistic school officials sought to rid the system of allegedly disloyal teachers, the teachers involved in this case were also viewed as undesirable for other activities and characteristics. Linville noted, "If a teacher happens to be a Jew, and a Socialist, and to be personally disliked by an official, they could be removed through the euphemism 'conduct unbecoming a teacher.'"[77] Still, loyalty remained the emphasis, and, for its efforts, Local 5 was itself accused of disloyalty. Cooperating with the mainstream Schoolmasters Association, the American Defense Society published and distributed a pamphlet titled "Unpatriotic Teaching in the Schools," which attacked Linville and the union for their opposition to loyalty oaths and their defense of the accused teachers. For a short time, copies were distributed in school libraries.[78] As the war ended and the First Red Scare ensued, New York teachers were further harassed, with members of Local 5 coming under particular scrutiny. Principals discouraged union membership by claiming that it was a Bolshevik organization, the president of the Board of Education accused Local 5 of publishing treasonous literature, and the local was barred from meeting on school grounds.[79]

Most telling was the Board of Education's 1919 suspension of Benjamin Glassberg for allegedly telling a student that teachers were prevented from revealing the truth about Russia. Local 5 immediately pledged its financial support to its embattled member and, as it did for other cases during the period, enlisted noted civil liberties lawyer Gilbert E. Roe to represent Glassberg. Through legal filings, Roe and the union forced the Board of Education to provide written charges and hold a hearing in the case. At the trial, the evidence against Glassberg consisted largely of testimony from eight students in Glassberg's class—testimony that was countered by other student witnesses. While political issues were certainly involved, so too were religious divides and anti-Semitism.[80] In his defense, Glassberg read a prepared statement maintaining his innocence but refused to answer questions about his political beliefs or ties to the Socialist Party. When the Board of Education formally ruled against Glassberg, Linville noted that the outcome had been preordained but the union would continue its fight.[81] The war hysteria and subsequent Red Scare had forced the issue of academic freedom on Local 5. The union's struggles only continued as New York's Lusk Commission aggressively investigated allegations of subversion in the schools in the early 1920s.

Linville's activities caused both local and national controversy, as Local 5 was more progressive than not only many New York teachers but also the mainstream of the AFT. AFT president Charles Stillman hoped to avoid controversy and was angered by Linville's defense of the accused teachers.[82] He sought credibility and mainstream status by emphasizing issues of professionalism and by comparing teachers to doctors and lawyers, just as the founders of the AAUP had done for professors. While Linville pushed for a progressive social agenda, Stillman and others wanted to avoid militant political stands or antagonism of school administrators. This dissension was complicated by Linville's control of the *American Teacher*, the New York–based magazine that had been accepted as the "official organ" of the AFT in 1916.[83] As its editor, Linville was an often-heard and frequently controversial voice in the union. Linville's action and articles on behalf of pacifist teachers painted the union as antiwar, even though the AFT had declared itself in support of American entry. Stillman and others worried that his political stances would harm the union's reputation and impair organizing efforts.[84] Still another problem was the emphasis on New York issues and cases, which differed from the concerns of other union members. As early as the fourth convention in 1919, the AFT considered removing the *American Teacher* from Linville's control, although Linville's supporters eventually defeated the motion.[85] Growing financial troubles brought on by drastic drops in membership and exacerbated by some members' refusals to pay for the *American Teacher* in protest over its progressive stances led the AFT to suspend publication of the magazine in 1921. When the magazine was restarted a few years later, production was moved to Chicago, and Linville was not involved.[86]

The prominent role of locals in the defense efforts and the divisions exemplified by the debates over the *American Teacher* limited the national response to issues of academic freedom, but the national AFT did not avoid the issue all together. Throughout this early period, national conventions recognized threats to teachers and professors posed both by charges of disloyalty leveled against the union and by individual animus. In 1918, the convention passed a series of resolutions that pointed to both the conflicted nature of the union's response and the larger struggles brought on by the war hysteria. One linked democracy in schools to the fight for democracy in Europe and called for an end to autocracy in school and college administration.[87] Another declared the union's loyalty to the war effort and condemned "the Prussian spirit of autocracy which exists in fields of American industry and American education."[88] The same convention argued that teaching German should be continued but warned that it must be taught carefully—and by teachers who were citizens "whose loyalty to American ideals cannot be questioned."[89] Just as the AAUP had, the AFT recognized the loyalty of teachers as a legitimate issue and declared its own patriotism.

Conclusion

World War I and the ensuing First Red Scare raised new and challenging questions for burgeoning ideas of academic freedom. As part of a larger national wave of hysteria, faculty members at institutions across the nation were pursued and persecuted for alleged disloyalty during the war and in its aftermath. Institutions were not content with dismissing professors for supposedly un-American statements and activities made during the conflict; instead, they retrospectively explored the patriotism of their faculty. Professors were dismissed for comments made and actions taken before American entry, and the purges continued after the war's conclusion. Others retained their positions but were silenced, had to shift their foci and activities, and otherwise felt the brunt of calls for 100 percent nationalism. The First Red Scare likewise affected colleges campuses, both through the attacks on individual professors and through larger campaigns against alleged infiltration of socialist and Communist thinking on college campuses. The period was one of restrictions, recriminations, and hostilities that only in retrospect did many condemn. Just as professors in Germany had pledged their loyalty to their nation's cause and staked their reputations on its claims, so too did many in American higher education. Indeed, the American professoriate was instrumental in the drive for war and deeply implicated in the efforts to enforce a specific kind of exuberant patriotism.

World War I brought both new challenges to academic freedom and faculty security, and new opportunities for engagement with the topics. Facing external pressures and a membership that was committed to the war cause, the AAUP reconsidered whether higher education really should offer an "inviolable refuge" from the war hysteria, ultimately asking for reason but accepting that limitations existed during the war. Though not yet active in higher education, the AFT experienced struggles that are further revealing. At the national level, the new union was committed to the war effort and repeatedly declared the patriotism of teachers. In New York, though, Linville urged restraint and then led the defense of those accused of disloyalty during the war and in its wake. This divide between individual locals and a national leadership would continue over the ensuing decades, with important implications for defenses of academic freedom and tenure. The NCLB, itself born in protest to the repression of the era, also addressed academic freedom but had few resources to support aggrieved faculty. Although occasional claims for freedom and sanity were made, the war hysteria revealed the tenuous nature of faculty positions and raised fundamental questions about the extent to which professors and their organizations were devoted to the protection of faculty rights.

4

COMPETITION AND COLLABORATION

As the extreme hysteria of the war and its immediate aftermath slowly receded, some believed that academic freedom and faculty protections had become entrenched in American higher education. An editorial in the New York journal *Review* claimed that violations of academic freedom were extremely rare and occurred significantly less frequently than they had only a generation earlier. It went so far as to declare that Stanford University's 1900 dismissal of Edward A. Ross would by then have been nearly impossible—and Brown University's 1897 removal of president Elisha Benjamin Andrews, even less likely.[1] Despite these and similar claims, academic freedom remained far from secured, especially for outspoken faculty. In the wake of intrigues over national politics remained pernicious battles over intramural speech: at Columbia University, James McKeen Cattell's criticism of president Nicholas Murray Butler would have been problematic regardless of his actions related to the war. The seemingly autocratic administrators and trustees lambasted by Thorstein Veblen and others returned to center stage, with multiple faculty running afoul of their institutions for their critiques of institutional practices. Complaints received by the American Association of University Professors (AAUP) confirm these challenges. Between 1915 and 1919, actions resulting in appeals to the AAUP were initiated from outside of institutions almost as frequently as they were from inside, but in the 1920s, fewer than 10 percent were initiated externally. Moreover, through the late 1910s and 1920s, administrators involved in AAUP cases charged that dismissed faculty were "troublesome" in half of the cases. More frequently than in later eras, the stated reasons for dismissals included disagreements over educational policy and faculty complaints about academic autocracy.[2]

Though concerns over faculty loyalty lingered, the AAUP's considerations of academic freedom refocused on prewar issues of professionalism, unionization, and procedural protections. Calls for tenure came to the fore, as most faculty worked on one-year contracts with little recourse for nonrenewal of appointment. Committee A on Academic Freedom and Tenure remained overwhelmed with cases and struggled under the burden of investigations and policy creation. Still, as the American Federation of Teachers (AFT) sought to organize college faculty, the AAUP found further need to emphasize its professional nature and declaim any link to or support of faculty unionization. Interest in the AFT increased on college campuses in the months and years after the war but soon waned amid institutional pressures, concerns over the appropriateness of faculty unionization, and continued allegations of socialist infiltration into higher education. In New York, the AFT's closest ally was the National Civil Liberties Bureau, which reconstituted itself as the American Civil Liberties Union (ACLU) in January 1920. The ACLU and New York Teachers Union (AFT Local 5) shared membership and cooperated in ongoing battles for teacher protections. With its emphasis on civil liberties, the ACLU was concerned about nationalism in the schools and attacks on leftist faculty, speakers, and students. It was also skeptical about the AAUP's ability to address these issues.

Arthur O. Lovejoy's 1919 address as president of the AAUP captured a number of the key tensions that dominated considerations of academic freedom until the middle of the decade. He advocated for faculty roles in institutional governance and warned that low faculty salaries were fostering efforts to unionize faculty. Lovejoy cautioned that money was influencing faculty research and pleaded for assistance with the "perennial and essential" academic freedom work of the AAUP.[3] Indeed, Lovejoy had recently been pressed into duty as interim chairman of Committee A, when University of Chicago zoologist Frank Lillie resigned and no one else would assume the position.[4] Though proud of the AAUP's work in the area, Lovejoy lamented both that it limited other groups' efforts and that professors almost never resigned in protest of a wrongful dismissal, as Lovejoy himself had once done. Perhaps most importantly, he called for the widespread adoption of procedural protections for faculty on continuing appointments, claiming that such protections would end improper removals while allowing for justifiable dismissals. He concluded his discussion of academic freedom by recommending that the association heed Massachusetts Institute of Technology mathematician and AAUP general secretary Harry Walter Tyler's suggestion that the AAUP initiate meetings with college presidents to pursue shared understandings of academic freedom policies and procedures.[5] Those meetings—eventually organized under the auspices of the coordinating body for higher education associations, the American Council on Education (ACE)—would result in the AAUP and Association of American Colleges (AAC) agreeing to the 1925 *Conference Statement on Academic Freedom and Tenure,* an important but contested step toward the 1940 *Statement of Principles on Academic Freedom and Tenure.*

Unionization, Professionalization, and Civil Liberties

Though professors such as John Dewey were early members of the AFT, faculty unionization began in earnest with the founding of AFT Local 33 at Howard University only weeks after the end of World War I. Walter Dyson, a founding member and officer of the Howard University Teachers Union, later recalled the faculty who, having "fought autocracy abroad," would "fight autocracy in the schools." The Howard local sought to effect change in the governance of the institution and supported efforts to provide faculty with greater voice in the administration and stronger protections for their speech and activities.[6] Local 33 was soon followed by AFT Local 41 at the University of Illinois, organized with a progressive political agenda and concerns over faculty salaries. As its founder, historian Arthur C. Cole, told the *Christian Science Monitor,* "Unlike the followers of most professions, instructors generally are without democratic voice in determining the conditions under which they perform their services to the public. This has caused widespread academic unrest."[7] By the end of 1920, faculty had formed 20 college locals in hopes of reforming their campuses and their communities.[8]

While few in number, these new college locals quickly drew the attention of the professoriate, raising issues of faculty rights and academic freedom. By 1919, the AAUP had staked its claim as a professional association, and its leaders—through, for example, Lovejoy's lengthy critique of faculty unionization in his aforementioned annual message—turned their attention to countering the inroads made by the AFT. Members of the Missouri University Teachers Union (Local 126) who were also members of the AAUP answered Lovejoy by arguing that unionization could bring faculty in closer contact with K–12 education and allow them to enter larger educational conversations. The Missouri faculty denied the charge that affiliation would bias investigators and argued that it would be a useful counter to the existing conservative bias on college campuses. They corrected Lovejoy's misunderstanding that AFT locals could be forced to strike in support of larger union causes. The members of Local 126 also contended that Lovejoy's position was based on an unfounded fear that the AFT hoped to replace the AAUP. Lovejoy privately responded by claiming that the Missouri professors were naïve and that unionization would be extremely damaging to the professoriate and the AAUP. Even if affiliation could expand the range of perspectives aired on campuses, it would come at the steep costs of reputational damages and the perception of bias. The cause of academic freedom would be hindered by its conflation with and contamination by trade unionism.[9]

Much of the professoriate shared Lovejoy's concerns, and the AAUP rejected organized labor. Still, the AFT attempted to make inroads into higher education and sought academic freedom for all teachers. At the national level, the AFT passed resolutions in support of academic freedom but itself struggled against allegations of radicalism. At its 1919 national convention, over some members' protests that the stance was too extreme, the union resolved that "no teacher should have his position placed in jeopardy because of opinions held or expressed either in or outside of the classroom on any social, political or economic problems so long as he does not advocate violence or the use of unconstitutional methods."[10] Yet, the following year, amid continuing Red Scare pressures, the union proclaimed its loyalty but avoided issues of teacher freedoms.[11] With few members from colleges and universities and an organizational structure that emphasized local activity, the AFT could do little to help protect aggrieved college faculty. When, for example, Madison State Normal School teacher Anna Mae Brady appealed to the union for assistance after her dismissal in 1920, AFT secretary-treasurer Freeland Stecker responded that the union national left such matters up to the locals. He cited the AFT's lack of influence and the likelihood that its assistance would be seen as outside intrusion.[12]

This inability to act on behalf of Brady was indicative of the larger struggles of a union that remained in a precarious position as antiunion sentiment continued even after the worst of the First Red Scare ended. Advances by the National Education Association (NEA), disagreements within the union, and teacher contracts forbidding union affiliation caused membership to decrease by 70 percent between 1919 and 1921. These struggles were even more profound on the college level, as all but one of the college locals founded by the end of 1920 folded due to a combination of antiunion sentiment and attacks from both inside and outside their institutions—attacks that implicated the very academic freedom and role in governance that their founders sought. At Howard, concerns that alleged Communism on campus would forestall necessary federal funding led the institution to crack down on progressive voices, ending the first faculty union. At Illinois, the small local failed to gain traction and ultimately closed amid pressures from a conservative governing board, a president who claimed neutrality but had previously argued that unionization was antithetical to the profession, and an administration that was believed to spy on progressive faculty. When, in 1923, a former member complained that the institution had dismissed key union leaders in a concerted effort to destroy it, the AFT had little recourse other than to forward the information to Henry Linville for inclusion in a book on the topic that he was co-authoring with Thomas Mufson under the auspices of the New York Teachers Union and the ACLU. Similar situations played themselves out at institutions across the nation, and political pressure and faculty apathy ultimately resulted in the end of this first wave of faculty unionization.[13]

Linville and Mufson's drafted but unfinished book highlights the New York Teachers Union's cooperation with the ACLU in pursuit of shared goals, including working for academic freedom.[14] The ACLU was overseen by a New York–based executive committee, which Roger Baldwin largely selected and frequently dominated, and managed by Baldwin and Forrest Bailey. Although a national committee existed, it was largely inactive, and the organization relied on correspondents for much of its work outside the New York City area.[15] This New York base fostered links with other area progressive organizations, especially Teachers Union. Linville was an early member of the ACLU's executive committee; and Teacher Union's counsel, Gilbert E. Roe, had long been involved in civil liberties issues, including serving as an attorney for the ACLU forerunner, the American Union Against Militarism.[16] Another important ACLU leader, Harry F. Ward, helped found Associated Teachers Union of New York (Local 71), a college teachers union that separated from Local 5 in April 1919. Academic freedom was not the primary focus of the ACLU, though the organization did address the issue from its founding. The ACLU's first statement of principles included that it should oppose efforts to enforce orthodoxy among teachers.[17] Together with a book by Leon Whipple, who had been purged from the University of Virginia for alleged disloyalty during World War I, Linville and Mufson's manuscript also points to the ACLU's early emphasis on publicity and propaganda as a means of furthering its goals for teacher freedoms.[18]

With limited resources, generating attention was its best hope for achieving change.

In the early 1920s, the ACLU tracked cases of professors dismissed for alleged Communist activity, the teaching of evolution, and religious expression, as well as the 1923 forced resignation of Alexander Meiklejohn from the presidency of Amherst College. The group also attended to prohibitions on liberal speakers at institutions across the nation. Typical among these were the University of Wisconsin's 1921 refusal to allow ACLU executive committee member Scott Nearing to address a student group and Clark University's 1923 decision to do the same.[19] The organization tracked violations of student freedoms, just as it did professorial freedoms, especially emphasizing the widespread challenges to the student presses. It also pursued other educational issues that demonstrated a broad conception of educational freedom: it considered college and university policies that discriminated against African American or Jewish students to be violations of civil libertarian conceptions of educational freedom.[20] The organization became particularly concerned about the encroachment of religion into public schools and colleges, as well as the mandated displays of patriotism that might interfere with students' or teachers' rights. Those battles, though, were yet to be fought. It was not until Linville and Ward's 1924 founding of the ACLU's Committee on Academic Freedom that the organization became more fully involved in defining and protecting teacher freedoms. Even then, though, confusion remained over how its efforts related to those of the already dominant AAUP.

A Preventative, not Protective, AAUP

Despite these additional entrants into the field, the AAUP remained the most active and important organization interested in professorial freedom and tenure. Its emphasis on professional approaches slowly earned it some standing with academic administrations, though challenges remained and were sometimes profound. In particular, threats to intramural speech rights were pronounced and often the most threatening to individual careers. Although the AAUP formally recognized the legal status of faculty as employees, it argued that faculty members' ability to participate in governance was a core aspect of the profession.[21] As Joseph A. Leighton claimed in the first report of the AAUP's Committee T on Place and Function of Faculty in University Government and Administration in early 1920, "Autocratic in legal structure, the best institutions are...more or less democratic in practice."²² For the AAUP, the most pressing organizational problem was the difficulty in finding suitable and willing professors to lead Committee A and undertake its time-consuming investigations. These two issues—challenges over intramural speech and the difficulty in handling the numerous complaints—encouraged the AAUP to pursue further cooperation with academic administrators at institutional and national levels.

These challenges posed by intramural speech concerns and investigative procedures are exemplified by the struggles of Washburn College's John Ervin Kirkpatrick. Kirkpatrick's difficulties with Washburn president Parley P. Womer dated to 1915, when Kirkpatrick informed legal authorities of gambling at the state fair. Womer feared that the Kirkpatrick had endangered fundraising and forbade him from making similar reports in the future. By the end of 1918, the situation had worsened, and Kirkpatrick led a small group of faculty complaining about Womer's autocratic administrative style, his attempts to inappropriately award students academic credits in hopes of appealing to potential donors, and the departures of several faculty members under suspicious circumstances. As faculty pushed Womer to enact reform, Kirkpatrick and Womer clashed over finances and Kirkpatrick's discussion of faculty salaries with a member of the institution's governing board, an act that Womer believed was tantamount to insubordination. The unrest centered on Kirkpatrick but was widespread enough for Womer to call a special meeting of the faculty, at which he claimed to have understood faculty concerns and pledged to institute a new era of cordiality, with significant provisions for shared governance and protections against unwarranted dismissals. Less than two weeks later, the institution's governing board agreed to rewrite the college's constitution and provide faculty with greater input into governance. At the same meeting, it dismissed Kirkpatrick without a hearing.²³

Kirkpatrick and his former colleagues founded a short-lived AFT local in hopes of pressuring the institution for redress. Womer, though, claimed that its existence justified his belief in Kirkpatrick's unfitness. At Kirkpatrick's request, the AAUP investigated, eventually finding that he had been inappropriately dismissed without either formal charges or an impartial hearing. In both private and open letters, Womer and Lovejoy battled over the situation at Washburn. Womer claimed that the AAUP had no authority to investigate and would be inherently biased in favor of faculty; he explicitly drew on the AAC's arguments in favor of institutional academic freedom and against "vexels" who disrupted harmony. Yet by the time the

AAUP was ready to release its report—18 months after Kirkpatrick's dismissal—all but two of the faculty at the college urged the association to refrain. They contended that the situation had improved, that new protections were in place, and that an AAUP report would only hurt the institution. The AAUP disagreed and used the report to argue against removals based on disharmony. Though Kirkpatrick felt vindicated, he was disturbed that the report did not attract more attention. For the remainder of the decade, he continued his efforts to improve institutional governance, efforts that ultimately cost him a second faculty position at Olivet College in 1926.[24]

Kirkpatrick was certainly not the only faculty member to face such concerns, and the substantial burdens on Committee A remained.[25] Each complaint required at least some correspondence to determine whether further investigation was warranted. When it was, the process could be drawn out over months or years, as it was in Kirkpatrick's case. The ongoing challenges to staff Committee A and repeated resignations of chairmen occasionally caused lapses in the association's work for academic freedom, including in 1922, when Henry M. Bates reported that his commitments as dean of the University of Michigan Law School had prevented him from fulfilling his responsibilities as chairman of Committee A. He resigned, noting that he had neither met nor even consulted with members of the committee during the previous year.[26] The association sought only established faculty to assume these roles, believing that their credibility would provide the investigations with legitimacy. Although consistent with larger concerns of respectability, this approach limited the pool to a smaller number of already busy professors. During these transitions—and even while the group was fully staffed—a great deal of the responsibility fell to Tyler, who had been named part-time general secretary in 1922 in part to handle the taxing correspondence that academic freedom work required of the professors' association.[27] Yet some in the association urged it to serve a more prominent defensive role and argued that it should investigate each alleged violation and provide redress for each aggrieved professor. These were not, however, the goals or purposes of the AAUP. As President Armin O. Leuschner argued in 1924, the association was not designed to serve a protective function, merely a preventative one.[28] Just as importantly, AAUP leaders were concerned that Committee A's work was too dominant; further emphasis on it, especially more aggressive and confrontational action, would only harm the association's reputation for judiciousness and detract from its other work. Torn between the desire for quick action and the need for thorough investigations before acting, the AAUP struggled with how best to promote adherence to its principles.

These difficulties and differences were highlighted in the aftermath of the dismissal of seven faculty members from the University of Tennessee in 1923. The AAUP initially declined to investigate after the nonrenewal of the annual contracts of Jesse Sprowls and A. M. Withers, but the dismissals of five additional faculty members, including local AAUP chapter president Asa A. Schaeffer, prompted action. Multiple issues were involved, including challenges to the teaching of evolution, the rights of faculty members to criticize university administration, and professors' freedom to express their opinions on issues of local importance. When Committee A released its final report in April 1924, it recognized that the seven dismissals were not technically illegitimate, as all contracts had been for one year. Though it raised concerns about the methods and timing of the dismissals, the investigative committee equivocated. It noted that there may have been cause for some of the dismissals and failed to assert professors' rights to question administrative policies. The report detailed the charges leveled against the professors but did not reach conclusions about whether they were unfounded, even noting differences of opinion within the investigative committee. Most interestingly, it repeatedly observed that requesting an AAUP investigation may have factored into several of the cases, but it did not challenge the administration over this aversion to the AAUP inquiry. In all, the report raised many more questions than it answered, providing enough information to show that there were troubles at the institution but also criticizing the professors and failing to reach conclusions about the specific cases.[29]

The *New Republic* responded with a harsh critique of the AAUP's "impotent silence" on important issues, arguing that the case had revealed the association's "vital weakness."[30] To the magazine's editors, the report highlighted the shortcomings of the association's focus on the technical aspects of tenure rather than on equity and justice to professors. The report's emphasis on the professors' alleged actions was to their disadvantage, introducing allegations and personal attacks to the broader public. Many within the association shared the magazine's concerns, and several executive council members requested changes ranging from minor alterations to a complete rewriting of the report. Winterton C. Curtis, a University of Missouri zoologist who had debated Lovejoy on unionization, threatened to resign from the AAUP if the report was not retracted.[31] Yet, his reaction was not unanimously shared. Some argued that the report should be left alone, either because they were untroubled by it or because changing it would raise further problems. Revisiting this one report could endanger the trustworthiness of all other Committee A work. For an organization intent on establishing the professional and reasoned nature of its efforts, the controversy was especially vexing.

Noting "radically divergent views," the AAUP reprinted the *New Republic* article in its *Bulletin*, along with letters to the editor of the magazine written by Lovejoy and Leuschner. If the report had been so flawed, Lovejoy and Leuschner asked, how was the writer of the editorial able to determine that the situation at the institution was so troubled? Lovejoy conceded that the committee may not have been clear in its findings and might have given the institution too much benefit of doubt, but he emphasized that AAUP investigations relied on fairness and judiciousness rather than defense of faculty.[32] At the ensuing annual meeting, Leuschner noted that no report had caused as much dissension. Others, such as Cattell, viewed it as the symptom of a larger problem. He questioned the desirability of "hanging out all the underclothing of the professor on the line for everybody," even if the professor was not at fault.[33] These issues were bound with larger concerns about the roles, responsibilities, and abilities of the AAUP. Finding respected professors who could undertake detailed investigations was difficult; revisiting reports would only make it more so. Recognizing these concerns, the convention passed a resolution clarifying the original report on the University of Tennessee. While claiming merely to correct the conclusions some drew from the report rather than admitting error, this resolution clearly stated that the dismissals were inappropriate and that the seven professors were denied fair hearings. Professors, it claimed, should be guaranteed rights to intramural speech and to appeal to the AAUP, both of which were missing from the original version.[34]

Reorganization and Mediation

In the middle of the 1920s, the AAUP considered several strategies for alleviating the types of problems that plagued the investigation into the University of Tennessee. The association tried dividing Committee A along regional lines, which would have ideally allowed for easier coordination, but was unable to enact the plan.[35] The association periodically considered hiring a paid investigator to undertake much of the work of Committee A or, alternately, paying the chairs of investigative committees for their work. Paid investigators could have allowed for additional inquiries and ensured the quality of the resulting reports, a particular concern following the Tennessee report. Concerns over finances, selecting the appropriate person, and the potential overemphasis on academic freedom undid this proposal. Still, in 1926, the burdens of working for academic freedom convinced the association that professional assistance was needed. Harvard University Law School professor John M. Maguire was hired to provide legal assistance to Committee A. He did not visit campuses or undertake investigations but did help prepare the final reports and was a crucial advisor on issues involving academic freedom for most of the next 20 years.[36]

More importantly, the need to reduce investigative work and calls for assisting aggrieved faculty led the AAUP to start mediating some conflicts. In its early years, the association's efforts for mediation were informal and ad hoc, with presidents or Committee A chairmen occasionally undertaking the work as part of the initial inquiry. In December 1923, Tyler began giving the issue more consideration, and, at the ensuing annual meeting, University of Michigan professor of law and Committee A chair Herbert F. Goodrich proposed a "Committee on Mediation," which could respond to appeals from universities for advice and could prevent dramatic violations. He argued that the establishment of a separate committee would both make the association more effective in individual cases and prevent the awkward situation of Committee A first mediating and then investigating if mediation failed. Though AAUP president Joseph V. Denney supported the idea, Tyler maintained that the work was best done informally.[37] In 1925, with the issue still under consideration, Lovejoy registered his protest to the separation of mediatory and investigative roles, arguing that they were necessarily intertwined. To Lovejoy, mediation included significant fact-finding and could be done most effectively as part of an investigation. The creation of a separate committee would both make Committee A look ineffective and taint it as aggressive and biased.[38] As an alternative, Tyler proposed the identification of local chapter heads or former Committee A or council members to whom cases could be referred for mediation. By the following year, mediation was a formal part of the process, although there is no evidence that the network Tyler had suggested was ever organized. Rather, it was left to the general secretary to intervene and recommend a personal conference between a Committee A member or local officer and an administration in hopes of making an adjustment in lieu of a full investigation. While this increase in the mediatory functions of the AAUP was intended to answer complaints that the organization did not do enough to assist faculty members with grievances, the backstage nature of these mediations failed to alter this perception.[39]

These structural changes in Committee A emphasize the heavy responsibilities of efforts for academic freedom and tenure. The association increasingly responded to calls that it intervene in more cases by working behind the scenes to help alleviate tensions and secure positions. Maguire also convinced the association to further supplement full-scale investigations and mediation efforts with statements of facts when these were not in question. These statements helped build "a body of common law" to support AAUP efforts.[40] Throughout this period, AAUP leaders assured members that the association's judicious and unbiased work was having influence, even as they privately noted some occasional shortcomings. Relying on testimony from administrators and pointing to behind-the-scenes efforts, Tyler, Lovejoy, and the succession of Committee A chairmen and AAUP presidents were convinced that the conservative and collaborative policy was the most effective.[41] Although it would be challenged at the end of the decade, this approach was most clear in the AAUP's work with the AAC.

The AAC's Commission on Academic Freedom and Academic Tenure

As the AAUP worked through these difficulties with its Committee A work and began to search for a collaborator, an evolving AAC emerged as a potential partner. In the years immediately following its 1917 critique of the AAUP's 1915 *Declaration of Principles of Academic Freedom and Academic Tenure*, the AAC paid little attention to academic freedom. Things began to change at the organization's 1921 meeting when the assembly heard from Committee A chairman Roy C. Flickinger, who spoke about the challenges faced by the AAUP, and the AAC and Council of Church Boards of Education formally established a joint Commission on Academic Freedom and Academic Tenure.[42] This commission increased AAC activity and, the following year, prepared a report specifically designed to be the basis for future joint understandings of academic freedom and tenure. Reporting for the commission, Oberlin College dean Charles N. Cole lauded Committee A's work and its setting the stage for collective action on behalf of academic freedom. Although the commission recognized that it could not enforce new standards among AAC members, it sought to further the cause of academic freedom by outlining ideals and promoting responsible measures for protecting both faculty and institutions from unjust actions or accusations thereof.[43]

The commission blamed problems involving academic freedom on both institutional conditions and individual faculty members, noting that they always implicated tenure issues (though not all violations of tenure implicated academic freedom). Colleges were often beholden to financial interests that found certain positions indefensible and could make the teaching of related topics untenable. Moreover, the commission concurred with the 1915 *Declaration*'s identification that student immaturity necessitated special care in classroom teaching but argued that the opposite often happened; professors too often responded to immaturity by commenting on topics beyond their expertise needlessly and without proper restraint. With direct reference to Tyler's 1920 article calling for organizations of administrators to work with the AAUP on shared understandings and codes of conduct, the commission proposed four conventions aimed to protect academic freedom and an additional four to protect academic tenure. As for academic freedom, colleges were to refrain from limiting professors' research unless it was so time-consuming that it prevented them from fulfilling their more important teaching responsibilities. Colleges were urged to allow freedom in teaching, except where student immaturity or previously agreed-upon institutional characteristics prevented the consideration of certain topics. When controversy resulted from teachers discussing topics unrelated to the course materials in their classrooms, the report contended that institutions were not required to support offending teachers. Finally, colleges were called upon to acknowledge professors' rights to free speech outside the classroom, though with the caveat that institutional reputations needed to be protected from serious injury. With respect to academic tenure, the AAC's commission acknowledged the value of "recognized permanency of greater or less degree" and called for its assurance following a probationary period, except in cases of disloyalty, immorality, or extreme neglect of duties. Dismissals during short-term and probationary appointments were to be allowed without cause, although a minimum of three months' notice was proposed. The report argued that fair hearings, including testimony from professional disciplinary experts, should be standard in cases of alleged incompetence and that the involvement of both faculty and governing boards was called for in dismissal proceedings except in cases of admitted disloyalty or immorality. Finally, while financial exigency was a legitimate reason to remove a tenured professor, it should be used only as an option of last resort.[44]

The AAC had earlier been critical of the AAUP's efforts, but the similarities between the AAC's conventions and the AAUP's 1915 *Declaration* are striking. Both organizations called for the establishment of academic freedom policies and, correspondingly, tenure as a means of protection. Both argued for professorial freedoms inside and outside classrooms but allowed for limitations due to student immaturity and recognized institutional doctrines. Both noted that professors did not give up the rights of other citizens, although their professional obligations did require that they be temperate and judicious. Both called for faculty involvement in reappointments and dismissals, probationary periods before the assumption of continuous appointments, a minimum of three months' notice on nonreappointment prior to tenure, and fair hearings including expert professional testimony prior to dismissals. Although the AAC decided not to create its own investigative committee analogous to Committee A, it did call upon the ACE to bring together the educational associations to cocreate principles of academic freedom, setting the stage for joint action.

These developments were important and portended future collaboration. In January 1923, Charles N. Cole again emphasized the need for faculty and administrators to work together to overcome the vagueness in standards and policies that led to controversies. Still, he reported that many of the AAC's member institutions had sectarian ties that could rightfully influence the perspectives aired on their campuses. At the same time, they did not consider themselves proprietary and thus could not conform to the expectations of the 1915 *Declaration*. Further, the AAUP's "Report on Academic Freedom in Wartime" had acknowledged limitations on freedom, and Cole argued that analogies between the national war issues and local religious concerns could be made. He asked, "What college or university would, under the banner of academic freedom, permit its professors to teach atheism, or advocate the substitution of polygamy or free love for the family, or urge the destruction of all government?" Cole's commission recognized the rights of institutions to set their own policies and impose corresponding restrictions. The conventions proposed the previous year were specifically designed to promote greater freedom by providing a balance between competing interests. The AAC's role was to lead these institutions to appreciate greater, though not unrestrained, freedom.[45]

The need for this advocacy of academic freedom was evident in the results of a survey of its member institutions that the commission had undertaken. The overwhelming majority of the one hundred respondents agreed that professors should have unrestricted freedom in research, but fewer than half believed that they should possess similar freedom in teaching. Just over two-thirds argued for restrictions based on religious, political, and economic beliefs, while a similar percentage believed student immaturity necessitated limits. The majority denied faculty members' rights to speak of controversial subjects in classrooms if they were unrelated to the course material. Respondents were more conflicted on the issue of external speech. Although almost 75 percent agreed that faculty members had the same rights to free speech as other citizens, a nearly identical percentage indicated that colleges had the right to restrict such freedom if they foresaw that it would offend their constituencies. While the overwhelming majority of respondents agreed with the ideas of tenure, due notice, and written charges before dismissals, only a narrow majority believed that faculty should be entitled to hearings by their peers prior to discipline. The vast majority believed in consulting faculty on appointments and dismissals, but only a slim majority agreed that faculty should have official roles in the process. The AAC membership recognized the importance of academic freedom, tenure, and faculty input on academic issues, but they also believed in limits to both faculty rights and faculty governance. Still, the membership acceded to the commission's recommendation of the formal adoption of the previous year's report.[46]

As Walter P. Metzger demonstrated, part of the shift in tenor and approach of the AAC in the early-to-mid 1920s was the shift in membership of the organization. Though the small conservative colleges that had founded the AAC were still central, they were no longer the only members of the AAC. It had expanded to include nationally respected private colleges and universities whose representatives helped move the organization away from an insular, protective view of academic freedom.[47] In 1923, the membership of the AAC expanded again, as the organization voted to allow liberal arts colleges of large universities to gain membership. Seven such colleges were admitted to membership by the following year's meeting, fundamentally affecting the AAC's work for academic freedom. Representatives of the University of Michigan and other large universities assumed leadership roles on the Commission on Academic Freedom and Academic Tenure. The AAC was becoming a viable and attractive partner for AAUP efforts to create agreed-upon standards for academic freedom.

Duplication, Cooperation, and the ACLU's Committee on Academic Freedom

Though the ACLU had expressed interest in academic freedom since its reorganization, its level of engagement was not enough to foretell that its first permanent committee on any topic would be the Committee on Academic Freedom, planned in the spring and summer of 1924 and announced later that fall. This new committee, which was led by Ward and Linville, was created with explicit recognition of the AAUP's efforts and an appreciation of both the value and shortcomings of its professional approaches. When first considering the idea, Baldwin reached out to the AAUP, asking for any materials on the topic and even if there was an agreed-upon definition of the term.[48] Ward and Linville then relied on the tripartite understanding of academic freedom arising from the 1915 *Declaration*.[49] Yet the ACLU also believed the AAUP's definition to be limiting, as it did not include issues of student speech, did not apply to external speakers, addressed only higher education, and emphasized tenure and procedural protections. A broader approach to academic freedom would include explicit attention to legislative initiatives that limited freedom, an extension of student and teacher rights to all levels of education, and an effort to counter militaristic propaganda in the public schools.[50] Ward and Linville, though arguing for this broad understanding, also defined their work more narrowly than did the AAUP. They believed that freedom of research was only rarely threatened and that only educational organizations could define and defend appropriate speech in classrooms. As such, the ACLU claimed it would focus its efforts on free speech issues, leaving the rest to the AAUP.

Still, in August 1924, when the ACLU invited faculty to join its new committee—for the purposes of legitimizing committee leaders' work—several potential members turned down the offer, citing their fear of interfering with Committee A's work. Even those who agreed to join sometimes saw the possibility of duplication, including Wellesley College professor Vida Scudder, who accepted the offer but knew that she would need to be able to explain how the ACLU's work would differ from that done "rather elaborately" by the AAUP. University of California professor Jessica Peixotto responded to the invitation with a more pressing concern: if Committee A was itself unsuccessful despite its efforts and knowledge of higher education, how could the ACLU possibly expect to succeed? In their responses, Baldwin and fellow ACLU leader John Haynes Holmes critiqued the

AAUP, its focus, and its lengthy investigative process. Baldwin wrote to University of Chicago law professor Ernst Freund that the ACLU regretted having to address academic freedom but felt compelled to do so because of its members' complaints about the AAUP's narrow scope of work and "dilatoriness." Holmes assured Scudder that there would be little duplication: Committee A undertook lengthy and meticulous investigations, but the ACLU would act quickly in response to an immediate threat. To Peixotto, he suggested that her very recognition of the AAUP's ineffectiveness demonstrated the need for the ACLU to act.[51]

In his correspondence with officers of the AAUP, Baldwin was more deferential. After explaining that he foresaw the ACLU committee focusing on student issues, he noted that there might be occasion for them to work on behalf of dismissed educators. These cases would, however, be rare at the collegiate level. He assured Allyn Abbott Young that the ACLU would not interfere with the AAUP and disclaimed any attempt to "embarrass" the association.[52] Young responded by welcoming the ACLU's efforts to ensure student freedoms and encourage free exchanges on campus, seeing little downside and a possible benefit. His support, though, was equivocal. In a postscript to his letter, Young argued that the ACLU should involve itself in professorial academic freedom cases only if the AAUP "falls down badly."[53] The AAUP's Tyler was more encouraging of the ACLU's efforts, noted the heavy workload of Committee A, and asked for the ACLU to maintain communication with Committee A. In his first communication with Baldwin a few days later, Committee A chair Goodrich actually encouraged the ACLU to intervene in a potential violation of academic freedom in Kansas.[54]

ACLU concerns over duplication and its desire for quick action demonstrated themselves in both the draft plans for the ACLU Committee on Academic Freedom and the public announcement of the new committee. So, too, did its alarm over nationalism and militarism in the schools and the belief that addressing educational liberties could bolster its broader civil liberties work.[55] In June, Ward and Linville coauthored "Freedom of Speech in Schools and Colleges," which offered the organization's "legal and publicity services" to students and educators who were attacked for their beliefs. In the event of a violation, the ACLU could assist by organizing protests immediately, publicizing the action in local and national media, and investigating the event so that additional details could be distributed. In doing so, they would offer a more aggressive approach than that of the AAUP, although one that also had the potential to cause difficulties. For the ACLU and other organizations, protesting and publicizing before gathering all the facts would prove troublesome in ensuing years.⁵⁶

Discord at Syracuse University the following spring helps demonstrate the difficulties facing the ACLU. In his May 1925 letter agreeing to serve as a local correspondent for the ACLU, Syracuse faculty member Hugh L. Keenleyside informed the organization that academic freedom was threatened at his institution. ACLU secretary Lucille B. Milner asked Keenleyside to investigate, but the professor declined both because he was involved and because his Canadian citizenship might leave any report that he made open to attack. Keenleyside did, however, outline the situation at the institution, including alleging restrictions on liberal student organizations, widespread faculty departures due to a domineering administration, and faculty dismissals based on advocacy for birth control and support of Robert M. La Follette's 1924 presidential campaign. Though the ACLU was convinced of problems at Syracuse, the organization was reluctant to act. Other pressing involvements were consuming its energies, and its leadership believed that they had little standing with a private institution. Thus, the ACLU encouraged prominent alumni to protest the limits on academic freedom and appealed to the AAUP to look into the matter. The latter consulted its local chapter and received assurance of "perfect academic freedom" at the institution. The ACLU was unable to pursue further action but privately derided the AAUP's decision not to investigate and further questioned its effectiveness. To the ACLU, the AAUP had, indeed, fallen down on its job.⁵⁷

Though the ACLU's interactions with the AAUP were conflicted, the important role that Linville played in both the ACLU and New York Teachers Union promoted a natural local alliance. This partnership was apparent in the two organizations' overlapping efforts for academic freedom in several cases involving high school teachers, most notably that of Benjamin Glassberg. In 1919, despite the protest of Teachers Union, the New York City Board of Education dismissed Glassberg for disloyalty, based on alleged comments about the State Department and the Russian Revolution. Glassberg secured employment at the socialist Rand School of Social Science but, retaining his desire to regain his former position, continued to appeal to state and local educational leaders for reinstatement. In 1923, state commissioner of education Frank Graves informed Glassberg that, although there were no legitimate grounds to deny Glassberg a position, his ties to Linville and the New York Teachers Union worked to his detriment. Graves informed Glassberg that his disassociation from leftist causes and radical politics was the only condition under which he would be able to teach again in New York schools.[58] The following year, New York City Board of Education member Arthur Somers, who five years earlier had overseen the dismissal, was more sympathetic. He blamed the firing on the excesses of the First Red Scare and unsuccessfully advocated Glassberg's cause at a meeting of the board. The ACLU blamed a combination of anti-Semitism and the American Legion's influence for the board's refusal to reinstate Glassberg. The organization appealed the decision, but the following summer Frank Dilbert, acting commissioner, denied it.[59]

Though involving K–12 schools rather than higher education, Glassberg's case is instructive in several ways. His 1919 dismissal was precipitated by charges related to disloyalty. Although the urgency of these issues had passed by the mid-1920s, patriotic groups such as the American Legion were still influential enough to affect the careers of heterodox educators. Some, including Somers, stepped back from the nationalistic fervor that had existed in the aftermath of the war, but others did not. In denying Glassberg's petition, Board of Education president George J. Ryan stated that he "would rather see 1,000 criminals pardoned than to take a chance of permitting one man with un-American doctrines to mould the character of our children."[60] Moreover, the case demonstrates the close ties between the ACLU Committee on Academic Freedom and Teachers Union, as Linville acted on behalf of both organizations and ensured the sharing of information. In 1924, the two organizations cosponsored a public rally in support of Glassberg following the Board of Education's refusal to rehear his case. Even though the state constitution proscribed appealing Dilbert's decision, the two organizations shared the expense as they collaborated to pursue legal redress. A victory for organizational collaboration, these joint efforts were a legal failure, thus ending Glassberg's career in New York City schools.[61]

The 1925 Conference on Academic Freedom and Tenure

As the ACLU increased its efforts and the AAC liberalized its positions, the AAUP continued its pursuit of shared understandings of and procedural protections for academic freedom. Its emphasis on professionalism and scholarly expertise precluded working with the AFT, and its preferred partner, the Association of American Universities (AAU), continued to demur.[62] At the 1921 AAUP annual meeting,

ACE president Samuel Capen encouraged the AAUP to consider the AAC as a suitable collaborator. With the endorsement of Committee A chair Frederick S. Deibler, who believed that partnering could reduce the burden on his overworked committee, the AAUP assembly endorsed the idea of working together with the AAC and other organizations under the ACE, as soon as opportune.[63] With shifts in the AAC's approach and membership, the timing was right by the end of 1923. Committee A chair Goodrich and the AAC's Cole quickly concurred that cooperation would be fruitful and that a revised version of the AAC's published report could serve as its basis.[64] At the AAC annual meeting a few weeks later, Cole reported that, during his meeting with Goodrich, the two had realized that their associations had "no fundamental difference of view" and that they should jointly work with other national associations to establish shared principles and policies.[65] The following autumn, Tyler, who had recently been elected president of the ACE, agreed with Goodrich's suggestion to organize a larger meeting of interested professional associations under the leadership of the ACE. He likewise agreed that the basic principles should be agreed upon ahead of time.[66]

On January 2, 1925, representatives from six additional organizations—the AAU, American Association of University Women (AAUW), Association of Land Grant Colleges (ALGC), Association of Urban Universities, National Associations of State Universities (NASU), and Association of Governing Boards of State Universities (AGBSU)—joined those from the AAC, AAUP, and ACE in Washington, DC, to act upon the groundwork laid by Cole and Goodrich, neither of whom was present. Tyler ran the meeting, which began with statements by representatives of the only three groups that had formally addressed academic freedom. AAUP president Leuschner reported on his association's interest and activity, while also advocating the benefits of cooperation among faculty, administrators, and trustees.[67] The AAUW's Mary Van Kleeck, a Smith College faculty member and labor activist who would later become an ACLU leader, raised issues about standards of scholarship, measurement of teaching, requirements for promotion, and women's advancement relative to that of men.[68] John R. Effinger, a dean at the University of Michigan and the new chairman of the AAC Commission on Academic Freedom and Academic Tenure, presented the four conventions that his association had agreed upon. These were then considered individually, with minor revisions and additions made by the assembled representatives. A subcommittee of Capen—by then the chancellor of the University of Buffalo—Lovejoy, and Effinger incorporated these revisions into a final version of the document, which was adopted later that afternoon and then referred to the individual organizations for approval.[69]

The final version of this document differed from the original AAC convention in small but important ways. The committee removed assertions indicating that teaching was the primary purpose of a college and that limitations on academic freedom due to the religious character of an institution were evidence of "weakness" and should be abandoned as soon as possible. Moreover, the strictures involving teaching were strengthened to include that educators were "morally bound" not to introduce irrelevant and controversial topics in their classrooms. In doing so, the committee placed the onus on the teacher, rather than merely indicating that the school was not obligated to help. The final convention on academic freedom underwent the most significant revisions and included some changes beneficial to faculty. Faculty free speech was no longer limited by the need to protect institutions. Rather, speech that raised serious concerns about a professor's "fitness" should be referred to a faculty committee for consideration. Although the clause left open the possibility that a faculty member's extramural speech could be used as a reason for dismissal, it shifted the emphasis and increased faculty input. The final convention further asserted that faculty members speak for themselves and tempered the need for professors to be "scrupulous" in making this clear in all external speech and writing by instead calling on professors to "take pains" to do so when necessary.[70]

The four conventions on tenure underwent greater revision. Most of the first convention's language dealing with initial temporary appointments, increasing ranks, and eventually indefinite tenure was replaced with the simple statement that the length and expectations of appointments should be agreed to in writing, thus undermining the potential for a set tenure track. The convention requiring three months' notice for nonreappointment was retained with the minor changes of encouraging notification at the earliest possible date and faculty reciprocation with early notice if they chose to leave. Immediate termination was still allowed in cases of "gross immorality or treason," a slight yet significant modification from the earlier "gross immorality or disloyalty to the country." Other dismissals remained acceptable when initiated with action of both a governing board and faculty committee, although a professor's right to "face his accusers" was inserted. Finally, the committee strengthened the protections afforded permanent faculty by revising the language on appointments during financial exigency, although without outlining the economic conditions that would make dismissal for financial reasons acceptable. In all, it made a case for academic freedom for faculty who operated within established bounds and made a strong case for tenure protections for established professors. At the same time, it was silent on how long a probationary period should be, thus avoiding comment on the continued existence of long-term instructors and assistants.[71]

One week after the conference, the AAC adopted this modified version of its own conventions. In presenting them, Effinger noted the benefits that would accrue when the various educational organizations each adopted identical statements on academic freedom and tenure.[72] Effinger's confidence was misplaced: no other organization officially adopted the 1925 *Conference Statement* as its overarching policy, and even the AAUP's eventual acceptance was provisional. The other organizations did not even go this far. The ACE later reported that it was the convener of the conference and was not itself in position to consider the issue. The AAUW argued that its committee was designed to investigate the topic, not adopt a report. The AAU, claiming that leading institutions already had the situation under control, referred the statement to individual member institutions, only a few of which specifically addressed it. The NASU and AGBSU similarly stated that such policy was beyond the scope of their activities, while the ALGC deferred consideration of the statement due to differences of opinion.[73] As Walter Metzger argued, the 1925 conference was "an AAC-AAUP affair through and through and the others were merely extras placed in seats to lend the *mise en scène,* an air of fullness."[74]

Though the inaction of other associations was disappointing to Tyler, it could be understood as a result of this emphasis at the conference on the AAC and AAUP. The AAUP's tepid support for the 1925 *Conference Statement,* though, is more striking and revelatory. After all, Tyler had been working toward a joint statement since 1917, and the association had been actively engaged in the preconference negotiations. As president of the ACE, Tyler called the meeting only when he believed that an agreement was forthcoming, yet the AAUP could not entirely support the resulting provisions for academic freedom and tenure. Perhaps the most contentious aspect of the 1925 *Conference Statement* was the inclusion of "treason" as reasonable grounds for immediate dismissal. In the aftermath of the violations of academic freedom during World War I, in which the AAUP was complicit, some members were concerned that the inclusion of such a term could lead to future difficulties. Dewey was particularly bothered, warning Lovejoy that use of "treason" in anything but a "purely technical" manner might result in faculty seeing a return of the excesses that characterized the war period. Lovejoy responded that he did not think that the word would be a problem, as he had insisted on just such an understanding at the meeting. Moreover, he reported that the term had been included at the specific request of the AAC representatives, who believed that their association would not endorse the statement if it was removed. In ensuing years, this single word would remain problematic and contribute to the ultimate articulation of the 1940 *Statement*.[75]

The compromise statement was problematic enough for AAUP leaders to consider appealing to the AAC for revisions, and Tyler refused to distribute the document to individual chapters for consideration.[76] At its December 1925 meeting, the association debated the statement but failed to adopt it, instead passing a resolution praising the effort and proposing another conference. Tyler apologized to Effinger for the faint resolution and, elsewhere, noted his disappointment that some members' belief that the statement was too weak had prevented the AAUP's full endorsement.[77] When the issue was raised at the annual meeting in 1926, Lovejoy argued that the document was merely a minimum standard, not a definitive statement on everything desired.[78] The AAUP then passed a resolution expressing its "general approval" of the 1925 *Conference Statement*, with the added caveat that it be interpreted based on the AAUP's previous statements. The AAUP would, in the next decade, argue that the statement was a historic step toward ensuring academic freedom, but it remained unsatisfied. So, too did the AAC, if for other reasons.[79]

In the years immediately after the 1925 conference, the AAC and the AAUP continued informal relations regarding academic freedom. Effinger's election as the president of the AAC encouraged AAUP leaders to believe that further advances were possible, although little formal action was taken. The associations sent representatives to each others' meetings and expressed appreciation for the collegiality experienced. Western College for Women president William W. Boyd, who replaced Effinger as head of the AAC commission in 1926, was an avid proponent of the 1925 *Conference Statement* and continued cooperation. He encouraged member institutions to adopt the principles formally and was disappointed when a survey of college presidents found that 86 of 97 institutions had not considered the conventions even though most respondents indicated support for the general principles. In 1927, Boyd's commission sent copies of the 1925 *Conference Statement* to presidents of all the AAC institutions, asking that they be distributed to each member of the institutions' governing boards. Few agreed to do so. While some indicated that their institutions were in sympathy with the resolutions, many did not want to introduce the issue to their boards. Perhaps most troubling for Boyd was that some who had initially voted to accept the resolutions were now opposed to them. Boyd determined that he had done all that he could to further the ideals of academic freedom and tenure. At its meeting in January 1929, the AAC agreed to Boyd's suggestion to discharge the Commission on Academic Freedom and Academic Tenure. It would be several years before the weaknesses of the 1925 *Conference Statement* and the increasing frictions of the 1930s would cause the AAC to reconsider the issues and again work toward joint understandings with the AAUP.[80]

Conclusion

These years after World War I were crucial for the development of academic freedom even though organizations advocating for it experienced difficulty finding their footing. Recognizing both that intramural speech issues were rampant and that it would never be able to address all of the cases it faced, the AAUP continued and expanded its emphasis on tenure, formal dismissal policies for faculty, and a role for faculty in institutional governance. These efforts at first appeared to have a salutary effect, as a 1921 Committee A survey of AAUP members revealed an increasing number of institutions with policies on tenure and dismissal hearings. The committee found that the principles it espoused were being accepted and adopted by increasing numbers of institutions, especially private institutions that were unencumbered by legislative interference. Noting the similarity in language between AAUP statements and institutional policies, the committee concluded: "It would seem, then, that gradually and with no blare of trumpets, the Association has been a potent influence in formulating an opinion in respect to the proper professional standing of the instructional staff of our colleges and universities; in determining what protection is necessary to promote research and the promulgation of truth; what procedure in terminating contractual relations is in keeping with the vital interest of the teacher or research student, and the dignity of the institution."[81] By working judiciously, reaching out to college and university administrators to cooperate, emphasizing the duties and obligations of faculty members, and demonstrating a willingness to issue reports denying faculty members' claims, the AAUP was establishing itself as a respectable voice in faculty issues.[82]

Though pleased with these individual institutional commitments, the AAUP recognized the need to create broader, overarching understandings and procedures. First on an ad hoc basis, and then under the umbrella of the ACE, the professors' association worked with the AAC to generate principles that could be widely espoused and shared. In 1925, representatives from these associations and additional higher education associations agreed to a set of conventions for both defining and protecting academic freedom. A unified stance on academic freedom and tenure was, however, not as easy to achieve, as only the AAC endorsed it at its ensuing meeting. The AAUP debated whether the statement was strong enough, considered attempting to renegotiate, and, finally, offered a tepid approval of the document as a minimum standard rather than final understanding.

The lack of unanimity on the 1925 *Conference Statement* highlights the profound difficulties remaining in the pursuit of faculty rights and protections. Committee A was inundated with work and unable to handle all of the cases it was asked to consider. As some inside the organization grew increasingly disturbed by the association's emphasis on lengthy investigations designed to promote policy development, the association began mediation to help ameliorate difficulties. More broadly, although the First Red Scare subsided, extremes in nationalism could still pose dangers to students and faculty. The inclusion of treason as a legitimate reason for dismissal in the 1925 *Conference Statement* exemplified its perniciousness and portended difficulty for progressive faculty in the years ahead. It was these progressive faculty who were most often the focus of the efforts of the AFT and ACLU. The latter, especially, increased its activity in the middle of the decade, offering a broad understanding of academic freedom for faculty, students, and speakers at all education levels. At the same time, it limited its activities to countering propaganda, opposing legislative restrictions on teaching, and protesting threats to extramural speech. Soon, it became the leading opponent of the threat of antievolutionism that had been growing in the South and Midwest in the late 1910s and early 1920s. And although the AAUP eschewed the "blare of trumpets," the ACLU and AFT maintained that public protest was an important strategy for helping dismissed teachers and faculty, one that it found more valuable than lengthy and judicious, even dilatory, investigations. This tension between quick action on limited evidence designed to aid individual faculty members and time-consuming investigations for larger procedural purposes would remain the key feature of organizational efforts to define and defend academic freedom until the AAUP and AAC endorsed the 1940 *Statement*.

5

Freedom of Teaching in Science

Deep in the March 13, 1922, edition of the *St. Louis Dispatch* was a short editorial comment on a recently resolved row in the Kentucky state legislature. The banality of the piece's heading, "A Close Call," was offset by a striking opening sentence that spoke to the amount and tone of national attention the situation had received: "Freedom of thought in Kentucky has been saved by a score of 41 to 42."[1] That score was the final tally of the Kentucky House of Representatives' vote defeating a bill to ban the teaching of evolution in the state's public schools, colleges, and universities; as the *Washington Post* reported, "Darwin Wins by One Vote."[2] Although the vote capped two months of fervent national interest in the proposed legislation, it did little either to quell the larger movement to ban the teaching of evolution in American schools and colleges or to subdue the attacks on faculty whose views offended fundamentalist Christians, especially in Southern and Midwestern states. Indeed, in his 1923 address as the president of the American Association of University Professors (AAUP), Ohio State University dean Joseph Villiers Denney called fundamentalism "the most sinister force that has yet attacked freedom of teaching."[3] Denney noted recent dismissals of faculty for their views on evolution but claimed that the danger was far more widespread and pernicious than even a dozen lost positions could indicate. Warning of "an un-American spirit of intolerance and fanaticism," Denney attributed the challenges to external religious groups that pressured colleges and to state legislators who proposed restrictive legislation.[4]

The leaders of the fundamentalist movement against evolution in schools lacked neither conviction nor bombast. William B. Riley, Baptist minister and president of the Northwest Bible and Missionary Training School, called the first meeting of the World Christian

Fundamentals Association (WCFA) in May 1919 "an event of more historical moment than the nailing up, at Wittenberg, of Martin Luther's ninety-five theses."[5] These leaders were also confident of their primary target. As Wheaton College (IL) president Charles A. Blanchard highlighted at the same conference, "infidelity, atheism, [and] anti-Christianity are making such inroads into higher and professional education of our time, it is the duty of all Christian preachers and parents and young people to know what the teaching of the schools in which they are interested is." His committee on education called on Christians to support only colleges that adhered to the biblical account of creation and to avoid all other "infidel, atheistic education."[6] Though some, including Thomas Theodore Martin, were as concerned about evolution in high schools, Blanchard's emphasis on higher education was not unique; the same year, in *The Crisis in Church and College*, George Wilson McPherson declared that "America has been an orthodox, an evangelical country, the home of robust faith and glowing Christian love, until some decades ago when our universities began to flirt with German, British, and French rationalism and infidelity, and New England Unitarianism, since which time there has been a growing unrest, a religious deterioration, a marked downgrade movement, all of which began in the university. The teacher was then as to-day, our problem, and our most responsible citizen."[7] Indeed, despite the popular image of antievolutionist attacks on public K–12 schools, much of the effort was actually aimed at restricting the teaching of evolutionary theory in colleges and universities.[8]

Of course, the WCFA was not the only organization involved in the controversies. Groups such as the Anti-Evolution League joined with its efforts, but the Science League of America and other groups were formed in opposition to the increasing threats of legislative interference with science education. College presidents acting on their own initiative or with an informal group of peers often played key roles at the state level. The AAUP founded a new committee to address the situation—Committee M on the Freedom of Teaching of Science—and worked with the American Association for the Advancement of Science (AAAS) to provide scientific opinions on the necessity of teaching evolution in schools and colleges. The most significant anti-antievolution organization was, though, the American Civil Liberties Union (ACLU), which sought test cases to challenge the constitutionality of the laws. Its role in John T. Scopes's famous 1925 trial in Dayton, Tennessee, is well known, but the organization's efforts did not end with the overturning of his conviction on a technicality. The ACLU continued to search for a test case, especially in Arkansas, where a 1928 law against teaching evolution in the state's schools and colleges was passed by a public referendum. These efforts, which appeared to bear fruit with the conditional agreement of an Arkansas Agricultural and Mechanical College science teacher to violate the law, fell apart and were eventually suspended in 1931. Although the immediate threat had passed, the issue remained ultimately unresolved until it returned to the fore in the 1960s.

FUNDAMENTALISM AND THE FEAR OF MODERNISM

While most American academics seemed able to reconcile their religious and scientific beliefs to include both a commitment to Protestantism and an acceptance of evolution, outside of academia the situation was less settled, and even some within higher education remained unconvinced. Concern over modernism and higher criticism (an approach to interpretation that considered the Bible a historical text) increased in the late nineteenth and early twentieth centuries. Organizations such as the American Bible League (later renamed the Bible League of North America) and individuals including Boston Theological Seminary professor Luther T. Townsend challenged new readings of the Bible, asserted the Bible's inerrancy, and foretold the coming collapse of evolutionary theory. *The Fundamentals,* a series of 12 edited booklets published by brothers Lyman and Milton Stewart between 1910 and 1915, emphasized the literal interpretation of the Bible and personal testimonies. The Stewarts further coalesced a movement that, amid the stresses of World War I and increasing anxieties over theological liberalism, surged onto the national stage in a more conservative form. The new movement, which was advanced by preachers such as Riley, Billy Sunday, and J. Frank Norris, was rooted in premillennialism and viewed the horrors of the war and the alleged German atrocities as evidence of a larger cultural and societal struggle. As historian George M. Marsden recounted in his influential *Fundamentalism in American Culture,* evolution was an emblem in the larger battle for the country's morality.[9] At the same time, the movement was diverse. Even some closely associated with it, including William Jennings Bryan, eschewed the term fundamentalism, opting instead to straddle between being purely inside the movement and at its borders.[10]

Complicit with and contributing to the troubles with modernism were institutions of higher education, which had been, according to opponents, overrun with German rationalism and diverted from their religious and moral purposes.[11] As Sunday famously claimed in 1916, "Thousands of college graduates are going as fast as they can straight to hell."[12] Sunday's and others' fears about the role of seminaries, colleges, and universities were emboldened by Bryn Mawr College psychologist James H. Leuba's study of the religious beliefs of more than nine hundred American college students and approximately the same number of faculty and scientists, published that same year. Leuba's work argued that students became less religious while in college; close to half of male students left college with "an idea of God incompatible with the acceptance of the Christian religion." He warned that students were "groveling in darkness" on religious issues and that scientists and faculty were even less likely to believe in Christian dogma than students, especially those faculty who were most renowned.[13] In the immediate postwar period and for much of the ensuing decade, fundamentalists such as Martin and Bryan repeatedly used Leuba's study as evidence of the destructive powers of higher education.[14]

Even before the war ended, though, the rhetoric around the dangers of higher education heated up. In his 1917 *Menace of Modernism*, Riley identified himself and all other citizens as "stockholders" in public higher education and claimed, "I never think of that great student body that throngs the halls of college and university...but to remember what soul-dangers they are sure to encounter."[15] He argued that modernism was destroying higher education and that faculty were both hypocritical and intolerant of religion. McPherson and others offered similar analyses shortly thereafter. With his 1921 lectures, "The Menace of Darwinism," populist politician Bryan focused these concerns on the issue of evolution, claiming it was the theory that led faculty to the moral and religious demise that Leuba had detailed.[16] Over the ensuing years, these claims against educators continued and were expanded. They focused first on denominational colleges and then moved more broadly across the higher education landscape. Bryan and others campaigned for legislative restrictions on teaching evolution, sought the dismissal of specific faculty, and called on college presidents to sign statements declaring their institutions' adherence to the book of Genesis.[17] And while the 1925 Scopes Trial captured the nation's attention and focused interest on evolution in the schools and colleges, the controversies persisted. Although Bryan died shortly after the Scopes Trial, others continued their assaults on modernist educators, including Sunday, who, in 1926, warned of "loud-mouthed, big vocabulary, foreign-lingo slinging, quack-theory preaching bolsheviki in the pulpits and colleges."[18] Moreover, the immediate aftermath of Scopes saw a surge in, rather than end to, the attempts to control college teaching in the South and Midwest.

Early Cases

The claims made by Riley, Bryan, and others concerned more than just evolution; the efforts they girded were more than just rhetorical. In the late 1910s and early 1920s, a series of controversies arose at specific institutions that threatened the careers of individual faculty members and institutional leaders. These began at religiously affiliated institutions before spreading more broadly, with the efforts of Martin, North Carolina Baptist layman D. F. King, and others to oust Wake Forest College president William Louis Poteat among the significant early cases. In a series of articles in the *Louisville Western Recorder* that warned of the "Three Fatal Teachings of President Poteat of Wake Forest College," Martin claimed that the long-serving executive of the leading Baptist institution in North Carolina was undermining Christianity both through his own teaching and because graduates of his college preached across the South. King likewise called for his ouster. At first, Baptists in the state defended Poteat, and the *Biblical Recorder,* the state's Baptist paper edited by a sympathetic Wake Forest trustee, refused to reprint Martin's attacks. Still, the issue remained present in the state, and, by early 1922, sentiment began to turn amid a massive fundraising campaign to support Baptist education. Poteat's efforts to clarify his belief in the compatibility of evolution and Christianity in the *Biblical Recorder* only intensified the pressure, eventually resulting in the editor banning discussion of evolution in its pages until 1925. Though Wake Forest responded to the controversy by investigating Poteat and declaring his fitness, controversy subsided only following Poteat's dramatic appearance before the statewide Baptist convention in December 1922. In a rousing speech, he demonstrated the depth of his Christian convictions while avoiding any mention of evolution. In doing so, Poteat protected himself from further serious attacks until 1925, when, in his delivery of the McNair Lectures at the University of North Carolina, he rekindled them by articulating his belief in evolution and warning of the dangers of religious extremism. By that time, the state legislature had begun to consider antievolution legislation, and controversies had spread to include concern over President William Preston Few of the Methodist-controlled Duke University and the writings of University of North Carolina professor Howard W. Odum. As historian George

Marsden noted, the efforts to oust Poteat were just the start of "The Battle of North Carolina."[19]

As Poteat's difficulties were beginning in North Carolina, similar battles were underway in Texas, battles that involved both Methodists and Baptists. In early 1921, Riley, Norris, and others forced John A. Rice's resignation from Southern Methodist University (SMU). They claimed that Rice's articulation of an oral tradition at the heart of the Old Testament in his *The Old Testament in the Life of Today* was heretical. Two years later, Norris—whom C. Allyn Russell described as a "fundamentalist, a sensationalist, a politician, and a controversialist"—joined with Methodist Rev. W. E. Hawkins in holding a mock trial of the state's Methodist institutions in conjunction with a WCFA meeting in Fort Worth. With testimony from students, including excerpts read from notes taken in SMU professor Mims Thornburg Workman's class, Norris and others condemned the spread of modernism and evolution in denominational colleges. Workman survived the pressure at the time, but ongoing fundamentalist attacks forced him to resign two years later, to the great irritation of students. That same year, the Northwest Texas Conference of the Methodist Episcopal Church began requiring that institutional presidents proclaim their faculties' unanimous agreement with all church doctrines before the institutions could receive any church funds. Concurrently, the North Texas Conference launched investigations into heterodoxy at both SMU and Southwestern University, though neither resulted in any sanction.[20]

Norris, a Baptist minister, was equally concerned with heterodoxy at Baptist institutions. In 1921, he used his newspaper, the *Searchlight*, and his popular sermons to force the removal of Baylor University sociology professor Grove Samuel Dow for publishing a text that told of a primitive human race, though Dow disclaimed belief in evolution. Norris's attacks on Baylor faculty continued for several years, first refocusing on zoologist Ora C. Bradbury and botanist Lula Pace, both of whom believed that some of the book of Genesis might be allegorical and that evolution might have been the manner through which God operated. Bradbury resigned under pressure, and Pace remained under assault until her death in 1925. Though these and other ongoing challenges resulted in several dismissals and further restrictions, they also revealed and contributed to divisions within the broader fundamentalist movements. Norris, especially, was a controversial figure whose claims and activities alienated many fundamentalists, while simultaneously galvanizing others.[21]

Of course, these issues were not limited to North Carolina and Texas, as Riley and others pushed on both public and private institutions to refrain from teaching any doctrine or idea antithetical to their beliefs. Dismissals continued throughout the South and Midwest, as well. The 1923 firings from the University of Tennessee—which led to so much controversy in the AAUP—implicated evolution, among other issues. In 1924, Georgia's Mercer College dismissed biologist Henry Fox for religious beliefs "utterly opposed to those held by Georgia Baptists," though not specifically for his teaching of evolution as a theory.[22] The following year, when Nebraska's Danish Lutheran Seminary removed its president, Carl P. Hojbjerg, for being an evolutionist, he responded, "it is my belief and I shall go on teaching it."[23] These and other specific inquiries into individual professors and entire institutions were joined by larger pushes to control the teaching in schools, colleges, and universities.

Legislative Interference

As with the efforts to constrain teachers and schools through loyalty oaths and related activities during the repeated Red Scares, state legislatures proved to be an attractive route through which to rein in what fundamentalists saw as destructive schooling practices. Between 1913 and 1930, eleven states passed legislation requiring that students read the Bible in school, and an additional six passed laws explicitly allowing such activity, with most of the legislation enacted after the war. According to the ACLU, which decried such legislation as inimical to freedom of religion, the laws were "developed under the influence of the influence of the [Ku Klux] Klan and the Fundamentalists.... Most of the laws require that the Bible should be read every school day; some specify the amount to be read. Many contain stringent provisions for their enforcement."[24] More famous and with greater relevance to higher education were the legislative efforts to prevent evolution and related ideas from being aired in public schools and colleges. From 1921 through 1929, more than 40 different bills and resolutions were introduced in 20 different state legislatures that would have either explicitly banned the teaching of evolution or offered similar restrictions that could have had the same result. Several of these were aimed more broadly than evolution and concerned larger issues of sectarian control rather than specific fundamentalist pressures, including the first, Utah's 1921 prohibition of "any atheistic, infidel, sectarian, religious or denominational doctrine."[25] More typical, though, were proposed bills that targeted evolution, including efforts in Kentucky and South Carolina the following year. The South Carolina bill—which would have banned money from public institutions teaching "as a creed to be followed, the cult known as 'Darwinism'"—died quietly during the reconciliation process.[26] The Kentucky situation, though, was anything but quiet.

The efforts in Kentucky were part of the larger national press against—and the first real legislative battle over—the teaching of evolution. They were triggered in 1921 when University of Kentucky president Frank L. McVey entertained an offer of the presidency of the University of Missouri and then used the ensuing outpouring of public support to bolster his efforts to increase the funding to and size of the institution. First in an editorial in the *Louisville Evening Post* and then in the *Louisville Western Recorder,* those concerned with the teaching of evolution at the institution pushed back. McVey believed that the difficulties would quickly pass. Instead, they took on new urgency in December when J. W. Porter, the pastor of the First Baptist Church in Lexington, spearheaded an effort to have the Baptist State Board of Missions intervene against the teaching of evolution. Though several major newspapers in the state supported the institution, Porter was able to build momentum in rural areas. He also garnered Bryan's support both in writing and talks that Bryan gave in the state in mid-January, including one before a joint session of the legislature.[27] Bryan lambasted evolutionists, referred to a professor teaching Darwinism as "the most dangerous man that could be met," and urged action.[28] His call was soon met with House Bill 191, introduced on January 23, 1922, with the aim of prohibiting the teaching of "Darwinism, atheism, agnosticism or evolution as it pertains to the origin of man."[29] Two days later, a slightly milder version was introduced in the Senate, launching a statewide debate over the limits that should be placed on schools and colleges.

McVey was wary of personally weighing in on the legislation alone and, instead, solicited leading educators and theologians to provide telegrams in opposition to the bill. McVey received almost fifty responses in the ensuing days and, after removing the two that supported the legislation, released them to the press.[30] Some of the responses were blunt, including former US commissioner of education Philander P. Claxton's claim that the bill was "unwise, absurd, ridiculous." University of Chicago dean Shailer Mathews called it disloyal, while his colleague Charles H. Judd called it a "folly."[31] Others, though, took a different approach, including Columbia University president Nicholas Murray Butler, who sarcastically offered that the bill was incomplete and should prohibit the use of the letters in the word "evolution."[32] McVey used these telegrams as the foundation of his opposition to the bill. He twice addressed the Senate and decried the destructive nature of the proposed legislation and the alternative proposals that were put forth. In an open letter to the people of Kentucky, he disclaimed the teaching of atheism or man's descent from apes at his institution. Instead, he sought to reconcile evolution and Christianity and demonstrate that concerns about the religiosity of the university were unfounded. Moreover, he contended that personal liberties and academic freedom would be violated by the passage of any of the bills under consideration. McVey's efforts contributed to the Senate shelving its version of the bill on February 19. Then, after tense debates and another visit to the legislature by McVey, the House version was narrowly defeated on March 9.[33]

In the aftermath, liberal theologian Alonzo W. Fortune argued that good had come from the controversy, opposing sides had been brought together, and the issue had been permanently removed from legislative meddling.[34] *St. Louis Post-Dispatch* columnist Clark McAdams saw the situation somewhat differently, opining that though McVey was successful, it was not a complete victory, merely the best that could be achieved in such dire circumstances.[35] Indeed, it was an equivocal triumph, and the issues remained unsettled, as Kentucky Wesleyan College's suspension of professor Ralph Demaree in 1923 demonstrated. Demaree's offenses were criticizing Bryan and telling students that there was no conflict between Christianity and evolution. He was reinstated for the remainder of the term only when he expressed regret and agreed not to discuss evolution in public again.[36] Moreover, antievolution legislation would again be proposed in Kentucky in 1926. The first state to pass such legislation was Oklahoma, where an amendment to a free textbook law including the provision that no textbook that teaches "the 'Materialistic Conception of History' (i.e.) The Darwin Theory of Creation vs. the Bible Account of Creation" could be used. It was adopted in early 1923 following a brief, unruly debate but was repealed two years later due not to concern over Darwinism but to the cost of the provision. Although the repeal generated controversy, stoked statewide debate over evolution in the schools, and led to a failed statewide referendum to reinstate the provision, Oklahoma educators remained quiet on the issue.[37]

Initial Organizational Responses

Amid the struggles over the evolution bills in Kentucky, the *St. Louis Post-Dispatch* warned higher education about the coming danger posed by Bryan and his supporters' efforts to rid academe of evolution, editorializing that university forbearance should be replaced by active opposition.[38] Yet despite the responses to McVey's plea for support, Poteat's own experiences at Wake Forest, and other college presidents' individual defenses of modernist teachers—including that of Goucher College president William Westley Guth, who refused a trustee's insistence that a bible instructor be dismissed for countering Bryan[39]—there was no organization of college presidents that was ready to take up a fight of the nature being described. The leading group comprised of university presidents, the Association of American Universities, avoided academic freedom and related issues from its start, claiming its focus was on graduate education. The Association of American Colleges (AAC) had argued for colleges' rights to prohibit professors' teaching of religious and economic doctrines in the late 1910s, and its Commission on Academic Freedom continued to maintain the appropriateness of sectarian influences on teaching. Though the AAC journal *Educational Review* published a stirring warning that fundamentalists were hampering academic freedom to the detriment of education and religion, the organization itself did not take such a stand.[40] Instead, in academic circles, the battle was initially left to the AAUP, already the leading voice for academic freedom, though one that still faced difficulties in its efforts to secure professorial rights to freedom in teaching, research, and extramural expression.

From its beginnings, the AAUP had wrestled with the appropriateness of doctrinal limitations on faculty teaching and extramural activities. Its 1915 *Declaration of Principles on Academic Freedom and Academic Tenure* claimed that institutions intended to promote specific religious doctrines in lieu of allowing academic freedom should necessarily make such purposes public. In 1919, its committee investigating Bethany College's dismissal of H. I. Croyle again asserted the need for doctrinal restrictions to be made known at the time of hiring, even though it was unclear whether Croyle was dismissed for ineffectiveness in teaching and lack of fit with the college community or for concerns over his modernist biblical teachings.[41] Three years later, following the battles in Kentucky and McVey's pleas for assistance, the AAUP's Dartmouth chapter requested intervention by Committee A on Academic Freedom and Tenure and cautioned that scientists needed to respond to the threats to academic freedom posed by fundamentalism.[42] The next month, the AAUP answered both by creating the new Committee M on the Freedom of Teaching of Science to address the situation and by writing to a Baptist conference to express its concerns. Each of these actions reflected uneasiness about both fundamentalism and larger organizational issues.

While Southern Baptist and Presbyterian groups had readily accepted fundamentalism, Northern Baptist and Presbyterian congregations were more conflicted, a circumstance that Denney seized upon. Writing as president of the AAUP, Denney appealed to the Conference of Northern Baptist Churches, noting that antievolutionists were creating "widespread anxiety" and could prove disastrous to higher education. Denney emphasized concerns about the professional status of faculty members and claimed that any efforts to restrict the teaching of evolution would diminish individual institutions and the respect for education as a whole. Truth in research and teaching were crucial, as was the standing of the professoriate. In his letter, Denney was careful not to address whether the theory of evolution was valid, as only the effects of restrictions on teaching were at issue. Denney's letter was read at the divided Indianapolis meeting of the conference and referred to its Committee on Resolutions before an election that saw the moderates defeat fundamentalists for control. The new moderator and other conference leaders then prevented the consideration of resolutions that might call for restrictions on the freedom of teaching. They also outmaneuvered conservatives on creedal tests, causing a deep and definitive break in the movement. The following year, when Presbyterians met in Indianapolis for their General Assembly, Bryan sought to become moderator but lost to the more liberal president of Wooster College, the Rev. Charles F. Wishart. Though Bryan launched a debate on the teaching of evolution from the floor, he was unsuccessful in his effort to have the assembly resolve against providing funds to any school that taught evolution.[43]

When Denney organized Committee M in June 1922, he viewed it as supplementary to Committee A and focused on proactively forestalling difficulties rather than investigating alleged violations.[44] Denney was able to find scientists, philosophers, and theologians willing to serve on Committee M, but, just as obtaining leadership for Committee A had proved difficult, so too was finding a chairperson for Committee M. He was pressed into serving as interim chair until 1924 and, in that role, led Committee M somewhat along lines that his letter to the Convention of Northern Baptist Churches might have suggested. He emphasized that the issue was not about evolution but rather freedom of teaching and the responsibility of professors to present their best understandings of the issues at hand. External pressures should not dictate classroom teaching. At the AAUP's 1923 meeting, Denney noted that Committee M had been very busy but had acted quietly. Rather than publicly advocating for freedom of teaching in science and potentially raising the ire of conservative churches, Committee M worked behind the scenes. Members wrote to state legislators who were considering antievolution laws, organized local committees in the face of potential violations, and used the issue to push for the ideals enumerated in the AAUP's 1915 *Declaration*.[45] At the meeting, Denney acknowledged that private institutions were legally free to restrict teaching but that they had the responsibility to enumerate limitations to both students and teachers; he approvingly commented on a sectarian institution's recent catalogue revisions clarifying just such limitations. If institutions were not committed to scientific truth, they should at least be honest about it.[46]

Throughout these efforts, the AAUP insisted that the prevailing issue was the right of professors to teach the latest scientific understanding at true educational institutions. When University of California zoologist Samuel J. Holmes, Denney's replacement as chairman of Committee M, reported on the group's work at the end of 1924, he was more willing to condemn antievolutionary belief as well as the intolerance that surrounded the teaching of evolution. Still, he continued to press for principles that were much larger than just the one issue. In a piece that the AAUP would distribute to legislators as part of its efforts to oppose fundamentalist encroachments on freedom in teaching, he termed antievolutionists' efforts to restrict freedom in teaching as "un-American" and argued for the necessity that scholars and educators, rather than the general public or segments thereof, determine what is taught.[47] The AAUP was not alone in these attempts to avoid involvement in the debates over evolution while also striving to protect freedom in teaching. The ACLU was similarly opposed to restrictions on teaching in science and similarly attempted to avoid the larger "warfare of science with theology" while arguing for academic freedom. This, though, was difficult, as was readily apparent in the event that would become known as "The Trial of the Century."

The Scopes Trial

The battle over the teaching of evolution was most famously fought in the Dayton, Tennessee, trial of John T. Scopes, a case with which the ACLU was intimately involved as an instigator, litigant, and publicist. In early 1925, Tennessee legislator John W. Butler proposed legislation prohibiting the awarding of state funds to any educational institution that taught "any theory that denies the story of the Divine Creation of man as taught in the Bible" or asserted "that man had descended from a lower order of animals."[48] It passed both houses of the state legislature with little dissent in 1925 and was soon signed into law by Governor Austin Peay. Although Oklahoma had passed its aforementioned textbook legislation and the Florida legislature had, also in 1923, passed a resolution condemning the teaching of evolution, this was the first law that prescribed penalties for any teacher or professor who violated such an ordinance. Still, the law was at first thought to be largely symbolic, and, at the bill's signing, Peay noted that it was likely never to be enforced. Only the reaction by the ACLU and the enterprising efforts of Dayton businessman George Washington Rappleyea provoked the drama that has since become part of American lore and a key, if ultimately inconclusive, event in the battle over academic freedom.[49]

ACLU leaders began tracking the legislation at its proposal and, according to Roger Baldwin's later recollection, were dumbfounded that it might be enacted. When Peay signed the legislation, the ACLU immediately distributed a press release offering to defend anyone charged under the law.[50] Upon reading the ACLU press release, Rappleyea convinced school superintendent Walter White and local lawyers Herbert E. and Sue K. Hicks, among others, of the desirability of staging a test case in Dayton, not primarily to challenge the law but as an entrepreneurial effort. A court hearing replete with national media and ACLU-sponsored lawyers offered the chance to attract publicity and money to the small town. The Hicks brothers agreed to prosecute the case and the group convinced Scopes, who had reviewed evolution as a substitute high school biology teacher, to participate. After receiving confirmation from the ACLU that they would fund the defense efforts, Scopes was arrested while Rappleyea and others communicated the news to the ACLU and to the media. The ACLU, interested in pursuing the constitutionality of the legislation and unaware of the extent of the drama that would unfold, offered to pay expenses for both the prosecution and the defense. Although the Hicks brothers, along with local co-counsel Wallace Haggard, refused the offer to fund the prosecution, the fact that it was made underscores the uniqueness of the case and the odd circumstances that led to its hearing.[51]

Despite the ACLU's crucial role in bringing about the Scopes Trial, the case did not proceed as the organization had hoped. Just as the AAUP tried to focus on academic freedom, not the issue of evolution, so, too, did the ACLU. However, the narrow emphasis on constitutionality that the ACLU foresaw quickly devolved into a battle between a literalist interpretation of the Bible and evolution. John R. Neal, who had been dismissed from the University of Tennessee amid controversy two years earlier, quickly volunteered as Scopes's local attorney and was accepted by the schoolteacher. The ACLU was divided over the representation it would provide, with many hoping for a religiously conservative lawyer who could focus narrowly while providing the defense credibility. Before the debate could be settled, Bryan, who was in Tennessee to speak to the WCFA convention, volunteered to work for the prosecution, setting the terms upon which the case would be fought and helping to force the ACLU's decision. In response, Clarence Darrow, one of the most renowned and controversial litigators of the era, volunteered to counter Bryan. ACLU leaders, including Baldwin, Forrest Bailey, and others, sought more conservative and respectable counsel. Even after Scopes indicated his preference for Darrow, many in the ACLU unsuccessfully worked to have him removed, with only Arthur Garfield Hays supporting the selection. Eventually the organization begrudgingly relented, and Darrow headlined a defense team that also included Neal, Hays, and divisive New York divorce lawyer Dudley Field Malone.[52]

Bryan's and Darrow's participation furthered the notoriety of the case and definitively marked it as a contest between science and religion rather than merely a challenge to the constitutionality of restricting teachers' freedoms. The trial is perhaps most remembered for Bryan's willingness to take the stand and Darrow's examination of his literalist biblical interpretation. By allowing for some interpretation on certain issues in Genesis, Bryan's testimony opened up the possibility of further interpretation and ill-served his goals. The defense work, much of which was planned by Hays but carried out by Darrow, was well received by Northern and urban audiences, many of whom believed that fundamentalist views had been thoroughly vanquished. Scopes was found guilty, however, as he had violated the law. Darrow's emphasis on religion and his thorough routing of Bryan played well in the national press but did not address the constitutionality of the law itself. Scopes appealed his conviction to the Tennessee Supreme Court as the ACLU searched for ways to remove Darrow from the continuing legal battles. In early 1927, almost a year and a half after the case was first heard, the Tennessee Supreme Court overturned the conviction on a procedural technicality. In doing so, it both prevented the ACLU from appealing the case to the Supreme

Court and allowed the Butler Act to remain law. While relieved of its struggle for control of the case, the ACLU had failed in its efforts to have antievolution laws ruled unconstitutional.[53]

The ACLU played a dominant role in the Scopes Trial, helping to provoke the test case, providing legal and financial support, and coordinating defense and publicity activities. As a result of its involvement, the organization gained some credibility and national recognition. Its fundraising efforts in relation to the case were so successful that they provided the association a budget surplus and stable funding for the first time in its history. Still, other organizations participated, although the ACLU was bothered by their limited roles.[54] The AAAS pledged its backing for ACLU efforts in opposition to the Butler Act and offered scientific testimony in support of evolution.[55] Under AAAS auspices, zoologist Winterton C. Curtis served as a defense expert. Curtis was involved with planning in Dayton and submitted an affidavit explaining the scientific evidence for evolution. While he did not do this as an official representative of the AAUP, he did serve on the association's executive council and Committee A. The AAUP was far less involved as an organization; only occasionally did it note the case or reprint the ACLU statements on it.[56] At its annual meeting two months later, Mathews noted that the case had highlighted ongoing conflicts between science and religion and critiqued Bryan's views, while lauding him for being honest about them. Still, most of his informal report, which he delivered in Holmes's absence, focused on the complicity of professors in the controversies over the teaching of evolution. Mathews, a modernist divinity school professor and dean, urged faculty members to treat religion respectfully, stop viewing themselves as victims, and accept responsibility for provoking some of the troubles.[57]

The teachers' organizations were also relatively quiet on the Scopes case. Despite the presence of Henry R. Linville, a biologist who had helped devise modern secondary school science curricula, the American Federation of Teachers (AFT) was struggling as an organization and could do little to address the issue, especially as it centered on regions outside its sphere of greatest influence.[58] At its 1923 convention, the AFT passed a resolution against legislative restrictions on curricula and textbooks.[59] In 1925, the union extended its support to Scopes and offered to help him in any way that it could.[60] Later that year, at Linville's urging, the convention passed a resolution further supporting his cause, although real assistance was not forthcoming from the organization. The National Education Association did not take even these steps, considering such action unwise.[61]

Beyond Scopes

While the Scopes case was one of the most memorable of the century and one that provided the ACLU its first favorable publicity in the mainstream press, it failed to end legislative restrictions on the teaching of evolution in schools or colleges. In the summer of 1925, Riley formed organizations to push legislation based on the Butler Act in California, Minnesota, and Oregon. In Florida, George F. Washburn formed the Bible Crusaders of America that November, and L. A. Tatum organized the Florida Purity League shortly thereafter; both sought to strengthen the state's 1923 antievolution resolution with new legislation to restrict the spread of evolutionist teaching and texts. Especially active in 1927, the antievolutionists in Florida were able to limit access to offending books but were effectively countered by private and state college presidents, the Florida Education Association, and others concerned about the anti-intellectualism implicated in the movement. In January 1926, Martin led the successful drive for antievolution legislation in Mississippi—legislation that was more restrictive than the Butler Act and banned both the teaching of evolution and the use of textbooks that discussed it. Undaunted by the defeat of North Carolina's Poole Bill opposing the teaching of evolution in schools in early 1925, Riley and Martin, along with their affiliated organizations, continued their lengthy efforts against evolution in that state. University of North Carolina president Harry W. Chase was instrumental in leading the opposition, as were McVey in Kentucky, Rollins College president Hamilton Holt in Florida, and University of Minnesota president Lotus D. Coffman in his state. Ultimately, a second Poole Bill was defeated in 1927, thereby arresting the controversy in the state. In all, 26 antievolution bills and resolutions were proposed in 19 state legislatures in the two-and-a-half years after passage of the Butler Act. Only the Mississippi act passed, but, in 1928, following unsuccessful legislative efforts to ban the teaching of evolution, Arkansas passed a similar prohibition by public referendum. More than 60 percent of the voters supported the referendum over the opposition of University of Arkansas administrators and faculty.[62]

Though often in leadership roles, college presidents were not alone in their efforts, as educational and affiliated organizations responded to these ongoing attacks. In September 1924, Maynard Shipley founded the Science League of America and launched a multiyear effort to counter antievolutionists, including sponsoring and participating in debates with Riley and writing numerous tracts, most famously the

1927 *War on Modern Science*.⁶³ In 1926, the AFT noted its work to lobby Congress in opposition to the Summers Amendment—which would have prohibited teaching evolution in Washington DC, schools—and claimed some responsibility for its defeat.⁶⁴ The AAUP also maintained interest in antievolution efforts, and Committee M continued some degree of work for several years. At the 1926 annual meeting, Vassar professor Woodbridge Riley argued that the AAUP needed to be more active in promoting freedom from legislative restrictions on teaching, specifically recommending the generation of additional publicity through syndicated newspaper articles. AAUP founder Arthur O. Lovejoy similarly lamented that the association had not done more to counter antievolutionists, and he introduced a resolution encouraging the association to lead interorganizational cooperation to oppose legislative interference with academic freedom and to encourage the separation of church and state.⁶⁵ Still, while referencing the ACLU as its source for information on antievolution efforts, the AAUP was looking to join with the AAAS, not a civil liberties group or teachers union.⁶⁶

Despite this recognition that more needed to be done, Committee M did not do much beyond lobbying against the restrictive legislation behind the scenes and issuing its annual reports to update members on legislative activities. In 1927, AAUP general secretary Harry W. Tyler collected information about local antievolution pressures but reported that efforts to assist chapters were rebuffed, as the issues were considered local in nature. In his Committee M report that year, Holmes recounted the recent efforts in Minnesota, Arkansas, and elsewhere, though without his earlier critique of scientists. In 1928, the association debated intervening—a small subcommittee was even authorized to meet with representatives of the AAAS to pursue joint efforts—but the AAUP continued focusing its efforts elsewhere. At the same meeting, the AAUP heard arguments that it would be more effective to drop the issue rather than granting it further publicity, as the situation was not as dire as the laws made it seem.⁶⁷ Committee M on the Freedom of Teaching in Science never again reported to an AAUP annual meeting.

As the Scopes Case appeal wound its way through the court system, the ACLU became increasingly eager to find another venue that would allow it to take a challenge to the United States Supreme Court. While publicly condemning the antievolution statute passed in Mississippi in 1926, the ACLU focused its efforts on Arkansas, where the 1928 referendum banned the teaching of evolution in public schools and colleges. With the approval of the AAUP and the

AAAS, the ACLU solicited educators willing to flaunt the law openly and risk prosecution. The organization initially received a favorable response from several people in higher education, and it appeared that a case might be found at either the University of Arkansas or Arkansas A&M. However, Virgil Jones, dean of arts and sciences at the University of Arkansas in Fayetteville, while supportive of the efforts, was not willing to risk his career for the case.[68] Horace Adams, an instructor at Arkansas A&M, offered to teach evolution, but he requested acceptance for graduate studies and a fellowship at the University of Chicago in exchange for sacrificing his position. Baldwin and the ACLU found this to be a reasonable exchange but were unsuccessful in securing funding and a position.[69]

Among those who were opposed to this offer was Lovejoy, who believed that providing Adams with graduate admission and financial support was equivalent to providing him an "asbestos martyr's robe" which would only raise questions about his motives. Indicative of the growing AAUP sentiment, Lovejoy further argued against pursuing a test case, as doing so would only enflame the issue.[70] In an article that appeared in *School & Society* and was later reprinted in the AAUP's *Bulletin,* Lovejoy addressed the Arkansas law and the larger issue of legislative restrictions on teaching. He argued that the issue under consideration was far more important than evolution but instead got to the heart of the American academic profession, to whether scholars could maintain their self-respect.[71] Still, Lovejoy believed that the Arkansas statute posed no serious threat to academic freedom. He found the law's language too vague to limit most teachers, including because it failed to define teaching and emphasized neutrality in the classroom—rather than scripture—as a justification. Since the law permitted teachers to maintain their own beliefs on evolution and only barred them from teaching that man descended from lower forms of life, Lovejoy argued that it was rather innocuous. In fact, he felt the emphasis on neutrality might help teachers refrain from dogmatism.[72] Preferring avoidance to a staged legal challenge, the AAUP retreated from the issue.

For a short time, the ACLU remained committed but struggled to find an appropriate situation through which to test the law. For several years, the organization continued to publicize that bringing a new case to the Supreme Court was among its top priorities, although it had little success.[73] In late 1931, the organization ended this quest when it received a report from the Arkansas attorney general that the law was not being enforced and was having no influence.[74] While history has subsequently demonstrated that limitations on teaching theories contradicting biblical accounts would return, for the time being, at least, the ACLU had come to agree with Lovejoy that the laws were no longer viable. Only with the unrest of the 1960s would the issue resurface for the organization, ultimately leading the Supreme Court to hear the ACLU's challenge of the Arkansas law in 1968.[75] Still, the efforts to restrict the teaching of science were important in helping to establish broader support for academic freedom.[76]

Conclusion

Believing that modernism and godlessness were ruining schools and threatening the morals of American children, fundamentalists challenged both public and private education in the 1920s, particularly on the issue of evolution. They focused their attacks on higher education and became powerful enough that, in 1962, Richard Hofstadter would compare the period to the recent Red Scare and note, "Today intellectuals have bogies much more frightening than fundamentalism in the schools; but it would be a serious failure of imagination not to remember how scared the intellectuals of the 1920's's were." He continued, "the sense of oppressive danger was no less real."[77] Hofstadter's claim might have been extreme—in many colleges and universities, fundamentalists held little sway. Yet, it maintained a great deal of truth, as attacks on professors and institutions could inhibit careers, or at least create difficulty and dissension. The legislative efforts to restrict the teaching of evolution were likewise troublesome for institutional leaders and constituents. They could generate pressure, raise concerns, and threaten institutional funding and operations. As McVey's responses in Kentucky and Poteat's in North Carolina demonstrated, the situation was serious for higher education and its presidents. At the same time, it was often underappreciated until it hit close to home.

McVey's activities in Kentucky are likewise important in that they point to both the role that institutional presidents played and the fact that they played them outside formal organizations. Though McVey drew on networks of educators, he did so on a personal basis rather than as a member of one of the burgeoning academic organizations. The organizational response from academe was left to the AAAS and its ally, the AAUP, which worked quietly despite Denney's declarations. Still, the ACLU, which had entered the academic freedom arena over its concern that the AAUP was ineffective, was more important and more active. The ACLU fostered the difficulties in Dayton, Tennessee, and sought to use them to demonstrate the unconstitutionality of restrictions on teaching. Yet its experiences with the case were not without conflict: it both achieved notoriety and financial benefit, and it became entangled in religious battles it sought to avoid. Moreover, it won the case on appeal, thereby losing the chance to seek its ultimate goal of a hearing before the United States Supreme Court. As a result, the ACLU refocused on higher education and sought new opportunities to have antievolution legislation declared unconstitutional. These efforts, though for a time promising, were ultimately forestalled, in part by an AAUP that both worried about propriety and believed that publicity would only embolden those whose goals fundamentally differed. As fundamentalists regrouped, higher education turned its attention elsewhere. Those battling over academic freedom first refocused on administrative pressures and then, in the ensuing decade, on the threats that they believed were posed by Communists and anti-Communists on and around America's college campuses.

6

EDUCATION, PROTESTS, AND BLACKLISTS

The 1925 *Conference Statement on Academic Freedom and Tenure* was an important step toward larger understandings and procedural protections. It demonstrated a growing awareness of the need for academic freedom in some circles, though not the full range of protections that the American Association of University Professors (AAUP) sought. Moreover, the battles over evolution that occurred throughout the 1920s demonstrated the persistent pressures and limitations. So, too, did institutionally based challenges to and infringements of academic freedom and tenure. Despite seeming progress, the AAUP found itself continually bombarded with claims of violations in the late 1920s and early 1930s, eventually forcing the association to reconsider its approaches to both handling initial complaints and acting once a violation had been found. Pressed by faculty who found the organization to be too conservative, the AAUP began what would later be known as censuring institutions, though the shift caused confusion both inside and outside the organization. Elsewhere, the American Federation of Teachers (AFT) reemerged after almost a decade of setbacks and tried to stake its own claims for academic freedom, though at first with limited success. And, despite its attention-garnering anti-antievolution efforts, the American Civil Liberties Union (ACLU), too, recognized the need for changes in its approach, which it reformulated and reconceived in the early 1930s.

Contributing to these organizational concerns were the ongoing struggles of individual faculty members pressured to conform to institutional and societal expectations. When they failed to do so—as in the case of University of Missouri faculty who allowed students to distribute a questionnaire on sexual beliefs or the Ohio State University professor who espoused support for racial understanding and social progress—they could face significant consequences. The

AAUP continued to recognize the prominent role that tenure violations played in the work of its Committee A on Academic Freedom and Tenure; by the early 1930s, it also recognized that the economic depression offered the potential to hide dismissals. All told, the late 1920s and early 1930s were years of significant challenges to academic freedom and tenure, as well as substantial repositioning among the organization most concerned with their protection.

A Reemerging AFT

For much of the early 1920s, the AFT's activities on behalf of academic freedom were limited as the organization itself struggled to maintain viability amid internal conflict, attacks from the National Education Association (NEA), and a testy relationship with the American Federation of Labor. While union locals could take action on behalf of aggrieved educators, as New York Teachers Union demonstrated, the national AFT dealt with more basic issues of maintaining membership and defending itself against external attacks. The AFT passed resolutions against loyalty oaths and antievolution legislation, lobbied Congress in opposition to restrictive textbook legislation, and otherwise showed an interest in—but had only limited ability to affect—the academic freedom of K–12 and college teachers.[1] In 1927, as the AFT was just beginning to reemerge, Henry Linville's Committee on Promotion and Organization called for the creation of a new Committee on Academic Freedom and Tenure to address the freedom of teachers both inside the classroom and in their private lives. Noting his New York experiences, Linville argued that numerous violations were left unaddressed, as the ACLU handled only those involving free speech, and the AFT had no mechanism appropriate for intervention.[2] Linville recognized that, although limited funds would hamper the committee's work in the short term, the committee could coordinate local efforts and look for cooperation from other labor and civic groups. When the convention approved the proposal, the committee soon undertook these activities, if on a limited basis. It reported on dismissals and locals' activities on behalf of aggrieved teachers and professors, requested information about academic freedom and tenure from local unions and state federations, and called for action from local unions and civic organizations. It hoped to generate publicity that would push others to act, as the AFT was not yet able to do so itself.[3]

In his report as the first chair of the committee, R. W. Everett noted that its goal was to overcome the union's tendency to "meet in annual convention, talk enthusiastically, resolve highly, and then go home and wait till the next Annual Convention."[4] It was a goal that remained difficult to achieve. At the union's 1928 convention, Everett's replacement, Amy Fox, reported her disappointment with the committee's work; she had been overwhelmed in the face of too many suggestions for activities. She proceeded to report solely on issues of tenure, creating a void filled first by a special convention subcommittee and then by the creation of a separate Committee on Academic Freedom with Linville as its chair. As he admitted in his report at the 1929 convention, Linville likewise struggled in this capacity. He did, though, take important steps in developing the union's national policy toward violations of academic freedom, including arguing that the inevitableness of conflict on economic and religious matters should dictate it. Based on the positive response to the ACLU's antievolution work and the lack of a comprehensive defense of academic freedom by any other group, Linville contended that the union should take a more active and public role. Its engagement could generate publicity, educate teachers and the general public about the importance of academic freedom, and help decrease future violations. Although he spoke favorably of the ACLU, he pointed to the AAUP's emphasis on tenure and questioned whether the AAUP was as committed to the principle of academic freedom as it was to securing faculty positions. Linville was followed at the convention by University of Chicago professor Paul Douglas, who was even more strident. He urged the AFT to be more militant in its work on behalf of teachers and professors, lambasted the AAUP's lengthy investigations as ineffective, and called on the AFT to overtake both the AAUP and NEA. Douglas's remarks were warmly received, but the AFT was not yet ready to pursue the militant approach he was suggesting.[5]

In 1930, Linville proposed a plan that served as the basis for the AFT's activities involving academic freedom until the middle of the decade, the primary component of which would be education. When the AFT learned of a potential violation, the chair of an enlarged permanent committee—composed of members from public and private institutions from kindergarten through universities—was charged with communicating with both the allegedly aggrieved educator and his or her institution to gather all relevant information as quickly as possible. A subcommittee of members knowledgeable about the local context could then investigate the situation and suggest action to the full committee, which might include referring the case to the ACLU for legal action, organizing a boycott, or dropping the case if the dismissal had been just and fair. Linville's basic proposal was approved, but the Committee on Policies refused to allow the formal referral of cases to the ACLU, as it did not want responsibility for whatever action the ACLU took. Though strong connections between the organizations would remain, leaders were fearful they could become encumbrances. The following year, Linville's committee itself backed away from another aspect of its proposal in deciding against instituting any form of a boycott or blacklist. Such action would be effective only if an organization were able to enforce it, and the AFT was not yet able to do so. As Linville explained, this decision was in direct response to the AAUP's recent debates and activities regarding increasingly aggressive action and the censuring of academic administrations that violated academic freedom and tenure.[6]

Throughout this period, the AFT emphasized its differences from the AAUP, taking particular delight in pointing to places where its activities had preceded the association's action.[7] Through Linville, the AFT somewhat misleadingly argued that the AAUP wrongly conjoined academic freedom to tenure, thereby emphasizing job protection rather than the importance of freedom in the educational process.[8] Although the union stressed educating teachers and the public about academic freedom, it retained its concern about individual teachers and professors who were dismissed, advocated for strengthened tenure laws, and called for locals to publicize cases and work for reinstatement of the wrongfully terminated. At the national level, more effort was expended on critiquing groups such as the Daughters of the American Revolution and the American Legion and on protesting the inroads that they made into education.[9]

"We Don't Patronize"

As the AFT was attempting to differentiate its approach from that of the AAUP, the AAUP was itself wrestling with how best to defend academic freedom and tenure while maintaining the professional status of the association and the professoriate. Long-standing concerns over staffing Committee A's investigative subcommittee continued and were joined by calls to more adequately address the needs of junior faculty, a group which had been explicitly excluded from membership at the association's founding but then allowed to join several years later. The AAUP advocated for a trial period prior to permanent appointments and, although it acknowledged the possibility for abuse, argued that college and university administrators should be given leeway in their actions regarding probationary faculty and temporary instructors. Edward Allen, a mathematician at Iowa State

College of Agriculture and Mechanic Arts—who himself had been removed from the University of Michigan over his political beliefs just after World War I—pushed the organization to reconsider the association's commitment to these members, first at the 1927 Annual Meeting and subsequently in correspondence with AAUP general secretary Harry W. Tyler. Allen argued that junior faculty members were silenced by the threat of dismissal and only those willing to heed their institutions' wishes were promoted. He believed that the current system, in addition to violating the rights of these junior faculty members and contradicting the principle of freedom, created a senior professoriate unwilling to take advantage of the freedoms, once granted. Allen accurately identified some of the enduring difficulties of linking tenure to academic freedom, but Tyler and others were largely dismissive of his concerns. Even though only a fraction of the complaints to the AAUP were brought by instructors and assistant professors, and Tyler would later become concerned by the existence of significant numbers of faculty who never reached permanency, at the time he believed the association was attending to their needs.[10]

A greater concern was the tension between the desire for an aggressive protective association and the goal of being a respected cooperating association. The appropriate faculty response to threatened or real dismissals was a enduring and serious issue. At the turn of the century, Arthur O. Lovejoy and others had resigned from Stanford in response to Edward A. Ross's firing; Charles A. Beard did the same from Columbia University upon the dismissal of James McKeen Cattell during World War I. In rare cases, faculty acted in unity, as they had at Trinity College during the 1903 Bassett Affair. These acts were relatively infrequent, however, and Lovejoy was among those who worried that they were becoming even rarer, especially after the AAUP's founding.[11] Questions likewise remained about whether faculty should be willing to accept a position that had been vacated by the inappropriate dismissal of another occupant. For the AAUP, these questions were tied up both in the purposes of Committee A's investigations and concerns over professional standing. Officially, the AAUP denied that their reports were creating a blacklist, including in 1916 when AAUP president John H. Wigmore rejected the idea that the AAUP would "defend its members by a 'We Don't Patronize' list."[12] The issue, though, could become clouded; part of the power of the investigative reports was to inform prospective employees of the tenuous nature of positions at offending institutions. Moreover, in 1919, when Geddes W. Rutherford learned that the position he had accepted at Washburn College had been created by the dismissal of John Ervin Kirkpatrick, he consulted Lovejoy and then, shortly before he was to begin, withdrew. In response, Washburn's president condemned AAUP interference.[13] Still, the organization disclaimed formal boycotting, leaving the faculty to make their own decisions based on Committee A reports.[14]

The issue again came to the fore in the wake of the University of Missouri's 1929 dismissal of one faculty member and suspension of second following the distribution of a survey inquiring into student attitudes about sexual behaviors, morals, and the economic status of women. A subcommittee of Committee A investigated and found the institution's action in violation of the AAUP standards on tenure and academic freedom.[15] Yet one member of the investigating committee, University of Chicago psychologist Louis L. Thurstone, was unsatisfied with publishing the report and relying on the consciences of individuals faculty members not to accept offers of employment at Missouri. Thurstone wrote to Tyler condemning "dignified and polite and impotent" reports, calling for them to be replaced by more direct activity.[16] He proposed that the institution be removed from the list of institutions whose faculty were eligible for membership in the AAUP, a list consisting of those institutions recognized by the American Council on Education (ACE). The institution could become approved again only either by reinstating the aggrieved professors and providing them with back pay or by waiting ten years. In the interim, any professor who accepted a new position at the institution would surrender his AAUP membership.[17] Tyler's critical response to the proposal emphasized the policy development that was done through the judicious investigative processes; he rejected Thurstone's calls for militancy.[18]

At the same time Thurstone proposed his plan for increased action, his University of Chicago colleague Ralph Waldo Gerard suggested even more aggressive action. Gerard not only called for boycotting institutions but also proposed the creation of a fund that would support wrongfully dismissed professors and any colleagues who resigned in protest. Gerard developed his plan in response to the Missouri situation, but he was also concerned about larger problems facing the association. He noted a generational divide among the faculty and argued that it was Committee A's ineffectiveness that caused many younger professors to avoid joining the organization. He offered his plan as a way of more successfully addressing the problems of academic freedom, especially in the area of individual remedy, while simultaneously appealing to younger faculty. Gerard's proposal had the support of Committee A chairman Anton J. Carlson, a physiologist at the University of Chicago, but was met with concern by Tyler, who questioned the wisdom of accumulating such a fund and the association's ability to administer it. AAUP president Henry Crew of Northwestern University was more direct. He asserted that the AAUP's power was based on its high-status membership and cautioned against any action that would suggest labor affiliation.[19] When the proposals were circulated to members of the executive council and Committee A in anticipation of the upcoming annual meeting, the responses were overwhelmingly negative and defensive, emphasizing the importance of professionalism, arguing that policies were more important than individuals, and decrying any hint of unionism. Several averred that most who appealed for help were malcontents; others highlighted that younger faculty were likewise often to blame for their own troubles. When Thurstone's and Gerard's proposals received limited hearing at the ensuing annual meeting, Crew and Tyler continued their defense of existing practices and, in Thurstone's mind, preordained rejection of the proposals. To these AAUP leaders, either the AAUP could work with administrators as a respectable organization or it could create a blacklist and alienate college and university presidents. Given that dichotomy, the choice was clear.[20]

Thurstone took the debate beyond the association by publishing a revised version of his plan in the new *Journal of Higher Education*. Although he questioned the effectiveness of the AAUP's reliance on publicity from its investigations to achieve change, he assured readers that his plan was conservative and free of any union connotations. Thurstone, Gerard, and Carlson then surveyed scientists gathered for a meeting later that spring and found that most believed the AAUP needed to be more aggressive in its work.[21] Tyler and others continued to resist the proposals, but widespread dismissals in Mississippi soon shifted the debate. At the request of Mississippi governor Theodore G. Bilbo, the Board of Trustees dismissed all of the presidents and vice presidents, many of the deans, and over one-third of all faculty members from the University of Mississippi, Mississippi State College for Women, and Mississippi Agricultural and Mechanical College. Bilbo boasted of his activity as just the start of a larger purge but denied political motivations. Professional education associations overwhelmingly disagreed, with numerous organizations condemning the action, including the Association of American Universities, the Association of American Medical Colleges, the American Society of Civil Engineers, and the Southern Association of Colleges and Secondary Schools. Each rescinded their approval or accreditation of the institutions.[22]

The AAUP held its annual meeting in the wake of this overwhelming condemnation of the Mississippi situation, but the extent to which the association would protest was unsettled. In his report as general secretary, Tyler commended the protests of the accrediting bodies and professional associations but noted that they were not technically blacklists: they did not affect personal affiliations or prohibit members from accepting positions at the offending institutions. Committee A's report noted the situation but claimed it was best left to other bodies, as the dismissals appeared to be primarily political in nature.[23] Yet despite these concerns, the AAUP membership took two steps that resulted in lasting changes to AAUP policy. First, the association changed its policy to allow for deviation from ACE's list of accredited institutions when determining eligibility for membership. It then passed a resolution condemning the Mississippi dismissals and calling on the schools to be dropped from the ranks of eligible institutions. When the council acted on this resolution, the AAUP had, indeed, initiated a form of a "we don't patronize" list. Current members at the institutions retained their membership, although under a different title, while no new members from the institutions would be accepted until conditions improved. Censure, as it would later be known, was now officially AAUP policy.[24]

The pervasive organizational condemnation of the Mississippi situation also led the AAUP to approach 17 other professional and learned societies about joint action on academic freedom, including asking if they agreed with the Thurstone proposals. Acting in direct response to a conference resolution, AAUP leaders hoped that few would agree. Such response would both justify the long-standing work of the AAUP—as opposed to the more recent action—and could help AAUP membership efforts. Leaders reasoned that if other organizations left the defense of academic freedom to the AAUP, they should at least encourage their members to join the professors' association. By the end of April, the overwhelming negative response had led the association to abandon its efforts for joint action and an academic freedom conference. The AAUP remained the primary advocate for professorial academic freedom, and, despite the Mississippi resolution, Tyler and others believed its restrained approach was vindicated.[25]

Pursuing Cases

Despite this perceived confirmation of the wisdom of a professional approach to academic freedom and tenure, ongoing controversies demonstrated that much work remained. Two 1931 dismissals in particular—those of sociologist Herbert Miller from Ohio State University (OSU) and English professor John Earle Uhler from Louisiana State University (LSU)—stand out and provide insight into both larger concerns and the varied approaches of the organizations most interested in academic freedom.[26] Miller's difficulties dated to the mid-1920s and related to intramural and extramural speech, as well as to his progressive and controversial teaching. While on sabbatical in Asia between 1929 and 1930, he was accused of fostering civil disobedience in India for praising Mohandas K. Gandhi's Salt March and of violating Japanese law for speaking on forbidden topics in Korea. Closer to home, he was criticized for taking white students to visit the historically black Wilberforce University, hosting events where white and black students interacted, and opposing compulsory militarism on campus, all of which contributed to accusations that he was an active Communist. Miller's May dismissal led to an outcry in scholarly and liberal communities. OSU professors, students, and deans protested both the procedure of and justifications for the firing. Faculty at other institutions similarly objected, as did organizations such as the National Association for the Advancement of Colored People, which was particularly appreciative of Miller's attitudes toward race relations. Others supported the firing, including the Ku Klux Klan, American Legion, and some local religious leaders who believed that academics had lost their faith.[27]

The ACLU was among the first to react, offering its assistance to Miller when his dismissal became public on May 26. ACLU National Committee member Norman Thomas met with Miller two days later, but the two decided that public ACLU involvement might only hurt his cause; the ACLU was itself suspect to some stakeholders. As such, the ACLU decided to work behind the scenes, encouraging protests but refraining from overt involvement. Even this proved difficult, however, as some responded to the organization's letter-writing campaign with concern that they lacked enough information to weigh in on the case. In doing so, they highlighted the tensions between acting quickly in response to an urgent situation and acting judiciously with full knowledge of the facts.[28] The AFT's Committee on Academic Freedom saw publicity as its best hope to help, although with broader aims in mind. As Linville reported to the 1931 convention, Miller's case could be used as the basis for a statewide campaign to educate both teachers and the general public about the need for academic freedom. Significantly, Linville believed that the case would allow for the further differentiation of considerations of academic freedom and tenure, emphasizing that the former was needed to provide true education and was unrelated to conditions of employment.[29]

Still, the AAUP proved to be the primary organization working on Miller's behalf.[30] A four-person investigative team visited OSU to interview involved parties, but OSU trustees refused to participate, and its president, George W. Rightmire, was less than forthcoming. In its resulting report, the committee declared that Ohio State authorities had abridged Miller's academic freedom and "violated every essential safeguard" championed by the AAUP. The committee found Miller's speech to be appropriate for a sociologist and less controversial than that of many others. It was unable to determine the effect of Miller's opposition to compulsory military training but did leave open the possibility that university officials acted against Miller in part to appease the legislature, which was evaluating OSU's budget.[31] The institution responded by claiming to implement new procedures to prevent similar controversies, but it continued to restrict faculty speech and placed additional limits on faculty tenure.[32] Despite this "heavy work" undertaken by the AAUP, Miller was not reinstated at the institution, though he soon accepted a position at Bryn Mawr College.[33] In this instance, Linville's claim that "inspired teachers rarely have to go without work"—made to justify separating considerations of tenure from those of academic freedom—proved accurate.[34]

Uhler's case, which likewise involved state and local politics, was inspired by the September publication of *Cane Juice*, his novel depicting the experiences and exploits of an LSU student.[35] While Uhler's intent was authoring a "lyrical story of Louisiana life," influential local priest F. J. Gassler termed it "nauseating," "monstrous slander," and "slimy animalism and mental filth."[36] In response to Gassler's protests and pressure from Governor Huey P. Long, the institution's governing board suspended Uhler on October 8 and dismissed him two days later. Though acknowledging Uhler's success as a teacher, the board claimed that *Cane Juice* offered an indefensible portrayal of the institution.[37] In response to a request from the novel's publisher and fitting with its emphasis on quick action, the ACLU intervened on October 9. In doing so, it disclaimed any interest in the book, expressing only concern that professors' rights to free speech be protected regardless of their medium.[38] The organization launched a letter-writing campaign and encouraged public protests from interested parties, including renowned authors and members of its Committee on Academic Freedom. Just as importantly, the ACLU saw the opportunity to challenge the dismissal in court, arranged for a cooperating lawyer, and prepared to support Uhler's legal efforts.[39] Uhler's employment on a one-year contract offered the ACLU two strategies: arguing for reinstatement or attempting to have his salary for the entire year paid. While it opted for the latter, it was concerned with larger principles of academic freedom rather than resolving Uhler's personal predicament, as the ACLU's Forrest Bailey bluntly informed him. Inopportunely for the ACLU, LSU quickly succumbed to the legal action by paying Uhler his owed salary, thereby depriving the organization of the test case that it sought.[40]

Other organizations noted the case but were not as involved. The AFT called for a public hearing on Uhler's dismissal and relayed the ACLU's efforts in the *American Teacher*.[41] The national union was not yet, however, a defense organization and, with no local in Baton Rouge, had to little offer. The AAUP's reticence is perhaps more noteworthy, especially considering the clear evidence of a violation—something that was increasingly difficult to find, as institutions became adept at hiding reasons behind dismissals. On the same day that LSU agreed to pay the remainder of Uhler's salary, Tyler wrote to future Committee A chair and future AAUP president Samuel A. Mitchell, an astronomer at the University of Virginia, agreeing that the AAUP should print a small statement about the case rather than undertake a full investigation. While the case was troublesome, the AAUP did not want to be linked to a professor who was so reckless.[42] Still, despite this avoidance, the AFT's powerlessness, and the ACLU's primary interest in a legal test case, Uhler's case ended with a satisfactory conclusion for the aggrieved educator. Seven months after his dismissal, LSU reinstated Uhler to his former position. While no official reason was provided, Uhler credited the ACLU's early publicity and legal efforts.[43]

THE GAG ON TEACHING AND THE ACLU COMMITTEE ON ACADEMIC FREEDOM

Even as it engaged with these controversies, the ACLU recognized the limitations of its centrally controlled approach that relied only on the Committee on Academic Freedom to provide an academic imprimatur for its leaders' efforts. Its activities had been inefficient, needed to be rethought, and needed to be undertaken by an enlarged and more involved committee.[44] This issue of reorganization took on more urgency in the wake of the ACLU's May 1931 publication of *The Gag on Teaching,* which the organization described as the first comprehensive treatment of restrictions on teachers and students to be published. The report delineated the multiple areas in which restrictions occurred and the multiple actors whom they affected. It emphasized legislative restrictions on teaching, compulsory patriotism, loyalty oaths, and the institutional limits placed on K–12 teachers and students. It also included explicit consideration of academic freedom in colleges and universities, noting that violations were widespread, occurred across institutional types, and implicated the same public pressures that caused governmental restrictions on K–12 schools. *The Gag on Teaching* also positioned the ACLU in relation to other interested bodies. It pointed to the work of both teachers unions and the AAUP, noting that the former faced resistance that inhibited their growth while the latter was regarded as a slow-moving body that released reports long after situations had concluded. Though it lauded the AAUP's recent consideration of a "more militant policy"—a direct reference to the process that would become known as censuring—it continued to view itself as the more flexible group that could respond quickly, arouse publicity, and pursue redress by appealing to the courts.[45]

The Gag on Teaching outlined organizational goals and circulated the organization's principles on academic freedom to a wider audience. These principles included claims for the end to legislation affecting school curricula; full freedom of expression and rights of citizenship inside, as well as outside, classrooms for faculty members; due process procedures and the reliance on professional academic authority before dismissal in cases involving academic freedom; and full freedom of expression for students, subject only to peer pressure from other students. In these, no distinction was made between higher education and K–12 education; issues of student expression were highlighted; and broad, widely applicable ideas—rather than specific, political issues—were emphasized. Elsewhere in the document, the ACLU identified its interest in threats that extended beyond mere civil liberties issues, including fighting propaganda and textbook censorship. Still, the group denied interest in intervening in internal administrative matters that involved personal animosity or procedural violations. It would leave these and related cases to the AAUP.[46]

Even though it was hastily compiled by the New York office without input from members of the Committee on Academic Freedom, *The Gag on Teaching* implied that the committee was responsible for its authorship, causing complaints and at least one resignation.[47] In response to this reaction and the larger realization that it needed an active and involved committee rather than a list of important names, the ACLU restructured its work for academic freedom. It reached out to new membership, both in New York and nationally, in hopes of expanding its capacity; and it attempted to diversify the committee's membership to include university presidents and school superintendents. While a number of executive invitees declined—including the University of North Carolina's Frank Graham, who regretted that struggles in his home state forced him to focus his attention there—others accepted. Just as significantly, the ACLU invited several members of the AAUP, including Lovejoy and City College of New York professor Holland Thompson, as part of a larger strategy to increase collaboration. Thompson was asked to serve as a liaison between the two groups in their efforts to form a "plan of cooperation."[48] With this impetus, the two organizations began to work more in concert, with the ACLU referring tenure matters to the AAUP and the AAUP referring those involving free speech but not academic freedom to the civil liberties organization.[49]

The Gag on Teaching posed difficulties beyond its implied authorship to include the very ideas espoused. The existing principles outlined in the volume aroused a great deal of criticism both within and outside the organization. Concerns over the leeway called for in classroom speech were especially pressing and, in 1931, the ACLU began a three-year effort to modify the principles, first under the leadership of William H. Kilpatrick, chairman of the Committee on Academic Freedom, and then under New York University philosopher Sidney Hook.[50] Finalized in April 1934, the new principles provided the basis for the ACLU's work on academic freedom for almost twenty years. They began with a defense of academic freedom based on the importance of unfettered experts in contested times, the historical role of educators as leaders, and the need for teachers at all levels to be trusted as authorities.[51] The new statement was organized in six main sections, three of which argued specifically against loyalty oaths, religious intrusion into public schools, and legislative restrictions on teaching. Another section argued for students to maintain all of their speech rights in school settings, including avoiding discipline for religious or political beliefs. As in the earlier version, any controls or limitations should arise only from their peers. Much of the document was devoted to the issue of "administrative control," including that in colleges and universities, "teaching should be quite free of all interference except for the requirements of standards of scholarship and effective teaching."[52] Excepting classroom propaganda, teachers should have the full ability to discuss any relevant opinions in their classes, including their own. If any controversy arose, the ACLU explicitly called for the AAUP or a similar organization to adjudicate.

The classroom rights for K–12 teachers were similar, though with concessions made for students' ages and the call for the final resolution of controversies to come from a broader panel of teachers, administrators, and the general public. Although the ACLU continued its call for citizenship rights, these rights were also qualified in a way that they had not previously been. Teachers and professors should be encouraged to participate in public life but with the caveat that such freedom of extramural expression was limited to that which did not negatively affect their teaching and research, conditions that remained undefined. The final section argued that these collective principles could be enforced only by active organizations of teachers and professors. Throughout, the ACLU demonstrated both its recognition that rights to academic freedom were not unlimited and its increasing appreciation of and respect for teachers' and professional associations, especially the AAUP.

During this period of expanding its committee membership and revising its principles, the ACLU continued to involve itself in several cases per year. It remained the leading advocate for student speech rights, offering legal support for leftist students at the University of Pittsburgh, campus paper editor Reed Harris at Columbia University, and others.[53] In 1934, it published a survey of restrictions on the uses of public school buildings by unpopular groups, argued that widespread discrimination existed due to prejudice and pressure from patriotic organizations, and offered its legal aid to those barred from speaking in school facilities.[54] The ACLU also retained its interest in violations of professors' academic freedom, most notably following Lienhard Bergel's 1935 dismissal from New Jersey College for Women for alleged incompetency. In a case that has remained controversial into the modern era, Bergel claimed that the true cause was the conflict between his department chair Friedrich J. Hauptmann's ardent Nazism and his own anti-Nazi beliefs.[55] ACLU meetings with college president Robert C. Clothier led to a formal institutional investigation consisting of 29 days of hearings. Representatives of an ACLU subcommittee attended each session and, at times, submitted questions to witnesses through Bergel's attorney, but the dismissal was ultimately upheld by the school's governing board. In its lengthy report, the ACLU lauded the thorough hearing but concluded that the board had been biased against Bergel and that his dismissal had, in fact, been politically motivated.[56] The ACLU was unsuccessful in its attempts to return Bergel to his position, but the experience did leave an impression on the institution. When Hauptmann quietly returned to Nazi Germany a few years later, Clothier and college dean Margaret Corwin kept it secret, recognizing that the ACLU's anticipated publicity could cause them difficulty.[57]

Continuing Pressure on the AAUP

Though actively involved in countering Bergel's and others' dismissals, the ACLU considered relatively few cases each year due to its focus on academic freedom and civil liberties over violations of tenure. Moreover, institutions were growing more adept at hiding the true reasons behind dismissals, rather than dealing with the negative publicity that organizations could generate when infringements became known.[58] The AAUP's Committee A, to which the ACLU referred some cases, found itself in a very different situation, and its late 1920s confidence that violations would decrease proved misplaced. In 1931, Mitchell reported that Committee A was busier than it had ever been before, with 63 new cases brought before it that year alone and a dozen earlier cases still pending. In the previous three years, only 63 new cases had been brought to the committee in total.[59] Mitchell blamed the increase on the effects of the Great Depression: faculty were being legitimately released due to financial necessity; institutions used the pretext of financial strife to dismiss faculty whose removal they sought for other reasons; and faculty who lost their positions found it difficult to secure new ones. These effects posed their own concerns, but all added to the work of an already burdened Committee A.[60] Investigations continued to be time-consuming, laborious, and expensive. Violations of tenure continued to be more frequent than violations of academic freedom, and the nature of the inquiries still delayed the publication of investigative reports. While the presence of John M. Maguire, hired to provide legal advice in 1926, helped facilitate Committee A's investigations, these inquires continued to rely on the work of already busy volunteers—volunteers whose services could be hard to obtain.[61]

This reliance on volunteers to carry out the bulk of the work forced the committee to be even more selective in deciding which cases to handle. Of the 75 total cases considered in 1931, Committee A carried out full investigations for only 9 and published short statements without visits on 7. The following year, during which 82 cases were brought to the committee's attention, full investigations were undertaken for 12, with 3 additional statements printed. While these numbers point to the committee's limited ability to investigate, Mitchell argued that the committee was growing more successful in its mediatory work and was increasing its ability settle disputes quietly to each party's satisfaction. In 1932, he noted that Committee A had changed procedures and recently begun to distribute some reports only to interested parties, giving the institution the opportunity to remedy difficulties discreetly. Although the number of new cases dropped to 36 in 1934, Committee A continued to handle many more cases than it had prior to the Depression, and the committee continued to increase its efforts to address situations quietly without publishing complete reports.[62]

One consequence of this inability to consider all cases was the decision to focus Committee A's efforts on institutions accredited by the ACE, the list used as the basis for potential membership in the AAUP. Suggested in the 1931 Committee A report and implemented the following year, this decision represented a change from the earlier plan of investigating dismissals regardless of institutional eligibility. In addition to limiting the AAUP's usefulness for educators at unaccredited institutions, this change caused some apprehension within the association. The primary concern was not that the organization was elitist, however. The continuing fear was that the AAUP might be thought to operate along union lines. It was therefore important for Committee A reports to emphasize that it remained committed to larger principles, not just members' rights, and was therefore willing to investigate dismissals of nonmembers. Mitchell's successor, Ohio State University historian Carl Wittke, was a supporter of unions but, in his 1934 report, pointed to this interest in nonmembers as proof that the AAUP was not one. He favorably noted that while the emphasis on eligible institutions was still in effect, a committee member had been sent to help mediate a case at an unaccredited institution.[63] The AAUP was not, he argued, "a closed corporation for the attainment of selfish ends for a favored few."[64]

Despite the efforts to differentiate the AAUP from teachers unions, some members argued that the association was ineffective and needed to act more like one if it wanted to protect academic freedom. While pointing to the ineligible list as evidence of strength, Committee A and AAUP leaders continually reiterated their belief that judicious investigative work provided the standing that allowed for greater gains than could militant action.[65] Yet as demonstrated by the 1933 events involving Rollins College—events that mapped closely to those at Washburn College more than a decade earlier in their impetus, outcome, and importance to AAUP claims for intramural speech[66]— the association's work remained complicated and contested. When Rollins president Hamilton Holt, who in the 1920s had led efforts against antievolution legislation in Florida, dismissed John A. Rice, who had in 1921 lost his position at Southern Methodist University due to antievolutionist attacks, Committee A's Lovejoy and Austin S. Edwards investigated at both Holts's and Rice's recommendation. They hoped to find an acceptable resolution for both parties. Before deciding on whether to submit a full report, the committee learned that three more faculty had been dismissed and two more had resigned due to conflict with the administration. In all, 11 faculty left during the 1932–33 academic year, many due to their efforts on Rice's behalf. The investigative committee ultimately found that Holt operated the institution autocratically, attempted to divide the faculty, was antagonistic toward the AAUP, and had dismissed faculty for disloyalty when they had tried to improve institutional governance.[67] Yet when the AAUP considered adding the institution to its ineligible list at the end of the year—which by that time included Battle Creek College and Harris Teachers College in addition to the Mississippi institutions—remaining members of the institution's AAUP chapter protested both at a lengthy council meeting and then at the 1933 annual meeting. They argued that the action violated the AAUP's charter, would damage the institution and its faculty, and would damage the AAUP itself. One member compared the AAUP's actions to those of superpatriots in the midst of the war hysteria. Shortly afterward, the AAUP overrode these concerns and placed the institution on the list. While some complained that the AAUP's actions were ineffective, they could hold real meaning to those involved.[68]

For its part, the administration of Rollins College challenged that the AAUP's investigation was "injudicious," a claim that was particularly stinging to an organization that prided itself on unbiased and respectable reports. Although the AAUP determined that the claim was true only in a legal sense and contended that its reports were scientific, the concern led the association to replace the less prescriptive instructions sent to investigative committees with more formalized and standardized procedures for Committee A.[69] These new policies, which took two years to formulate, identified Committee A's continuing inability to handle all cases of alleged violations. As such, the committee investigated only those cases that it considered important to the larger association and continued to emphasize accredited institutions. The policy stressed that the investigations were to be unbiased, were intended to uncover all relevant facts, and were not designed to benefit incompetent teachers (as long as they were treated fairly). Although the burden of proof was on the complaining faculty member, this did not grant institutions the license to dismiss staff indiscriminately and then provide reasons upon request. Investigating committees were to emphasize mediation whenever possible but not at the expense of the association's principles. Moreover, all publicity was to be avoided, as it would interfere with investigative activities. With this policy, for the first time the AAUP claimed that junior faculty should be considered permanent after three to five years and could then only be dismissed for just cause, though being considered unworthy for promotion was deemed a reasonable justification for nonrenewal. In offering these ideas, the AAUP was slowly moving toward a redefinition of tenure proposals and an abandonment of the dual track of tenurable and non-tenurable that had been implicitly condoned in the 1925 *Conference Statement*. These last two issues were particularly relevant to the AFT's increasing involvement in higher education and its attractiveness to junior faculty.[70]

The nonrecommended list became known as the "ineligible list" in 1935 but continued to raise concerns in the AAUP in the ensuing years, in part due to disagreement over its meaning. At the 1935 meeting, then–general secretary and Northwestern University law professor Walter Wheeler Cook claimed that it was not a blacklist, as had been widely reported, and that it only indicated dissatisfaction with an institution's current administration. Contrary to common belief, AAUP members who accepted positions at institutions on the list would not lose their membership; new members would just not be accepted from ineligible institutions.[71] When University of Buffalo chancellor Samuel Capen, Association of American Colleges (AAC) member and former ACE leader, described the action as a "blacklisting" at the ensuing AAUP meeting, the AAUP tried to mitigate the confusion by printing a clarification alongside his talk in the *Bulletin*.[72] Carlson explained that the use of such a list was analogous to the medical profession setting standards for medical schools: educational professionals were setting similar standards and using "moral coercion" to benefit the organization and its efforts.[73] Still, the act remained misunderstood and controversial, resulting in the 1937 decision to "censure" administrations rather than institutions. The AAUP would henceforth identify institutions whose administrations did not meet its standards, but professors at them would again be eligible to join the association.[74]

Conclusion

From the late 1920s through mid-1930s, the three main organizations interested in academic freedom—the AAUP, the ACLU, and the AFT—continued to reconsider and rework their efforts to achieve its establishment in American higher education. Each responded to both internal and external pressures and struggled with how best to meet desired goals amid limited resources, misunderstandings of purposes, and disagreements over the best paths forward. Through its Committee A, the AAUP was the most consistent voice for academic freedom and tenure, yet the challenges it faced were real. Depression-related financial struggles led more colleges to dismiss faculty members, and Committee A was able to investigate an even smaller percentage of cases than it had just a few years earlier. The controversies in Missouri and Mississippi led to the creation of the non-recommended list and provided the AAUP with a new, if misunderstood, publicity tool. Still, the association failed to satisfy critics who wished it to serve in a more protective role and undertake more aggressive action—at the same time that many of its leaders remained troubled by supposition that it was a professors' union. Ongoing challenges may have prevented the AAUP from achieving all that some hoped, but the association was still able to make progress toward its goals of academic freedom and tenure, all the while facing stern criticism from within and without. Both criticism and praise would only increase amid threats from the AFT and efforts to replace the 1925 *Conference Statement* in the late 1930s.

Through its emphasis on legal action and publicity, the ACLU's work complemented that of the AAUP. While it did not have the respect of the professors' association, the civil liberties group did offer flexibility and a network of lawyers interested in establishing a legal basis for civil liberties. The ACLU also broadened the consideration beyond issues of professionalism to include students, religious discrimination, and the rights to use school facilities. Willing to undertake unpopular political stances and challenge entrenched interests, the ACLU achieved success in some individual cases. As the Uhler case at LSU demonstrated, though, the successes were not always the ones for which they hoped. Elsewhere, as with Miller's dismissal from OSU, the ACLU's very reputation limited what it could do for an aggrieved educator and pushed it behind the scenes. When cases involved the ongoing challenges to intramural speech and easier-to-demonstrate violations of tenure, the ACLU was even more hampered and, with its revised principles, noted the acceptability of some limitations. The AFT reemerged as a national presence by the end of the 1920s and continued its legislative lobbying on behalf of teachers in Washington, DC, and beyond. Under Linville, its Committee on Academic Freedom was beginning to work on the national scene, advocating increased acceptance of basic standards of academic freedom as necessary for education rather than as tied to employment. Though its work for specific educators was limited and deferred to locals, by the middle of the decade, the AFT was changing. It would, as it moved beyond the educational approach later in the decade—and after Linville left the union in a controversy over Communists in his local—become the most militant, if not most judicious, advocate for academic freedom.

The activities of these organizations and the lingering issues involving appropriate responses and attempted cooperation foreshadow some of the concerns that would dominate academic freedom in the late 1930s. The AAUP continued to face internal and external criticism over its approach to academic freedom. The ultimate insufficiency of the 1925 *Conference Statement* led the AAC and the AAUP back to the negotiating table to rework principles and protections. In the midst of increasing economic strife, the AFT continued its recovery and became a more active participant in the ongoing battles. The need for greater protection led to other entrants into the field and a push for greater cooperation. The concerns over Communists, which were implicated at Ohio State in 1931, greatly expanded and became one of the most pressing problem for advocates of academic freedom. These issues were still emerging, however, as were the principled and pragmatic shifts in the activities of some of these associations interested in establishing academic freedom.

7

Toward a Less "Dangerous Occupation"

The mid-to-late 1930s were years of political activism, ongoing economic struggles, labor strife, and increasing fear over the impending war in Europe. On college campuses, they were characterized by a student movement that was more robust than had ever been seen in the United States—one that has yet to be matched in terms of the proportion of students involved.[1] It was also a period of Communist intrigue, as superpatriots and Hearst newspapers warned that Soviet agents and their American counterparts were undermining the educational system, corrupting students, and destroying society. Shrill warnings by Elizabeth Dilling, the Daughters of the American Revolution, the American Legion, and others demonstrated that allegedly Communist professors were at the heart of the concern. Political repression of teachers spread across the country, as did legislative investigations into radicalism in education and movements to require faculty members and teachers to sign oaths pledging their loyalty to the US Constitution and the country. The oaths were, according to American Federation of Teachers (AFT) secretary-treasurer Florence Hanson, "a menace to intellectual freedom probably exceeding all other threats" and were routinely denounced by Hanson's and other educational and professional associations.[2]

The more mundane concerns over institutional politics and violations of tenure remained and proved decisive for some faculty—to the American Association of University Professors (AAUP), these were the most important issues—but the public battles over academic freedom in the mid-to-late 1930s were often fought over leftist politics. As historian Ellen W. Schrecker argued, although leftist faculty had more freedom than ever before, restrictions remained and politically motivated actions could end careers.[3] The leftward move of a portion of the academy and the related controversies over Communism did more than just affect individual faculty on college campuses: they affected the activities and approaches of the organizations working to define and defend academic freedom. The AFT and the American Civil Liberties Union (ACLU) each struggled with how best to handle the real or alleged Communist Party affiliation of some of their members, with each ultimately acting against them. Yet in the late 1930s, some of the very AFT members who would later be expelled or otherwise removed from power for their leftist politics were at the center of the organization's efforts for academic freedom and its increasingly aggressive stance. At the same time, larger political challenges brought new entrants into the field, pushed educational and related associations to try to work together, and simultaneously kept them from doing so. The Progressive Education Association (PEA), which sought to form a national umbrella organization to mount a staunch defense of teachers' freedoms, was unable to gain traction. In the face of organizational rivalries and its own emphasis on quick rather than judicious action, the PEA failed to foster a united front and further undermined its own efforts.

This tension between quick reaction and thoughtful investigation had been long standing within the arena but reached new heights in the rivalry between the AAUP and AFT, the two organizations that were the most important late in the decade. As the AFT challenged the AAUP in academic freedom cases and increasingly appealed to instructors and junior faculty, the AAUP reacted. Its leadership was fearful of the inroads the AFT was making in higher education and believed that the union sought to take over the AAUP. This recognition added urgency to the AAUP's efforts to rework the 1925 *Conference Statement on Academic Freedom and Tenure,* made the Association of American Colleges (AAC) more amenable to the reconsideration, and ultimately affected the principles that would result. The 1940 *Statement of Principles on Academic Freedom and Tenure* was the specific outgrowth of these activities, the legacy of 25 years of organizational interactions, and the basis for both modern policies regarding and modern conceptions of academic freedom and tenure. The procedural protections that it called for were in response to the primary understanding arising from the continually draining work of Committee A on Academic Freedom and Tenure. As AAUP associate secretary William McGuffey Hepburn contended at a regional meeting of the AAC in 1937, without tenure, teaching is "a dangerous occupation."[4]

Legislative Inquiries and Loyalty Oaths in the Middle of the Decade

The dangers to teachers and faculty came from a variety of sources in the 1930s, including efforts of state legislatures and the US Congress. Beginning with US Representative Hamilton Fish Jr.'s investigations into alleged Communist activities in schools and colleges in 1930, governmental bodies repeatedly inquired into student and faculty subversion, though they rarely found much before the end of the decade. Fish's committee interviewed almost three hundred witnesses in a dozen cities, eventually warning of subversion at a handful of universities, although without substantiating evidence. In 1933 and 1935, the Wisconsin legislature investigated radicals at the University of Wisconsin, focusing first on students and then the institution's president, Glenn Frank. When drugstore magnate Charles Walgreen removed his niece from the University of Chicago in 1935 to protect her from alleged indoctrination, the state's senate probed the institution as the first step of a planned larger inquiry. Despite sensational allegations by Dilling and others, university president Robert Maynard Hutchins and esteemed but controversial professor Robert Morss Lovett successfully defended the institution broadly and Lovett specifically. Hutchins believed that the defense would serve as a "brake on further assaults on academic freedom," but such assaults continued the following year in New York, where state senator John J. McNaboe led an investigation into Communist subversion at Cornell University. McNaboe similarly sought to extend his hearings more broadly but found little support and soon faced ridicule.[5]

Alongside these investigations was an increased push for loyalty oaths in state legislatures and, to a lesser extent, Congress. Encouraged by groups such as the American Legion and the Daughters of the American Revolution, 16 different states considered implementing loyalty oaths in 1935 alone. By the following year, 21 states had loyalty oath legislation on the books, some dating back several decades but most implemented during the 1930s. Legislation in many states applied to college faculty, in addition to public and private K–12 teachers. In Washington, DC, the House of Representatives considered a resolution calling on all states to pass loyalty oath requirements for educators. Though the resolution failed, Congress did pass the so-called "red rider" in 1935, thereby requiring teachers to attest that they had not taught or advocated Communism prior to receiving each paycheck. These requirements were panned by educators both for imposing burdens on them that were not placed on others and because they were deemed ineffective. Still, they largely obeyed them. Harvard University president James B. Conant, for example, famously but unsuccessfully was among the many college and university presidents who opposed the oaths in Massachusetts, then enforced them after they became law. University of Michigan president Alexander Grant Ruthven lamented that educators were singled out but still sought to avoid antagonizing the legislature.[6] He simultaneously warned of subversives who propagandized under the banner of academic freedom, noting, "Here is to be found the real threat to academic freedom—that irresponsibility will be given protection in its name. The reactions of laymen to this absurdity in education are apt to be violent, hysterical and misguided."[7]

Numerous educational and related organizations joined individual educators in opposing these legislative interventions. In 1935, the AAUP formed Committee B on Freedom of Speech. Composed of University of Chicago physiology professor Anton J. Carlson, Harvard law professor Zechariah Chafee, and Arthur O. Lovejoy, the committee released a report two years later calling the oaths "the manifestation of an essentially un-American temper on the part of a fraction of our citizenship." Though Committee B sought to coordinate activities with other professional associations—including the American Council on Education (ACE), the American Academy of Arts and Sciences, and the Social Science Research Council—its efforts were short-lived, as the association focused on other pressing concerns.[8] With its overriding concern for governmental encroachment on civil liberties, the ACLU was even more involved than the AAUP. Along with its efforts to protect freedoms of students and the rights of leftist speakers to use school buildings, the ACLU focused its academic freedom activities in the mid-to-late 1930s on attempting to forestall the oaths and inquiries. The ACLU protested the Fish Committee even after it had run its course. In 1933, it led the effort to preempt a loyalty oath in New Jersey. At the time, it helped keep the legislation from being voted on, though similar legislation was passed two years later. In its new principles, released in 1934, the ACLU included the specific claim that the oaths were discriminatory, harmful to education, and should be "vigorously opposed"; in 1936, it formed a special subcommittee to help teachers and professors under investigation as a result of these laws. Its state affiliates were often involved in the specific local efforts for repeal. Still, it did not directly challenge the loyalty oaths in court. Though believing they were problematic and illegal, the ACLU was unsure that the courts would agree.[9] The AFT was likewise engaged, commissioning Henry Linville's 1935 analysis and critique of loyalty oaths and, under the leadership of its legislative committee, challenging the "red rider" legislation in Washington, DC. In 1937, these lobbying efforts bore fruit, as the loyalty oath for educators in the nation's capital was repealed.[10] In these efforts to counter loyalty oaths and legislative inquires, educational associations occasionally found common ground and put aside their differences for shared goals. The AFT, for example, worked with the ACLU and occasionally, as in Washington, DC, found itself on the same side as the more conservative and influential National Education Association (NEA). Some, though, doubted that any individual organization could counter the array of forces that opposed academic freedom and, resultantly, sought greater coordination. At the forefront of that movement was Frederick Redefer, executive secretary of the PEA.

Failed Efforts at Collaboration and Intervention

Founded in 1919 to promote the "new education," the PEA called for carefully studying students' development while attending to their health and well-being, connecting the school with the home, and using educational institutions as laboratories for experimentation. Through the publicity of its annual conventions, the exposure provided by the journal *Progressive Education*, and the credibility offered by honorary presidencies of Harvard University's Charles W. Eliot and Columbia University's John Dewey, the PEA established itself as an important voice on educational issues, though one that was small and often faced financial difficulties. When, at its 1932 convention, George Counts challenged the organization to fulfill its promise of restructuring American schooling and society, the PEA entered a new era of increased vitality toward social reconstruction.[11] At the same meeting, the association's Committee on Social and Economic Problems, led by Counts, argued that teachers must achieve academic freedom, retain full rights of citizenship, and fight the encroachment of business and patriotic groups on school curricula.[12] This interest in academic freedom became a primary emphasis of the association in the mid-1930s and frequent topic in *Progressive Education*, including Howard K. Beale's "Dare Society Deny Its Teachers Freedom?" in early 1934. Based on the research that resulted in *Are American Teachers Free?*, Beale offered a rousing critique of patriotic groups, public utilities, business interests, community attitudes, and educators themselves. He bemoaned the wrongful dismissal of teachers but noted: "The real problem, however, is not to prevent dismissal, but to protect the teacher from innumerable repressions, short of dismissal, which prevent his full self-expression or deny him the privilege of intellectual honesty."[13]

A few months later, when North Carolina junior high school principal James M. Shields lost his position shortly after both his organizing of schoolteachers and the publication of his novel critical of the local schools and community, the PEA took the opportunity to act on these beliefs. Lacking any organizational mechanism, Redefer personally wrote to the superintendent and the school board for information about the case, encouraged the state teachers association to investigate, and communicated with local PEA members on Shields's behalf. After these efforts failed—his letters to school officials went unanswered, the teachers association indicated it would be several months before it could report anything, and even members of the PEA advised that investigating would be inflammatory—Redefer saw an opportunity to pursue his larger goal of uniting national educational associations interested in academic freedom. An initial meeting specifically about Shields's case led Redefer to invite other organizations to send unofficial representatives to an informal discussion of existing organizational policies and activities, principles of academic freedom, current mechanisms for defense, and the possibility of forming an umbrella organization to protect K–12 educators. In these efforts, Redefer specifically targeted the influential but conservative NEA, which he believed could be shamed into participating. He sought to push the NEA to live up to its recent statement in support of academic freedom while also helping to liberalize the organization, a goal of progressive educators in the era.[14]

In a pair of meetings in late 1934, representatives from multiple organizations met with Redefer, Shields, and Beale to discuss academic freedom and the possibility for joint action. At the first meeting, they relayed their organizations' beliefs, principles, and efforts, with most admitting that their organizations had little ability to defend aggrieved educators. The group agreed that principles needed to be established and that no single organization was adequately able to promote and protect academic freedom for elementary and secondary teachers.[15] At the second meeting, representatives from the ACE, ACLU, AFT, American Association of University Women (AAUW), National Congress of Parents and Teachers, National Council of Religion in Higher Education (NCRHE), and several NEA departments joined Redefer, Beale, and Shields to discuss the possibility of greater coordination. Three subcommittees were quickly formed, each discussing one of three proposals: a statement on academic freedom written for the meeting by Ohio State University professor Boyd H. Bode; "A Framework for a Code of Ethics for Teachers," presented by Milwaukee State Teachers College president Frank Baker; and Redefer's "Proposal for the Establishment of a National Commission on Academic Freedom in Public and Private Elementary and Secondary Schools." Bode's document called for the recognition of the importance of academic freedom for students, argued that teachers' rights derived from those of students, and contended that propaganda was contrary to student needs. In addition, teachers and students must have all rights of other citizens outside of classrooms. To Bode, the problem was not just internal academic freedom for teachers but educational freedom more broadly. The second proposal, the code of ethics, called for hiring teachers on merit, granting tenure after a short probationary period, and offering the right to appeal a termination to an impartial body. Further, although educators should avoid personal attacks on other teachers, honest criticism of teaching methods and philosophies was an important part of the profession, as was teachers' control over their own ethical standards. Quickly approved with few modifications and later distributed in pamphlet form, these two documents outlined basic principles around which national organizations could interact.[16]

The more important document—Redefer's proposal on the creation of a national commission—was not nearly as well received. The original version called for an active body of representatives from the participating associations that would coordinate activities, carry out an active educational campaign, investigate alleged violations, interpret principles of academic freedom for schools and communities, and appoint juries of professionals and laymen to adjudicate difficult cases. To Redefer's severe disappointment, a much less ambitious plan was approved. The committee called for the creation of what became the National Advisory Council on Academic Freedom (NACAF), which would meet twice a year to share information and promote educational efforts about the importance of academic freedom. When representatives of the AAUW, ACLU, ACE, NCRHE, NEA, PEA, and Phi Delta Kappa (a professional organization for educators) finally met again ten months later, disappointments continued. Few organizations had formally considered Bode's and Baker's statements or even deliberated joining the coordinating body. Two that had considered the latter, the National Congress of Parents and Teachers and the AAUP, had decided against participating, although the AAUP did agree to provide information to the group. Eventually, the ACLU and NCRHE joined the AFT, NEA's Department of Classroom Teachers,

Phi Delta Kappa, and PEA in the new, less ambitious NACAF. It was an organization that would be burdened by a lack of funds—the initial proposal of a $5,400 annual budget was reduced first to a $200 donation per organization and then to a mere $25 per organization—as well as, in Redefer's terms, "very evident jealousies" among the interested organizations.[17]

The six participating organizations of the NACAF moved forward with plans to hold semiannual meetings to share information on cases and consider ways that they could more effectively promote academic freedom. In 1935 and 1936, member organizations worked together to oppose loyalty oath laws in New York and shared information about violations of academic freedom. While the initial plans called for a group to address only primary and secondary education, it soon relayed information on cases in colleges, as well, including dismissals from Cedar Crest College, Lock Haven State Teachers College, and City College of New York.[18] These considerations of postsecondary education were still not enough to entice an AAUP more interested in differentiation than collaboration to join the coordinating body. Moreover, the NACAF failed to gain a foothold in the debates over academic freedom and struggled against competing organizational interests and "lethargy."[19] Participants soon began questioning whether the NACAF was still in existence. By 1938, merely getting the group to convene was considered a success, though not an important enough one to keep Phi Delta Kappa from withdrawing due to a lack of interest among members.[20]

The slightly smaller committee undertook one major project before dissolving at the end of the decade: an examination of the apparatus available to protect academic freedom at state and national levels. The results were disappointing. The mechanisms for protecting aggrieved professors and teachers were so inadequate—and the local and state considerations of academic freedom were so lacking—that the NACAF declined to distribute its findings. Furthermore, the study itself caused consternation. AAUP leaders were particularly frustrated with the survey and considered refusing to reply, both because of perceived flaws in the methodology and mistrust of the council's intentions. Many others did not respond at all.[21] While the NACAF offered a venue for sharing information and some hope for greater collaboration, it was unable to overcome the lack of action, commitment, and dedication of the member organizations. The PEA's efforts to create a unified front for academic freedom had failed.

Although the NACAF was unsuccessful in its attempts to coordinate defense mechanisms for academic freedom, it did prod at least some action from other organizations, including the NEA. In November 1935, the NEA established a five-member Committee on Academic Freedom designed to oppose legislation restricting academic freedom and to investigate alleged violations thereof.[22] Despite being given a mandate to "cooperate with other reputable and recognized national organizations" on the topic, it never joined the NACAF and by the end of the decade had lapsed.[23] Neither this new group nor the NEA Department of Classroom Teachers' own Committee on Academic Freedom, which was formed in 1932 and participated in the NACAF, was as active as the NEA's Committee on Tenure. The latter group primarily sought improved teacher tenure laws but, under the leadership of Indiana school superintendent Donald DuShane, soon investigated alleged violations of tenure, as well. While most of this work involved elementary and secondary education, postsecondary issues were also occasionally considered, including an investigation into dismissals from Lock Haven State Teachers College that revealed the difficulties that DuShane and his committee faced in their work.[24]

In May 1935, the Lock Haven governing board decided against renewing the appointments of four instructors and the dean of women. None was provided a legitimate hearing or received an official reason, although the board later declared that financial exigency led to the removals. Following a superficial investigation that did not include interviewing the aggrieved educators, the Pennsylvania State Education Association's (PSEA) Commission on Professional Ethics quickly accepted the official explanation. Believing the inquiry to be illegitimate, the NEA Committee on Tenure initiated its own investigation. Its study found that the college hired six new educators during the summer after the dismissals, including the son of a board member. It further discovered that the five dismissed teachers had each appealed to the board prior to their dismissals, complaining of difficulties within the institution's administration. As a result of these findings, DuShane's committee called on future tenure legislation to apply to college professors and expressed an interest in studying the issue at the college level. The ensuing NEA national convention approved the report over the objections of officials from the PSEA, whom DuShane contended both tried to suppress the results and remove him from the Committee on Tenure in hopes of preventing future investigatory work. Considered dangerous and outside the NEA mainstream by many in the organization, the Committee on Tenure was hindered in its efforts for teacher rights. Despite being the largest educational association in the nation, the NEA remained only a peripheral player in the efforts for academic freedom for the rest of the decade.[25]

The NEA was not the only organization to respond to the NACAF by founding a new body to address violations of teachers' freedoms. At its February 1935 meeting, the PEA passed a resolution in support of the NACAF and a second that warned of the efforts of patriotic groups to limit freedoms, called for teachers to have the right to discuss controversial topics, and authorized its board to pursue "this fundamental concept of Americanism."[26] Based on his experiences with the NACAF and relying on this resolution for justification, Redefer founded the Commission on Educational Freedom (CEF) later that year.[27] Initial response was underwhelming: solicitations for membership attracted only 350 of 9,000 PEA members.[28] One respondent who refused to join the commission noted that it amounted to "an invitation to stupid martyrdom." Another was concerned for very different reasons, questioning whether the commission would protect Communists, whom he believed were intent on destroying democracy under the guise of freedom.[29] With this unsure footing, the CEF soon began work on what became a 48-page study guide addressing broad issues of academic freedom and civil liberties for teachers, including various definitions of the concepts, discussion questions, and case studies that it believed could help address shortcomings in teacher education. This confidence was misplaced. The CEF mailed copies to deans of teachers colleges and schools of education, but it was never adopted by teacher educators and no copies were ever sold.[30]

More damaging than the failure of the study guide was the haphazard manner in which defense work was approached. The CEF rarely met, faced funding concerns, and was largely run by Redefer and Teachers College professor Goodwin Watson. Its main activity was trying to generate publicity in cases such as those at Lock Haven, the University of Kansas City, and elsewhere, though its efforts were often secondary to those of more involved organizations and even the PEA was unsure if it had any positive effects. Its negative effects soon became apparent. In May 1937, Watson sent an urgent plea requesting that members intervene on behalf of "four live cases," alleging that administrators at four institutions were dismissing teachers and professors for union membership, for liberal political activities, and for questioning the policies of the administration.[31] The response was resounding: advocates of academic freedom quickly questioned Watson's judiciousness, objectivity, and tact. One, New York University professor Philip W. L. Cox, claimed that Watson was wrong about the situation in the Scarsdale, New York, Edgemont School. If Watson's information on the other situations was "as superficial, unfair and contrary to fact," then the CEF was "encouraging many foolish and futile protests."[32] The information was, in fact, not much better. By the end of June, evidence appeared that the requests for intervention had been inappropriate in at least three of the four cases, leading some to question whether the commission was doing more harm than good for academic freedom and the broader goals of the PEA.[33]

In response to these challenges and a threatened libel lawsuit by the principal of Edgemont School, the PEA reorganized the CEF that fall and removed Watson from its chairmanship. As Ohio State University professor H. Gordon Hullfish, Watson's replacement, later wrote, the commission was to have "a more ambitious, and yet a more cautious, approach."[34] It was to set up regional and local committees to investigate and defend academic freedom while the national committee would carry on educational activities. Members' participation in cases would only be encouraged with the approval of the PEA president. Although all PEA members were automatically granted membership in the reorganized CEF, participation lagged further. A call for donations resulted in fewer than two hundred replies. Efforts to establish local and regional academic freedom committees were largely unsuccessful, as were attempts to organize summer sessions on academic freedom. The defense of teachers threatened with dismissal was further doomed by the lack of the funds needed to undertake the type of thorough investigations necessary to prevent the recurrence of earlier difficulties.[35] By 1940, the PEA Board of Directors agreed to Hullfish's suggestion that the commission be discontinued. In its five years of activity, the group was unable to rouse its own members' support, failed in sustaining an effective coordinating body, and generated more controversy over tactics than support for its principles.

Protests and Politics in the AFT

Though the AFT took part in the NACAF, its solo efforts for academic freedom were more significant. Indeed, as the ACLU increasingly focused its efforts on legal challenges, students, and schools as public forums, the AFT became the second most prominent association in pursuit of academic freedom but one that harbored aspirations of becoming the leading voice for both teachers and college faculty. In the early 1930s, its Committee on Academic Freedom focused on informing the public about the educational need for academic freedom, but some began calling for the union to do more, including

Florence Hanson, who in 1933 argued that the AFT's primary role should be to protect teachers' positions.[36] She and others sought more militant defense of aggrieved educators and a shift from Linville's disassociation of academic freedom from tenure. Yet before the AFT was strong enough to heed her call, it began a long internal fight that centered on Linville's New York Teachers Union (Local 5). Longstanding concerns over factionalism in Local 5 led Linville and others to attempt first to limit Communist members' influence and then to disband and reform the local. When both New York–based and national efforts failed, eight hundred members of the local, including Linville and almost the entire leadership, left to join the new Teachers Guild, a rival teachers union unaffiliated with the AFT. The years of struggle, which included accusations that Linville both abandoned his democratic principles and failed to defend the academic freedom of his opponents, left the New York Teachers Union under the control of a more radical group than ever before—leadership that would play important roles in fights over academic freedom. These years also foreshadowed the events to come. In 1936, Yale University Divinity School professor Jerome Davis was elected president of the AFT. During Davis's three-year presidency, the AFT fought for academic freedom in ways that the union had been previously unable to do. At the same time, the New York concerns over factionalism moved to the national stage.[37]

AFT locals passed resolutions supporting academic freedom and opposing the Hearst newspaper attacks on teachers and alleged Communists in schools. New York Teachers Union remained in the forefront of defense work, undertaking, for example, a successful campaign for the reinstatement of Brooklyn College instructor Morris Schappes and several colleagues in 1936. The effort, which drew on local labor unions, student activists, the ACLU, and other organizations, featured widespread public protests and focused on the Communist Schappes, though it benefited from the cover provided by the concurrent dismissals of non-Communists. To its organizers, it demonstrated the benefits of aggressive action. National efforts, at first led by Local 5 member Ben Davidson as chair of the renamed and expanded National Academic Freedom Committee (NAFC), increased, as well. Davidson called for assistance from members across the nation, worked with the Legislative Committee to lobby against loyalty oaths, arranged for cooperation with the ACLU, and otherwise sought to counter superpatriots' efforts to control school curricula. He formed a series of subcommittees on specific topics, including tenure, higher education, and the Hearst press. Davidson also began the larger shift toward a protective role for which Hanson had advocated. In the effort, he was somewhat aided by the new National Defense Fund, an idea suggested by Hanson in 1933 that was subsequently begun with a small number of voluntary contributions in 1935. These funds, though, soon proved inadequate. Cooperation from locals could be difficult to acquire, but defending aggrieved professors and teachers was coming to the fore.[38]

During Davis's presidency of the AFT, the rise of more elaborate and consistent national activity proved important to the work for academic freedom. So, too, proved Davis's personal experiences as a leftist educator who was involved in one of the most famous academic freedom and tenure cases of the era. In June 1936, Davis learned that the Yale Corporation had responded to the Divinity School faculty's request that he be reappointed to a three-year term, rather than be promoted, by issuing him a one-year terminal contract. Ignoring Yale president James Rowland Angell's warning not to publicize the case, Davis requested both AFT and AAUP involvement the following fall. The AFT's effort was multi-pronged but centered on two groups, Davidson's NAFC and the Reappoint Davis Committee, which was formed by the vice president of the AFT's College Section with Davis's approval. The latter was chaired by Amherst College economist Colston Warne and included Arnold Shukotoff, a professor at the College of the City of New York and key leader of Local 5. These efforts were vigorous but also conflicted: While investigating the situation, both Warne and Shukotoff publicly condemned Yale's actions—the former as one of the authors of a report on the case that was included in the *New Republic*'s exposé titled "Yale on Trial." Their combined activities as investigators, vocal defenders of Davis, critics of the institution, and campaigners for redress raised serious questions about the impartiality of their work and contributed to Yale's reluctance to engage with them. Moreover, Shukotoff soon appropriated the title "College Committee on Academic Freedom" for the group, setting it apart from Davidson's NAFC and exceeding his authority.[39] Davidson repeatedly complained about Shukotoff's activities, usurpation of power, failure to communicate, and lack of cooperation. And, though the executive committee called on Shukotoff to work more closely with Davidson, in 1937, he replaced Davidson as head of the NAFC.[40]

The College Committee made the first use of the AFT's Defense Fund, though it received less than half of what it requested—and even this was enough to overdraw the account.[41] Still, Shukotoff built on the successes of Schappes's defense, organized petition drives, circulated information, and generated publicity and union support on Davis's behalf. Its lengthy investigative report, released in May 1937, alleged that the effort to silence Davis dated to 1925 and included warnings not to participate in labor activities, denunciations of his protests against legislative inquiries into Communism, and expressions of concern that promotion would lead Davis to increase his controversial political activities. The report refuted both the institution's initial claim that financial concerns were at the root of the termination and its later justification on the basis of Davis's ineffectiveness as a teacher and scholar. Calling the dismissal a "clear case of the violation of academic freedom," it declared that "Prof. Davis is being dropped because his economic views, his researches into the nature of the present social order, and his activities in the labor movement offended wealthy alumni and members of the Yale Corporation."[42] The union saw this report as an important statement on Davis's behalf, a warning about the influences of unrestrained capitalism on higher education, and a broader plea for the importance of academic freedom. A month later, the union organized a picket of 250 educators on Yale's campus demanding and eventually receiving an audience with the Yale Corporation. When, two weeks after the picket, Yale provided Davis with an extra year's salary, the union considered it an admission of guilt and validation of aggressive action.[43]

The situation, though, was not so simple. Other organizations had likewise weighed in on the case, including the PEA, which agreed with the AFT that Davis' academic freedom had been violated and the NEA's Committee on Tenure, which argued that his tenure had been infringed upon.[44] Neither, though, based their reports on thorough investigations of all parties and neither was as integral as the AAUP, which in October 1936, reached out to Angell in an effort to rectify the situation quietly—an effort that was scuttled when the public campaigns on Davis's behalf made it untenable. Moreover, despite AFT claims that its publicity brought the AAUP to the case, Warne had initially asked the AAUP to delay its investigation. The publicity that he and others generated damaged relations between the two organizations and, at first, inhibited AFT vice president Maynard Krueger's efforts to organize college faculty who were also members of the AAUP. The publicity almost prevented the AAUP from undertaking the investigation at all. Yet Committee A did investigate: it gathered testimony from Yale administrators and faculty, and concluded that Davis's academic freedom had not been violated but that his tenure had. Demonstrating the high stakes and contentious debates, the report proved highly controversial among AAUP leaders. Some found the draft version appropriately restrained and objective; others were deeply troubled by its deference to Angell and its inability to address all outstanding issues, including the allegations published in the *New Republic*. New AAUP general secretary Ralph E. Himstead believed that the repeated use of the word "employee" to describe Davis's relationship to the institution did a disservice to larger principles of faculty participation. He was among those who argued that the case highlighted the need for the AAUP to place greater emphasis on defined probationary periods before tenure. Lovejoy threatened to dissent from the findings, believing that the report needed to be much more definitive in its assignment of blame to Angell and Divinity School dean Luther Weigle. These debates reflected both the content of the report and the context; AFT activity had focused a spotlight on the case, and the AAUP knew its report would be viewed in light of the union's militant stand. The tension was between assertiveness and judiciousness in what Lovejoy believed was the most important case yet handled.[45]

The revised version of the Committee A report, published in May 1937, did not offer an endorsement of Angell and Yale University but remained restrained and tempered. Its body presented evidence that Angell and Weigle acted inappropriately while the Divinity School faculty was preparing to vote on Davis's promotion. Weigle's actions contributed to the faculty's decision to recommend a three-year contract rather than a full professorship, thereby undermining the appropriate faculty role in the process. Still, the committee did not conclude that Davis's academic freedom had been violated, as only indirect, rather than direct, pressure had been applied on the faculty. While the Divinity School faculty understood that it would be inopportune to vote for Davis's promotion, they still had the opportunity to do so. Angell's opposition had been influenced by Davis's extramural activities, but the committee was unable to find evidence that that opposition was decisive. Still, based on his 12 years at the institution, Davis was not adequately treated with a one-year terminal contract. His tenure had been abridged. The AAUP council responded by resolving that academic tenure was not safe at Yale, and, therefore, neither was academic freedom. Without the former, the latter was inherently vulnerable.[46] Due to the attention and public protests that Davis and the AFT had provoked, the AAUP did not believe his return to Yale was feasible but instead sought an additional year's salary. Despite Angell's disinclination to do so due to the AFT picket and the union's other activities, the institution provided the salary in hopes of improving morale in the Divinity School and repairing relations with the AAUP. In ensuing months, both Yale officials and AAUP leaders were incensed that the AFT repeatedly claimed credit for the payment, even though its activities had almost precluded it. Davis complained that the AAUP did not do more to assist him, while the AAUP continued to contend that his and the AFT's actions had fundamentally damaged the cause. Still, the AAUP recognized that the AFT posed a new danger, especially since some in the association believed AFT claims of victory and admonished the AAUP for not having done more.[47]

When, on the basis of his work in the Davis case, Shukotoff replaced Davidson as the head of the NAFC in 1937, he further expanded the AFT's emphasis on the protection of teachers and faculty. His was an activist and expansive approach that used union tactics and sought to mobilize locals in their efforts on behalf of specific educators. He surveyed locals to learn how best the NAFC could support their work, as well as to gather information about specific violations, policies, and practices in their areas. He proposed—and the convention passed—a resolution calling on locals to have standing academic freedom committees able to respond to violations while also undertaking educational work. As had long been the case in the AFT, numerous resolutions condemning specific violations of academic freedom were likewise proposed and passed at the annual conventions. Echoing an idea from Davidson, Shukotoff proposed the creation of a separate tenure committee, which, when organized under Philadelphia teacher Sara T. Walsh, was charged with studying and working to extend teacher tenure and the statewide legislation that could support it. Indicative of its efforts—both in their intent and the difficulty in undertaking them—was the short-lived bulletin, *Academic Freedom,* which highlighted on-going cases and broader efforts to establish principles.[48]

The NAFC also drafted, circulated, and rewrote new principles for work on academic freedom. First presented at the 1938 convention and then finalized the following year, these principles explicitly linked academic freedom to democracy and argued for the need for freedom across school settings. They called for teachers to have the ability to study and publish on any topic of their choosing, as well as full freedom of expression in the classroom, tempered only by the requirements that they identify opinions as such and take into account students' immaturity. They emphasized that teachers should have full rights of association and should maintain all of the citizenship rights and freedoms enjoyed by others, including participating in political and community activities. The principles then emphasized that the AFT would seek to ensure the "effective participation" of teachers in educational, curricular, budgeting, hiring, and promotion decisions, as well as in "the determination of their working conditions." They were approved conditional to the addition of a statement on the need for appropriate proceedings before dismissals, including formal charges and hearings, with the right to be represented and to question witnesses.[49]

Most importantly, under Shukotoff, the NAFC further increased the number of cases it considered to 25 in 1938 and 48 the following year. These cases, many of which involved allegations that teachers and professors were dismissed for their union activities, together demonstrate both the work of the NAFC and the limitations that it faced. For the first time, the NAFC was able to support this work with money from a permanent, rather than ad hoc, National Defense Fund, created at Shukotoff's request after his difficulty paying the expenses associated with Davis's case. With the allocation of one cent of each AFT member's dues per month, the NAFC became solvent and began distributing money to help defend individual educators. The money was limited and intended to supplement locals' efforts, rather than underwrite entire campaigns, a situation that both posed difficulties for small and vulnerable locals and precluded working to support members-at-large who lacked a local with which to affiliate. The fund was also not designed to sustain teachers dismissed from their positions; a 1939 effort to create such a resource on a voluntary basis netted only ten dollars. Still, over three years, almost $6,500 was distributing for defense efforts, though not always without controversy. In addition to allegations of the misuse of distributed funds and confusion over the types of activities that could be supported, the assignment of funds to certain cases was problematic. Frequently, considerations included how it might affect organizing, as it did in 1937, when the NAFC weighed whether to protest dismissals in Louisiana and West Virginia. The latter case was further problematic, as the AFT was unsure how to balance its support for educators' rights to serve on school boards with protests against a college faculty member who, as a board member, was responsible for troubling dismissals. AFT decisions around academic freedom work could be even more political and the AFT was reluctant to distribute Linville's analysis of and protests against loyalty oaths after he left the union. Reports such as those written in the Davis case and, for example, following the dismissal of Philip O. Keeney from Montana State University, may have been strong statements for academic freedom and tenure, but they were also expensive to publish and difficult to sell. Postage costs made it prohibitive to distribute them at no charge. Still, Shukotoff and others viewed their efforts for academic freedom, and especially the several lengthy reports that were produced, as crucial to organizing in higher education. Shukotoff further understood that he was in the midst of a battle for the divided AFT—he was on the left edge of a local that would be purged in 1941—and that his efforts for academic freedom were aimed at both external critics and internal adversaries.[50]

Formalizing Tenure Procedures

Though important, the Davis case was just one of a number of incidents toward the end of the decade that helped set the stage for modern policies regarding academic freedom and tenure. Indeed, both the 1915 *Declaration of Principles of Academic Freedom and Academic Tenure* and 1925 *Conference Statement Conference Statement on Academic Freedom and Tenure* had included discussions of tenure, but the negotiated latter statement had retreated from some of the assertions of the former. In not insisting on a set probationary period, the AAUP had allowed for the continuation of a permanent class of untenured assistant professors and instructors. More broadly, formal tenure procedures and protections were rare into the 1930s.[51] In 1932, the AAUP's temporary Committee W on the Conditions of Tenure surveyed almost three hundred member institutions and found that most academic appointments were for fixed terms, usually a year. Even at the full professor level, initial appointments were for a fixed term at just over half of the responding institutions. Of these, the overwhelming majority were for one year. Though some institutions indicated the expectation of permanency for faculty at the highest level, and occasionally even at lower levels, fewer than half had formal procedures for dismissal, and only a quarter had provisions including faculty input. Only eight institutions had formally adopted the 1925 *Conference Statement*.[52] Three years later, when Rice Institute surveyed 78 leading institutions on the status of tenure, fewer than 50 percent reported formal written policies. Just more than a third had informal policies, although there was great variety in what these policies included and little evidence that faculty had any real protections.[53]

In the face of these results, Rice did not initiate a formal tenure policy, but other institutions soon did, one of which was implicated in its own high-profile alleged violation of academic freedom. In March 1937, Harvard University issued economics instructors J. Raymond

Walsh and Alan Sweezy terminal contracts after their department's faculty failed to recommend their promotion. Although three others were also dismissed from the department, Walsh's and Sweezy's well-known Marxist beliefs and activity in the Cambridge Union of University Teachers (AFT Local 431) drew attention to their cause—attention that Local 431 and the AFT furthered, including through the publication of the pamphlet *Harvard's Liberalism: Myth or Reality*. The union questioned President Conant's defense of the dismissals as based, first, on the quality of Walsh's and Sweezy's work, and, later, because other younger faculty had been suggested for promotion ahead of them. Behind the scenes, union members were among those who organized a petition—eventually signed by 131 junior faculty members—to nine senior professors at the institution asking them to request investigations into the dismissals, academic freedom, and concerns about administrative authority. When the nine relayed the request, Conant acceded and appointed them to investigate and report on both the specific dismissals and the larger issues of promotion. The resulting committee, which included eight professors after one of the original nine died, found that neither Walsh's nor Sweezy's academic freedom had been violated but that they had still been mistreated. Internal communication problems and Conant's desire to reform appointment policies to end the existence of perpetual junior faculty had combined to deprive them of their positions. The committee raised concerns about Conant's desire to shorten appointments for junior faculty and quickly replace them if they were unlikely to be promoted, either due to their own shortcomings or the lack of senior-level openings in their departments. It further questioned the bases for such decisions, noted the importance of diversity of opinions and methods within departments, and argued for the necessity of faculty who carried on work similar to that of Walsh and Sweezy. Each of these pointed to further problems with the dismissals, and the committee ultimately called for Walsh's and Sweezy's reappointment. Conant rejected the request as unworkable, and neither Walsh nor Sweezy returned to Harvard.[54]

The committee's second report, issued in early 1939, addressed broader issues of tenure and promotion policy at the institution, noting that they were similar to those affecting other institutions, as well as the more general problems of younger professionals on probationary appointments. The report called for a normalization of tenure procedures, an eight-year up-or-out policy to prevent permanent instructorships, the elimination of the rank of assistant professor, and a standard salary structure. Departmental faculty committees would formally consider junior faculty members' teaching and research and weigh in on potential promotions, as would external reviewers. When a version of the plan was approved, Conant quickly and bluntly implemented it by dismissing ten junior faculty members, including Ernest Simmons, the president of the union local. The formalized procedures, which grew out of concern over the treatment of Walsh and Sweezy, would likely not have helped them.[55] These reports were significant at Harvard but also reflect larger trends and concerns. Lovejoy, who lauded the initial report as the most similar to a Committee A report that he had ever read, argued that it highlighted the need for the AAUP to address the length of probationary appointments, something that the AAUP committee investigating Davis's dismissal had previously noted.[56] It would soon do so through its collaboration with the AAC on the 1940 *Statement,* collaboration that was informed by Harvard's new policy and a similar effort at Yale.[57]

As other institutions also took up formalizing tenure and promotion procedures, broader changes ensued, yet difficulties remained and could become intertwined with policy creation. The problems experienced by specific faculty members could contribute to new policies, even though aggrieved individuals did not always benefit from them. In 1937, for example, the Howard Teachers Union (AFT Local 440) protested the dismissal of Arthur Callis, its president and an AFT vice president. It was unable to secure Callis's reappointment, but the resulting controversy led the institution to reconsider and formalize its tenure procedures. Union members participated in key, though informal, roles in the process.[58] And, as at Harvard, the implementation of new, formal tenure procedures elsewhere caused faculty to lose their positions. One such example is Eric A. Beecroft, who was dismissed by the University of California at Los Angeles in January 1940, two months after the campus instituted a new tenure procedure. In Beecroft's case, though, his hardship was short-lived. In his last report as chair of the NAFC, Shukotoff noted that despite the dismissal—which Shukotoff blamed on Beecroft's liberal progressive activities—Beecroft had assumed a new position at the institution's Berkeley campus.[59] Formalized tenure procedures were being established, though not without complications.

Ralph E. Himstead and the AAUP

Despite the aggressive work of the AFT and the engagement of other organizations and individuals, the AAUP remained the dominant voice on issues related to academic freedom and tenure. Even the slight dip in the number of appeals to Committee A in the middle of the decade did little to diminish the organization's work, as each case required substantial correspondence and work. As Hepburn reported in late 1937, the committee had handled more active cases during the previous summer than it had in any prior break in the academic year.[60] The numbers would only grow, from 42 new and 58 total cases in 1937 to 52 and 94 in 1938, 60 and 104 in 1939, and 54 and 108 in 1940.[61] The high numbers of ongoing active cases reflect both the demands of the work and the presence of Himstead, a Syracuse University law professor who became the first full-time general secretary of the association in 1936. A perfectionist who labored over each piece of correspondence and was hesitant to approve reports or otherwise finalize investigations, Himstead frequently complained about the burden of Committee A work and talked about the need for sharing the work with others. Still, he was reluctant to delegate or release the work, causing needless delays in an already lengthy and deliberative process. The open cases are also indicative of the further increase in efforts for negotiation and mediation, rather than investigation. Although Himstead regularly argued that protecting faculty and seeking individual redress was beyond the scope of the AAUP, the association did increasingly work to such ends. His appointment as a full-time general secretary was, in part, aimed at such action. In the late 1930s and early 1940s, the AAUP attempted to achieve compensation or redress in almost two-thirds of the cases it received, a 50 percent increase from the period prior to Himstead's arrival. Even at the height of these negotiations, though, only a minority received compensation and extremely few retained their positions.[62]

Though time-consuming and expensive, the investigations were important and continued—the AAUP decreased the number of issues of its *Bulletin* from eight to five in 1938 to free up more funds for other core work, especially that related to academic freedom and tenure.[63] During Himstead's first nine years as general secretary, the association inquired through correspondence in 36 percent of the cases and informally on campus in 17 percent. It undertook formal investigations in fewer than 10 percent.[64] In many of these cases, the investigative committee failed to find clear evidence that academic freedom had been violated. Far more frequently, a faculty member's tenure had been abridged, continuing a long-standing trend in findings. In addition to the aforementioned Davis case, the AAUP *Bulletin* published reports or notes on 17 cases between 1936 and 1940. Together they covered a range of issues, including the 1935 dismissal of Glanville Hicks from Rochester Polytechnic Institute, which Hicks blamed on his leftist politics but the president blamed on financial necessity. The committee was unable to determine the true cause, but it did find the institution's system of one-year appointments to be highly problematic and inimical to best practice. The *Bulletin* published a short notice that an instructor at Washington State College was improperly dismissed when his recently published novel offended key administrators and, in doing so, made a claim for the necessity of artistic freedom for faculty members. It warned of the inappropriateness of removing someone on an approved leave and of local chapters becoming involved in cases after the dismissal of associate professor Charles F. Metz from Park College. The administrations of seven institutions were censured: the University of Pittsburgh in 1936; North Dakota Agricultural College in 1939; and John B. Stetson University, Montana State University, St. Louis University, the University of Tennessee, and West Chester State Teachers College in 1940.[65] And while this increase in activity emphasized the continued need for Committee A's efforts, it offered evidence of progress, as well. Only the greater establishment of principles of academic freedom and tenure encouraged faculty to come forward when either one was violated.

These violations—and the difficulty of handling them—highlighted the ongoing need for Committee A's work while, at the same time, raised continuing issues of how best to handle it. For some, they raised the possibility of working with other organizations on shared goals, both in individual cases and more broadly. The AFT reached out to the AAUP several times in the aftermath of the Davis case, hoping to coordinate activities, share resources, and otherwise work more closely. Though willing to meet, the AAUP was wary of entanglements with the union both for philosophical reasons and out of the aforementioned mistrust generated by the Davis case. The AFT was, to the AAUP leaders, biased, too aggressive, and unable to disassociate itself from its larger political goals. Lovejoy, a longtime opponent of faculty unionization, argued that the appropriate cooperation would be somewhat different: the AFT confining itself to K–12 and junior college issues, leaving higher education to the AAUP. Even when the AAUP reluctantly agreed to send representatives to meet with the AFT, the two organizations viewed the results differently. The AFT trumpeted their cooperation and similarities, while the AAUP believed that the meeting highlighted their incompatibility. The latter formally voted not to publish the meeting minutes or any comparison of the two organizations' work. Himstead complained that dealing with the AFT was delaying more important work, and, increasingly, AAUP leaders were wary that the union was trying to supplant, rather than work with, their association. The fear was not without merit. Davis foresaw the AAUP becoming the AFT's higher education wing, and Shukotoff wrote about this vision in his organizing materials.[66]

At the same time, the pressure on the AAUP to define, defend, and extend its activities increased. Responding to the difficulties caused by the AFT and larger concerns of the professoriate, the 1937 annual meeting concluded with an almost daylong symposium and forum titled "What the American Association of University Professors Is and What It Is Not." Participants discussed the differences between the association and a union and debated the appropriate roles for the AAUP to play. Some expressed hope that the association would become more active, thereby minimizing the gains made by the AFT. Others lauded unions more broadly but argued that any move toward unionization would diminish the AAUP's standing and effectiveness. Tyler, the former general secretary who participated via letter due to illness, disclaimed the term "employee" and called the AFT's approach "so fundamentally contrary to our own that mere reconciliation of the two would be as futile as mixing oil and water." The letter was a piece that Himstead would contend should be "required reading," but it was just one of the many that demonstrated both the AAUP's concern for its appropriate professional role and the larger professoriate's consideration of AFT-style organizing.[67] For the AAUP, the AFT provided an impediment, as some were drawn away from the AAUP to affiliate with labor. At the same time, others saw the rise of the AFT as evidence of the AAUP's value as a professional association.

The 1940 Statement

If, in the late 1930s, the AFT was the AAUP's primary rival in efforts to appeal to faculty, the AAC was its primary counterpart in attempting to reform policies and principles. Yet before the AAUP and the AAC could work together to rewrite the 1925 *Conference Statement,* the AAC had to re-enter the field after having discontinued its Commission on Academic Freedom and Academic Tenure in 1929. In 1934, the AAC took this step, noting both the recent dismissals of several college presidents and the economic-related dismissals of college professors. At the organization's 1934 annual meeting, executive secretary Robert L. Kelly argued that the AAUP was not concerned with the former and was perhaps too interested in the latter. The renewed commission consulted with the AAUP, hoping to avoid difficult situations between professors and college presidents. While Kelly assured members that it would not look to antagonize relationships and would not have the power to undertake its own investigations, he did note that founding the commission was a "precautionary measure" in case issues arose.[68] Although the commission's reestablishment foretold the possibility of handling difficulties and working together toward mutually beneficial ends, the potential for conflict was also clear. The selection of the new commission chairman, Wesleyan University president James L. McConaughy, who believed that the AAUP was too quick to find fault with college administrations and who was considered imperious even by those who shared his perspectives, guaranteed that this conflict would occur.[69]

Walter Wheeler Cook, AAUP general secretary from 1933 to 1935, helped initiate cooperative work, including telling the 1935 AAC annual convention that they were "partners in this common enterprise" and calling for greater consultation between the organizations.[70] This sentiment was somewhat shared by the commission, which urged the AAUP to communicate with the college association in the case of impending trouble at a member institution. It also requested that the AAUP include college faculty, not just university faculty, on investigative committees involving AAC institutions. Four months later, McConaughy reported to the AAC that the AAUP had contacted the commission about three cases, two of which were quickly settled. The third appeared to be of little concern.[71] While this initial report indicated promise for future work, relations between the two groups quickly deteriorated. McConaughy was hopeful of intervening in AAUP investigations and preventing negative reports of AAC institutions, but his overbearing personality caused a rift that threatened future cooperation. Representatives from the two associations convened their first official meeting toward the end of 1935. In a gathering that Walter P. Metzger termed "explosive," McConaughy castigated AAUP efforts as unfair to the AAC and charged that the professors' association was unsympathetic to colleges. Though the intervention of other college presidents allowed the cooperation to continue, it remained plagued by difficulties related to McConaughy's demands and personality.[72] By early 1937, these efforts around cases were beginning to break down, despite some early successes in sharing information and reaching settlements. In April, as the AAUP prepared to release its report on Park College, McConaughy complained that the AAUP was violating an agreement not to pursue cases that he did not believe warranted investigation.

Himstead denied any such agreement, and other AAUP leaders worried that McConaughy sought veto power over AAUP activities. In the ensuing weeks, the AAUP abandoned thoughts of undertaking joint investigations and decided to limit the information that they would share with the AAC. Amid ongoing tensions, McConaughy attributed the AAUP's hesitance to cooperate to some of its own members' push for greater aggressiveness. Although McConaughy's personality was a significant part of the problem, AAUP leaders did need to move cautiously to avoid alienating its members in light of the AFT's more militant actions.[73]

Yet a second strand of the two associations' work—rewriting the 1925 *Conference Statement*—continued and appeared to receive a boost when McConaughy stepped down from the commission's chairmanship to assume the AAC's presidency in 1937. The effort was spurred by institutions' resounding failure to adopt the 1925 *Conference Statement,* worries about its tone, and the lingering concern over the inclusion of treason as a justification for dismissal. When the AAC first suggested convening to meet and reformulate the statement, many AAUP leaders feared that the AAC sought to restrict freedoms through further definition and also to make it easier to dismiss faculty in times of financial difficulties. AAUP president Carlson, though, recognized the opportunity to reinforce the principles and help increase protections, and the AAUP agreed to do so. When, amid the swirling controversies over policies and protections in the aftermath of the Davis case, Brown University president Henry M. Wriston took over the commission, the AAUP seized the opportunity to work with someone whom it viewed as progressive and favorable to academic freedom. Still, the negotiations remained tense and Himstead remained distrustful. Indeed, the negotiations almost broke down multiple times, including even before the first official meeting in 1937, when Himstead accused the AAC of failing to submit its promised proposed revisions. McConaughy's continuing involvement in the conferences further fostered ongoing difficulties but was not entirely unwelcomed by Himstead, who viewed him as typical of the domineering presidents who headed small denominational colleges. He believed that McConaughy's approach would prevent the AAUP from naïvely giving away too much.[74]

When the proposed revisions were presented at the first conference, many proved uncontroversial and basic agreements on many principles were reached. Two issues, one involving academic freedom and one involving tenure, were much more difficult to manage. As some in the AAUP had feared, the AAC sought to revise the provisions for freedom in extramural utterances, a key point of contention in the many cases that had been brought to the AAUP. While maintaining 1925 language assuring professors' rights to speak freely outside their fields, the presidents called for limitations to faculty expression on their topics of expertise. Recognizing professors' influence in society and the likelihood that any professorial speech would be linked to a faculty member's institution, the proposals called for restrictions based on institutional commitments and professional integrity. In response to these proposed limits, the AAUP's John M. Maguire agreed to redraft the language and submit the revised statement to both parties. The resulting suggestions noted that faculty rights came with "special obligations" of restraint, responsibility, and attention to the welfare of their institutions. It was met with vehement opposition within the AAUP negotiating committee, with one member, Ralph L. Dewey, suggesting that the AAUP might as well "cave completely."[75] Importantly, both Maguire's draft and the reaction to it were informed by the recent controversy at Yale. Maguire believed that Davis was in the minority of "inconsiderate" faculty whose needs did not outweigh those of the responsible majority. Cook, Ralph Dewey, and William T. Laprade, Duke University historian and Committee A chairman, philosophically disagreed and also recognized the difficulty posed by Davis's case. They countered that such backtracking on extramural utterances would further the AFT's cause to the AAUP's detriment.[76] Still, as it had agreed, the AAUP brought Maguire's draft to the next meeting, held in 1938, and was able to negotiate a modification to lessen its impact somewhat by replacing a series of "musts" with "shoulds." More promising for the AAUP, the primary concern was seemingly resolved when Wriston suggested—and AAUP representatives readily agreed—that enforcement of the provision should remain in the hands of individual professors themselves.[77]

Just as important were the concerns over tenure, which had become pressing. Himstead, especially, had come to believe that the separation of tenurable from long-term but temporary faculty, as recognized in the 1925 *Conference Statement,* was inherently problematic; he lobbied for a single agreed-upon track with a set probationary period. With the difficulties of the Depression as a backdrop and the specific experiences in the Davis case as a further spur, he was able to convince his colleagues of the need for a defined probationary period. With the rise of the AFT, which was arguing for a three-year probationary period, Himstead and his colleagues agreed to argue for a five-year probationary period—substantially shorter than ten years early AAUP leaders would have considered, but close enough to the AFT's proposal that it might prevent junior faculty from abandoning the AAUP for the union. At the 1938 meeting, AAC representatives acknowledged the benefits of tenure and sought flexible, rather than set, timelines. In the end, though, the AAUP and AAC agreed to a modified six-year tenure clock as standard practice, with provisions for faculty to earn credit for service at prior institutions.[78]

In ensuing months, the AAUP readily endorsed this compromise statement but, this time, the AAC demurred. When Wriston introduced the proposed statement to the AAC convention several months later, he argued that it was an improvement over the 1925 *Conference Statement* and supported its endorsement as a nonbinding statement of principles. In describing the specific provisions, he highlighted that self-enforcement on extramural speech was not a substantial change—Himstead had informed him that only Davis's case had raised the analogous provision from the 1925 *Conference Statement,* and the AAUP had determined it was not implicated. Wriston also argued that the self-enforcement clause provided protection for professors but, significantly, also provided protections for institutions. Echoing A. Lawrence Lowell's contention from the trials of the World War I period, he noted that without any control over teachers' extramural speech, colleges could not be held responsible for what they said.[79] Wriston further acknowledged that his own views on the probationary path to tenure had changed due to the difficulties associated with the Depression. Hoping to protect instructors from unemployment during dire financial times, institutions retained faculty on repeated appointments even though they were undeserving of promotion. The proposed policy would force colleges and universities to "do the most difficult of all things—namely make up their minds."[80] These arguments were not enough to sway the conservative president of Earlham College, William Cullen Dennis, a participant in the negotiations who almost derailed the process several times.[81] Dennis attacked the new provisions, leading to a proposed amendment to strike the self-enforcement statement and to the ultimate deferral of action on the proposed statement for a year. At that time, the AAC approved a revised version excluding both the provision for self-enforcement and a set probationary period prior to tenure.[82]

The revisions offered and approved at the 1940 AAC convention almost ended the negotiations and precluded the 1940 *Statement.* Himstead was particularly incensed by the elimination of a set probationary period in the AAC version, claiming that the revision undercut the entire statement, jeopardized academic freedom, and threatened to leave some faculty without any security for their entire careers. He blamed the revisions, in part, on Conant's new involvement in the commission and Conant's larger emphasis on up-or-out procedures, rather than on those based purely on length of service. In his correspondence with Wriston, Himstead questioned the AAC's commitment to the process and argued that since the AAUP had already given ground on extramural speech issues, it was incumbent upon the AAC to give way on a set probationary period.[83] The two sides eventually agreed to meet in November 1940 in hopes of settling lingering disputes and rescuing the process. In Wriston's absence, Himstead worked with Dennis to find a solution to the complaints about the self-enforcement provision. In response to Dennis's demands for an impartial tribunal to determine if extramural utterances could be the basis for dismissal, Himstead offered the use of hearings as described in the included tenure procedures. The final document included the clause on self-enforcement agreed upon in 1938 but with the interpretation that faculty speech could be rightfully considered as long as due process was followed. While Himstead viewed the change as insignificant at the time, the addition of the explanatory footnote allowed extramural utterances to be considered as a basis for faculty termination. The two sides likewise agreed to reinstate a fixed probationary period—though Himstead conceded an additional year to set the standard at seven years—with the AAC recognizing that Wriston had accurately identified institutional benefits.[84]

In 1941, both the AAC and the AAUP endorsed the 1940 *Statement of Principles on Academic Freedom and Tenure*. In so doing, the two associations eliminated the notion of treason from explicit consideration and agreed that professors should have the right to free extramural speech—but, as Wriston noted, with the "unequivocal recognition of special obligations on the part of the teacher as a citizen."[85] While educators were granted freedom in teaching, their classroom discussion of controversial topics unrelated to the subject matter was not protected. Professors had the right to research and publish, though they needed institutional approval if they were to receive payment for such work. To safeguard these freedoms, written terms of appointment, a fixed probationary period of no more than seven years, and due notice for dismissal prior to tenure were endorsed; financial exigency as an excuse for dismissal was to be "demonstrably *bona fide*." Finally, teachers dismissed for cause were to be provided due process, including hearings before both faculty committees and governing boards when possible. Although the two associations did not have the authority to bind institutions to these provisions, they subsequently became the basis for almost all ensuing academic freedom and tenure policies and procedures.[86]

Since the initial agreement between representatives from the AAC and AAUP, more than two hundred additional organizations have endorsed the 1940 *Statement,* providing evidence of the widespread support for the document in the academic community. This does not, however, mean that the principles and procedures were unproblematic. The AAC and AAUP have added footnotes to the statement several times, demonstrating the need to clarify the meanings of ambiguous (and gender-specific) language. The tenure provisions and fixed probationary period somewhat standardized promotion and dismissal practices, though the prominence of contingent faculty in the modern era has reinstituted a form of the two-tier structure that Himstead found troubling and that the set probationary period was intended to end. Moreover, as debates in recent decades have shown, there is no unanimity of belief in the appropriateness of tenure in a changing academy. Indeed, the agreement failed to protect the most radical and endangered of faculty by allowing extramural considerations to be considered in dismissal hearings.[87] The 1940 *Statement* was the crucial step toward establishing academic freedom and tenure, even if it did not guarantee all for which some might have hoped.

Communism, Anti-Communism, and Academic Freedom at the End of the Decade

As the negotiations leading the 1940 *Statement* took place, an array of actors from across the political spectrum continued and expanded their attacks on subversion in education. Dilling undertook a series of inquiries into radicalism in American higher education, each time claiming to uncover the Communist indoctrination that she so frequently alleged. Walter S. Steele's *National Republic* offered repeated warnings of "The Enemy Within Our Gates," and, in its pages, Dan W. Gilbert argued that radicals hid behind academic freedom as they corrupted "the youth of the land with communist, free love and other un-American propaganda." He continued, "According to the radical idea of 'academic freedom,' 'sewer psychologists' have an inalienable 'right' to draw pay from American parents while they spread propaganda among students of tax-supported universities!"[88] With Gilbert, Hearst's newspapers, and others helping to stoke fears, legislative inquiries continued and expanded, including in Florida, where the legislature investigated alleged subversion at the Florida

State College for Women. More centrally, under the leadership of US Representative Martin Dies, the House Un-American Activities Committee inquired into Communist infiltration across the nation, examining whether teachers and faculty were indoctrinating students and considering whether the activist student movement was evidence of a larger plot to disrupt the nation. It heard testimony about subversion among college leaders, inquired into reports of Communist teachers in Detroit, and queried how University of Kansas student Don Henry transformed from an apolitical student to a radical who lost his life while fighting against Fascism in Spain. It also spurred the further development of state and local investigations, such as that undertaken by the Tenney Committee in California.[89] The most damaging of these investigations, that by the Rapp-Coudert Committee in New York, was launched in 1940 following the substantial controversy of English philosopher Bertrand Russell's appointment to a faculty position at City College, an appointment that was withdrawn and defunded in the face of charges that Russell's views on marriage and free love would corrupt impressionable students. Pressured by the investigation and its findings of widespread Communist infiltration, the New York Board of Education launched its own inquiry, ultimately dismissing 20 faculty members for conduct unbecoming, causing another 11 to resign, and simply not reappointing others. Among them was Schappes, who had survived the earlier attempt to dismiss him through the help of AFT Local 5 and the support of the ACLU. By 1941, though, the alignment of anti-Communist forces was different and the defense of leftist educators less successful. Found guilty of perjury based on his testimony denying knowledge of active Communists at his institution, Schappes served 13 months in prison.[90]

Concerns over radicalism affected both the freedom of heterodox educators and the ways in which organizations sought to define and protect such freedom. At the heart of many of the debates was whether Stalinists were committed by their affiliation to preordained ideas and activities or whether they were intellectually free to pursue authentic research and undertake teaching. The extant divides and concerns were heightened when the Soviet Union signed its nonaggression pact with Adolph Hitler's Germany in August 1939, thereby irreparably fracturing the political left. These concerns over Communists also helped shape organizational responses to the challenges facing educators. In March 1939, Columbia University professor Franz Boas formed the American Committee for Democracy and Intellectual Freedom (ACDIF) in recognition of the threats posed by the rise of fascism in Europe and reactionary pressures in the United States. The ACDIF sponsored public discussions about the dangers of anti-Semitism and warned of racist and anti-Semitic teaching in American schools. It also opposed the work of the Dies Committee and warned of the dangers of the war in Europe. The organization hosted a discussion entitled "Science, Education and Civil Liberties" at the 1939 World's Fair in New York, supported the rights of leftist students, and was lauded by activists including Davis and PEA president W. Carson Ryan.[91] The ACDIF's National Committee included numerous prominent educators and advocates of academic freedom, including Milwaukee State Teachers College's Baker and University of North Carolina president Frank P. Graham, the AAUP's Carlson and Samuel A. Mitchell, and the AFT's Harold Groves and Paul H. Douglas, both of whom urged the union to be more militant in its defense of academic freedom.[92] The ACDIF was not, however, universally welcomed by supporters of academic freedom. In May 1939, John Dewey announced the formation of the Committee for Cultural Freedom (CCF), which was specifically opposed to Boas's organization. While the ACDIF condemned fascism, anti-Semitism, and racial discrimination, its failure to condemn Communism led Dewey and other prominent academics to reject the group. The CCF counted educational leaders—including the AFT's Counts, the ACLU's John Haynes Holmes and William Kilpatrick, and the AAUP's Lovejoy— among its supporters. Indeed, the AAUP as an organization refused to endorse the ACDIF's manifesto as it mentioned only the totalitarianism of Germany and Italy but was silent on that of the Soviet Union.[93]

The existence of these organizations points to the anxiety not only over totalitarian governments and policies in Europe but also over potential threats in the United States. These same fears led to decisive changes within two of the organizations that had been most prominent in supporting academic freedom for leftist educators, the AFT and the ACLU. During Davis's presidency, the AFT had undertaken its most aggressive action for academic freedom and tenure, but factionalism and mistrust continued to plague the organization. In 1939, Counts defeated Davis with the backing of liberal and Socialist anti-Communists in a meeting that began as the nonaggression pact between Germany and the Soviet Union became public. He spent the next year consolidating support, and, in 1940, the anti-Communist slate of candidates swept the organization's executive council, setting the stage for the 1941 revocation of the charters of New York Teachers Union, Philadelphia Teachers Union, and New York College Teachers

Union, as well as the concurrent removal of constitutional protections for Communists and others "subject to totalitarian control." These activities were highly contested within the union—particularly by the majority of its college faculty members who voted against the expulsions—but were justified by Counts and others based on their belief that the locals were dominated by Communist cliques that used the locals to their own political ends.[94]

The repercussions of these struggles affected academic freedom both directly and indirectly. Though the NAFC had initially campaigned for Russell's appointment at City College and the union had protested against legislative inquiries in New York and elsewhere, things soon changed. When Shukotoff was removed from leadership of the NAFC in 1940, he began impeding the efforts of his replacement, Alice Hanson. When his local was expelled from the union, he and Bella Dodd continued to challenge the AFT and ultimately set up their own academic committee under the auspices of the New York Federation of Teachers. Hanson soon accused them of interfering with her work to the detriment of aggrieved educators, just as the AAUP had done a few years earlier. Moreover, Dodd was among the driving forces behind the protests of legislative inquiries in New York and the defense of radical teachers. When her local was expelled, AFT efforts on their behalf subsided. The union's executive council resolved against the tactics used by the Rapp-Coudert Committee but did not question its legitimacy. The AFT's charges against its locals further spurred the efforts, and AFT members and former members testified against Communists in the schools. Political divides in the union had again influenced the AFT's work for heterodox educators, and Communists no longer received the support that the AFT had once provided.[95]

In the late 1930s, the ACLU continued to entertain cases of academic freedom, as it had in the preceding years. Uninterested in mere violations of tenure, the organization tracked alleged cases involving freedom of speech or political activities of teachers, offering its services in a handful of cases each year. As in previous years, the work was heavily orchestrated out of its New York offices, with the Committee on Academic Freedom providing advice and consent rather than direct action. During the final years of the decade, the organization supported the legal efforts of librarian Keeney at the Montana State University and Russell in New York, among others. However, the ACLU noted that colleges and universities remained adept at hiding causes for dismissal, and, with its own emphasis on civil liberties, it left most cases to other organizations. Exemplifying its continuing interest in larger educational and religious issues, the ACLU remained the organization most interested in student rights; was active in pursuing legal action in support of Jehovah's Witnesses who refused to salute the American flag in schools; and published revised versions of *The Gag on Teaching* in 1936, 1937, and 1940.[96] Yet, just as the AFT struggled with Communist intrigue, the ACLU's long-standing defense of the rights of Communists, including Communist faculty, wavered just prior to World War II. Although the organization continued to be interested in academic freedom, Red Scare pressures and growing concerns over the autonomy of Communist Party members led the ACLU to several controversial actions—including barring Communists and supporters of other totalitarian groups from holding leadership positions in the ACLU. Also significant was its tepid response to the Rapp-Coudert Committee's investigations. Some influential members, including Sidney Hook—the drafter of its principles on academic freedom—and Reinhold Niebuhr, argued that Communist Party members were unfit for teaching positions, while others remained committed to ideals of free political association for teachers. The New York branch of the ACLU supported the teachers under investigation by providing occasional legal assistance. Ultimately, however, the national organization protested some of the methods of the Rapp-Coudert Committee but, like the AFT, not its right to investigate. In light of the investigations, the ACLU conceded that any educators who committed perjury, used false names, or were deceptive about their involvement in political activities had failed to live up to scholarly standards and could rightfully be dismissed. Further, it argued that while neither membership in a legal organization nor espousal of controversial beliefs was grounds for dismissal, such membership or beliefs could be considered as part of larger investigations into disruptive behavior. Uncertain about the appropriate response to the Communist threat, the ACLU ultimately retreated from its strongest stands in support of academic freedom.[97]

Conclusion

The years before World War II were years of both hope and disappointment, of advances and backtracking. They saw some of the strongest defenses of academic freedom for heterodox educators that had ever been undertaken, yet some of the very individuals and organizations that rallied for the academic freedom of some educators occasionally hesitated when called upon to defend the rights of others. The AAUP continuously fended off challenges both that it was too much like a union and that it should act more like a union; it was viewed as both too aggressive and not aggressive enough. The AFT significantly increased its defense activities, created a National Defense Fund, and committed to the cause in new and important ways. Yet the same forces that brought about these strides eventually splintered the union. The purge of Communists in the early 1940s demonstrated the conflicted state of academic freedom. The ACLU, which emphasized legal activity and public protest, similarly struggled with Communism, eventually offering lukewarm support for appropriate investigative procedures rather than a defense of fundamental rights and core values. Even the 1940 *Statement*—the most promising development of the years prior to World War II and a crucial accomplishment for establishing ideas central to modern American higher education—ultimately failed to protect the faculty members most in need of protection. Procedural protections and tenure could do little to affect hiring decisions or otherwise guarantee freedoms for those at the lowest ranks, especially when the professoriate was conflicted about the extent to which some of its members should have freedom to pursue their political ends.

The increased pressures on academic freedom led educational and related organizations to understand that that they could not protect academic freedom on their own. Defending academic freedom was expensive and time-consuming, and its foes—including some patriotic and business groups—were well-funded and well-organized. At the same time, the educational organizations struggled to overcome their own interests to work together. Individual frictions and personal jealousies interfered with the achievement of common aims. Desirous of independence, occupied with other tasks, and worried about competition, organizations' frequent efforts at sustained collaboration were often only partially successful. The multiple investigations that frequently resulted both exacerbated tensions, as they did in the Davis case, and further pointed to the need for better cooperation toward shared goals. Yet the goals were not always shared, and the competing notions of appropriate professorial behavior and organizational politics inhibited a united front for academic freedom and tenure.

Still, great strides were made, due in part to the very conflict over professional and union approaches for academic freedom and tenure. Most significant, the AAUP and AAC cooperated on the development of new principles and policies for academic freedom amid the ongoing rivalry between the AAUP and the AFT. The Davis case and the surrounding concerns helped shape the issues that were considered, the language that was used, and the compromises that were agreed upon. They were an incitement to act and a brake on concessions. Ultimately, the widespread endorsement of the 1940 *Statement* was a vital step in the development of modern higher education. Never before had academic freedom been so widely recognized as a core value—and never before had the basis for permanent academic employment been so fully articulated and agreed upon. Conditions of faculty work were fundamentally changed. Yet, even as the AAUP and the AAC were negotiating the procedural protections and conditions of employment that would mark academic life in the ensuing decades, the very real threats to heterodox faculty were revealing themselves. Though the protections changed the form and nature of employment, offering security to those who could survive up-or-out tenure policies, they were not enough to protect the most challenging of faculty either in the moment or in the trying years ahead.

Conclusion

Academic freedom has been called the "glue that holds the university together," "a fundamental value for a university in a free society," "the raison d'être for the professorate," and the "basis for the high moral ground from which the university community speaks."[1] In the 1957 *Sweezy v. New Hampshire* decision, United States Supreme Court Chief Justice Earl Warren wrote that without it, "our civilization will stagnate and die."[2] Yet, despite the widespread acknowledgment that faculty freedoms to teach, research, and pursue the full rights of citizenship are core aspects of American higher education and fundamental to the creation, preservation, and dissemination of knowledge, such was not always the case. It was in the decades leading up to World War II that American academics established modern understandings of academic freedom and the procedures that would come to protect it. Academic freedom went from being widely panned as a claim for special privilege to a recognized, if not always secure, feature of academic life. Tenure transformed from an informal understanding for a select few to formal policies endorsed for many; the existence of a perpetual staff of instructors and assistants was renounced by both the professoriate and institutional leaders. It was through the activities of individual educators such as John Dewey and Arthur Lovejoy—and, more importantly, the associations that they led and served—that these understandings developed, were refined, were negotiated, and were ultimately endorsed. The period was one in which, according to inaugural Association of American Colleges (AAC) president Robert L. Kelly there existed "a more or less blind American faith in the efficacy of organizations," and some of those organizations proved vital to establishing academic freedom.[3]

The path from the AAC's denouncing of the American Association of University Professors' (AAUP) claims for professorial rights to becoming its partner in the landmark 1940 *Statement of Principles on Academic Freedom and Tenure* was neither direct nor easy. Both parties experienced shifts in membership and contests over how best to serve their members' interests. Yet, over the course of 25 years, these and other associations interested in the topic coalesced around a set of ideas. With the AAUP as the central organization but others both feeding off and contributing to it, educators and civil libertarians came to understand that college and university faculty needed to retain their freedoms to teach, undertake research, disseminate their findings, and exercise their rights as citizens. Yet, as multiple organizations noted by the late 1930s, these rights were not without limits. Freedom in classroom teaching did not mean that all topics could be discussed without concern for their relevance or the audience. Freedom in research did not negate the need for a scholarly approach. Retaining rights of citizenship did not mean that faculty could not be held accountable if their speech or activities raised serious concerns about their fitness for their positions. As the hysterias around war and Communism demonstrated in the era and have since, violating these restrictions could be met with severe consequences.

Despite its leading role in defining and promoting both academic freedom and tenure, the AAUP was frequently criticized for its measured approach to cases and its failure to achieve the reinstatement of dismissed faculty members. Investigative reports appeared months after dismissals, often generated little publicity, and seldom had an effect on the specific cases under consideration. This impotence and dilatoriness, as it was at times called, was a key factor in other groups becoming involved in these issues, though with their own interests, agendas, and motivations. The involvement of these additional organizations, in turn, influenced the future understandings and protections. Still, while the criticisms of delays may have been appropriate, the professors' association neither viewed itself as nor claimed to be a defense organization. Early in its history, it specifically disavowed interest in individual cases. Only members calls for militancy and the pressures of the Depression pushed it to work for specific redress. While some urged for action along union lines, leadership demurred. Instead, the AAUP maintained its emphasis on professional status by quietly working with administrators to prevent dismissals, many of which involved violations of tenure but not academic freedom. The AAUP believed it could provide its greatest service to professors as a whole—and eventually to individual professors—by avoiding confrontation as much as possible and resorting to public statements only after careful consideration and the exhaustion of other options.

Other organizations were far more interested in quick action and public protest, even as the AAUP argued that such activities interfered with its ability to resolve cases successfully. The American Civil Liberties Union (ACLU) identified this publicity as a central element of its plan of action in 1924, and the American Federation of Teachers (AFT) assumed an activist defensive role as the 1930s progressed. Working together and on their own, the two organizations publicly protested firings, called on members to participate in letter-writing campaigns, and urged other liberal and labor organizations to object to wrongful terminations. The Progressive Education Association (PEA) similarly implored the members of its Commission on Educational Freedom to send protest letters to schools and colleges as soon as it received word of an alleged violation. These vigorous activities could be problematic, however, as the ACLU, AFT, and PEA each generated concern by protesting dismissals based on allegations rather than determinations of fact. Quick public protests could not only alienate administrators but also could offend members and damage organizations when the actions were discovered to be unwarranted. For the PEA, these missteps could not be overcome.

The tensions between protecting individuals and pursuing principles, as well as between pursuing quick public action or deliberate investigation and quiet mediation, were most apparent in the battles between the AFT and the AAUP in the late 1930s. The Jerome Davis case and the AFT's appeal to younger faculty placed pressure on the slower-moving AAUP, ultimately contributing both to its efforts to again negotiate with the AAC and to the 1940 *Statement* that resulted. Both the AAUP and AAC believed that their negotiations could limit the AFT's further influence in higher education, a shared goal for organizations that believed unionization was antithetical to professionalization and would forestall disinterested research on contested social, political, and economic issues. The 1940 *Statement* that emerged from these principled and politicized challenges established a professional notion of academic freedom. It also offered a set of protections that were built around the security of positions and based on an understanding that faculty were the best arbiters of faculty members' fitness for continuation. These were simultaneously important claims that affected faculty work and faculty workers, and incomplete agreements. They remained open to some of the same stinging criticisms that Alexander Meiklejohn offered of the 1915 *General Declaration of Principles of Academic Freedom and Academic Tenure*: protecting academic freedom primarily through tenure procedures and security of position does nothing to offset repression through hiring decisions, and relying on faculty to police their ranks presumes characteristics and ethics that may not be present.[4] Certainly, the experiences of World War I and the repeated Red Scares demonstrated that challenges to freedoms could come from within the professoriate. Additionally, although the 1940 *Statement* called for academic freedom for probationary or temporary faculty, no mechanisms were in place for its enforcement. Moreover, the seeming end of perpetuating annual appointments was not an unambiguous good for instructors and assistants who found themselves without renewals under a new system that forced institutions to make decisions based on permanency rather than continuation.

Despite the validity of these criticisms—and the related concerns about effects of these new understandings and policies on the most heterodox among the faculty[5]—the alternatives under consideration were likewise limited. By the time the AAUP and AAC were coming to final agreement, the AFT had backed away from its most activist stances, restricted its efforts to its members, and was moving toward the AAUP's approach rather than offering a viable alternative for the professoriate as a whole. The ACLU, whose legal work offered some opportunities and which occasionally pursued cases others neglected, came to see its efforts as supplemental to the AAUP's rather than a replacement for them. It recognized that certain limitations in public speech and classroom teaching were valid. And both the AFT and ACLU had begun to act against their Communist Party members. Indeed, AAUP leaders commented on the AFT's actions, noted that such was not their association's policy, and suggested that they might work to the AAUP's benefit.[6] Yet, as the difficulties of the ensuing years demonstrated, the AAUP was similarly unable to protect the most politically heterodox of its faculty in the face of the "tyranny of public opinion."

In 1941, Roger Baldwin considered the ACLU's work for academic freedom and noted strengthened tenure provisions, greater public acceptance of academic freedom, fewer overt administrative restrictions, and more engaged professional associations. He noted, "If we failed in precise objectives, so did everybody else who opposed restrictions on academic freedom. Yet it is obvious that academic freedom in every aspect is vastly stronger today than twenty years ago."[7] He was right. Professional societies, voluntary associations, and teachers unions were unable to accomplish all that some had hoped. Educators could still be dismissed for violating conventions and expressing unorthodox political and social perspectives. Individual administrators could use their power and influence to limit freedom or damage careers, as could the faculty who attacked their colleagues for political, personal, and professional reasons. Still, through the efforts of the AAC, AAUP, ACLU, AFT, and others, the concept of academic freedom was far more accepted than it had been prior to the organizations' foundings. The procedural protections of tenure had perhaps come even further. Enactments of these protections were and are, however, ultimately dependent on the individuals and institutions involved in specific situations.

And, yet, if academic freedom is a core value and tenure is its primary protection, the modern era has placed new and pressing challenges to American higher education and those who teach and research in it. Concerns over appropriate extramural speech in the immediate aftermath of September 11, 2001, garnered national headlines and resulted in both a few known individual difficulties and broader restrictions involving potentially sensitive research. They remained amid both the wars in Iraq and Afghanistan and enflamed tensions related to the Middle East. Unrelated but similarly political battles involving stem-cell research, global warming, and other highly charged issues have further affected academic freedom for those working in important but contested areas. The modern emphasis on externally funded research has likewise led to uncertainty about the control of research products, the ability of faculty to publish their findings, and the ways in which professorial work can be externally dictated. Efforts to compel faculty to release their research data to attorneys during litigation in tobacco, automotive safety, and other cases have further raised the specter of infringement in ways that no statement from the profession could possibly counter. The new possibilities for communication and expression that modern technology has provided have also raised concerns about institutional restraints in the digital age. Intramural speech, a perpetual source of conflict, has in recent years come under new threats as institutions sporadically close faculty senates or act against outspoken critics. In a handful of cases, the United States Supreme Court's *Ceballos v. Garcetti* ruling, which allows for government-imposed restrictions on work-related public employee speech, has been used to uphold discipline imposed on college faculty. Though the specifics might be new to the modern era, long-standing concerns over public pressures, legislative interference, institutional prerogatives, and faculty behaviors remain.[8]

Most importantly, the mass casualization of academic labor in the modern era has resulted in more than 60 percent of the instructional staff in American higher education working not only without tenure but off the tenure track altogether. The return of an overwhelmingly contingent labor force has sweeping implications for academe, for its staffing, and for whether and how it is able to enact its espoused values. The erosion of tenure—the "means" to the "certain ends" of protecting academic freedom, attracting highly talented scholars to the professoriate, and allowing institutions to fulfill their duties to students and the public[9]—threatens fundamental principles and weakens higher education's ability to serve society. At the fiftieth anniversary of the 1940 *Statement,* Walter P. Metzger noted that Depression economics of the 1930s had caused widespread hardship in higher education and that "the competition for nontenure positions tended to turn new PhD's into scramblers for openings that demanded heavy workloads at cut-rate pay, and turned the currently employed into supplicants for continued favor." This "plight of the academic underclass" was one of the factors that helped push the AAUP to negotiate with the AAC and to insist not just on the protections of tenure but also on a standard tenure clock that would bring an end to both permanent contingency and the "career-long purgatory" of unending probationary periods.[10] In the modern period, we have returned to the two-tiered system of a tenured and tenureable elite and a larger mass of faculty without the protections, security, and support that undergird the academic enterprise. In short, through erosion, rather than by commission, the agreements between faculty and administrators, and between higher education and society, are being renegotiated. Faculty working conditions are reverting to the models that the AAC and AAUP agreed to abandon more than seven decades ago—and that more than two hundred endorsing organizations have likewise eschewed.

NOTES

INTRODUCTION

1. 1940 *Statement of Principles on Academic Freedom and Tenure*. Available at http://www.aaup.org/AAUP/pubsres/policydocs/contents/1940statement.htm.
2. "The Professors' Union," *New York Times*, January 21, 1916.
3. "The Place and Function of the Proposed Association," *Association of American Colleges Bulletin* 1, no. 1 (1915): 49. In ensuing references to the journal, including to those after its name was changed to the *Bulletin of the American Association of Colleges*, the association's name is shortened to *AAC*.
4. Ellen Schrecker, "Academic Freedom: The Historical View," in *Regulating the Intellectuals: Perspectives on Academic Freedom in the 1980s*, ed. Craig Kaplan and Ellen Schrecker (New York: Praeger, 1983), 25–43, 29.
5. Richard Hofstadter and Walter P. Metzger, *The Development of Academic Freedom in the United States* (New York: Columbia University Press, 1955). This work was republished as two distinct volumes in 1961, and, unless the jointly authored introduction is cited, all references are to the separate volumes to clarify attribution: Richard Hofstadter, *Academic Freedom in the Age of the College* (New York: Columbia University Press, 1961); Walter P. Metzger, *Academic Freedom in the Age of the University* (New York: Columbia University Press, 1961).
6. Ellen W. Schrecker, *No Ivory Tower: McCarthyism and the Universities* (New York: Oxford University Press, 1986).
7. See Mary O. Furner, *Advocacy and Objectivity: A Crisis in the Professionalization of the Social Sciences* (Lexington: University Press of Kentucky, 1975); Thomas L. Haskell, *The Emergence of Professional Social Science: The American Social Science Association and the Nineteenth-Century Crisis of Authority* (Urbana: University of Illinois Press, 1977); David R. Holmes, *Stalking the Academic Communist: Intellectual Freedom and the Firing of Alex Novikoff* (Hanover, VT: University Press of New England, 1989).

8. Walter P. Metzger, "The 1940 Statement of Principles on Academic Freedom and Tenure," *Law & Contemporary Problems* 53 (Summer 1990): 3–77; Matthew W. Finkin and Robert C. Post, *For the Common Good: Principles of American Academic Freedom* (New Haven, CT: Yale University Press, 2009); Carol S. Gruber, *Mars and Minerva: World War I and the Uses of the Higher Learning in America* (Baton Rouge: Louisiana State University Press, 1975); Sheila Slaughter, "The Danger Zone: Academic Freedom and Civil Liberties," *Annals of the American Academy of Political and Social Sciences* 448 (March 1980): 46–61.

1 ACADEMIC FREEDOM IN DEVELOPMENT

1. John H. Wigmore, "President's Report for 1916," *Bulletin of the American Association of University Professors* 2 (November 1916): 9–52, 14. In ensuing references to the journal, including to those after its name was changed to the *American Association of University Professors Bulletin*, the association's name is shortened to *AAUP*.
2. Although Hofstadter and Metzger appropriately cautioned that emphasizing cases can create a martyrology of faculty whose freedoms were violated, cases still offer some of the best evidence of key ideas in development. Richard Hofstadter and Walter P. Metzger, *The Development of Academic Freedom in the United States* (New York: Columbia University Press, 1955), ix–x.
3. Richard Hofstadter, *Academic Freedom in the Age of the College* (New York: Columbia University Press, 1961), 3.
4. Ibid. See also Ralph F. Fuchs, "Academic Freedom—Its Basic Philosophy, Function, and History," *Law and Contemporary Problems* 28 (Summer 1963): 431–46, 431.
5. The extent to which freedom existed in medieval universities remains contested. See Fuchs, "Academic Freedom"; William J. Courtenay, "Inquiry and Inquisition: Academic Freedom in Medieval Universities," *Church History* 58 (June 1989): 168–81; Charles Homer Haskins, *The Rise of Universities* (Ithaca, NY: Cornell University Press, 1957), 51, 54; Hofstadter, *Academic Freedom*, 12; Russell Kirk, *Academic Freedom: An Essay in Definition* (Chicago: Regnery, 1955), 13–18.
6. Samuel Eliot Morison, *Three Centuries of Harvard, 1636–1936* (Cambridge, MA: Harvard University Press, 1936), 19; Hofstadter, *Academic Freedom*, 86–91.
7. Hofstadter, *Academic Freedom*, 178; William J. Hoye, "The Religious Roots of Academic Freedom," *Theological Studies* 58 (September 1997): 409–28, 410–14.
8. Hofstadter, *Academic Freedom*, 209–74.
9. Roger L. Geiger, "Introduction to the Transaction Edition," in *Academic Freedom in the Age of the College*, ed. Richard Hofstadter (New Brunswick, NJ: Transaction, 1996), vii–xxiv; Roger L. Geiger,

ed., *The American College in the Nineteenth Century* (Nashville, TN: Vanderbilt University Press, 2000); James McLachlan, "The American College in the Nineteenth Century: Toward a Reappraisal," *Teachers College Record* 80 (December 1978): 287–306.
10. Thomas Jefferson to Mr. Roscoe, 27 December 1829, in *The Writings of Thomas Jefferson* 7, ed. Henry A. Washington (Washington, DC: Taylor & Maury, 1854), 195–97, 196.
11. Wayne Hamilton Wiley, "Academic Freedom at the University of Virginia: The First Hundred Years—From Jefferson through Alderman" (PhD diss., University of Virginia, 1973), 99–106; Gordon E. Baker, "Thomas Jefferson on Academic Freedom," *Bulletin of the AAUP* 39 (Autumn 1953): 377–87; Hofstadter, *Academic Freedom*, 240–41.
12. Thomas Jefferson to General Robert Taylor, 16 May 1820, in *The Writings of Thomas Jefferson* 15–16, ed. Albert Ellery Bergh, Andrew Adgate Lipscomb, and Richard Holland Johnston (Washington, DC: Thomas Jefferson Memorial Association of the United States, 1905), 252–56, 256.
13. Hofstadter, *Academic Freedom*, 263–69.
14. Michael Sugrue, "'We Desired Our Future Rulers to Be Educated Men': South Carolina College, the Defense of Slavery, and the Development of Secessionist Politics," *History of Higher Education Annual* 14 (1994): 39–72, 52.
15. Geiger, "Introduction," xix.
16. Kirk, *Academic Freedom*, 21; Hofstadter, *Academic Freedom*.
17. Kirk, *Academic Freedom*, 21–22; Christopher J. Lucas, *American Higher Education: A History* (New York: St. Martin's Press, 1994), 304–5; Erving E. Beauregard, *History of Academic Freedom in Ohio: Case Studies in Higher Education, 1808–1976* (New York: Peter Lang, 1988), 19–29; Clement Eaton, *The Freedom-of-Thought Struggle in the Old South*, rev. ed. (New York: Harper & Row, 1964), 222; Hofstadter, *Academic Freedom*, 260. Known controversies existed at Bowdoin College, Centre College, Dartmouth College, Denison University, Dickinson College, Franklin College, the University of Georgia, Harvard University, the University of Iowa, Jefferson College of Mississippi, Kenyon College, Lane Theological Seminary, Miami University, the University of North Carolina, Oberlin College, the College of South Carolina, and Western Reserve College.
18. Eaton, *Freedom-of-Thought Struggle*, 228–29. On the history of textbook struggles, see Joseph Moreau, *Schoolbook Nation: Conflicts over American History Textbooks from the Civil War to the Present* (Ann Arbor: University of Michigan Press, 2003); Jonathan Zimmerman, *Whose America? Culture Wars in the Public Schools* (Cambridge, MA: Harvard University Press, 2002).
19. Eaton, *Freedom-of-Thought Struggle*, 237.

20. Monty Woodall Cox, "Freedom During the Fremont Campaign: The Fate of One North Carolina Republican in 1856," *North Carolina Historical Review* 45 (October 1968): 357–83; Michael Thomas Smith, *A Traitor and a Scoundrel: Benjamin Hedrick and the Cost of Dissent* (Newark: University of Delaware Press, 2003), 63–87; C[ornelia] P. Spencer, "Old Times in Chapel Hill, No. XVII: Prof. Hedrick's Case," *North Carolina University Magazine* n.s. 10, no. 1 (1890): 43–56.
21. "Fremont in the South," *North Carolina Standard*, September 16, 1856, reprinted in *Benjamin Sherwood Hedrick*, ed. J. G. de Roulhac Hamilton and Henry McGilbert Wagstaff (Chapel Hill, NC: University Press, 1910), 8.
22. "An Alumnus," in Hamilton and Wagstaff, *Benjamin Sherwood Hedrick*, 9–11, 10; Cox, "Freedom During the Fremont Campaign," 376n76.
23. In Hamilton and Wagstaff, *Benjamin Sherwood Hedrick*, 12–15, 12.
24. Ibid., 16–17, 17.
25. Ibid., 22–23, 23.
26. Ibid., 27–29.
27. Ibid., 29–30, 30.
28. Cox, "Freedom During the Fremont Campaign"; M. T. Smith, *Traitor and a Scoundrel*.
29. Hamilton and Wagstaff, *Benjamin Sherwood Hedrick*, xx.
30. Kemp P. Battle, *History of the University of North Carolina*, vol. 1, *From Its Beginning to the Death of President Swain, 1780–1868* (Raleigh, NC: Edwards & Broughton, 1907), 655.
31. Swain to Manly, 7 October, 1856, in Hamilton and Wagstaff, *Benjamin Sherwood Hedrick*, 26–27, 27; Swain to Manly, 7 October, 1856, in ibid., 27–29.
32. Mary Ellen Hedrick to Mrs. Rankin, 29 December 1856, Folder 15, Benjamin Sherwood Hedrick Papers (#325), Southern Historical Collection, Louis Round Wilson Special Collections Library, University of North Carolina at Chapel Hill.
33. Harrisse was embroiled in his own dispute relating to student discipline and his critique of the administration's handling of his complaints about it. He was not retained at the end of the year in a case that has been linked to that of Hedrick but which had its own catalysts. Battle, *History of the University of North Carolina*, 1:657–59.
34. Charles Phillips to W. C. Kerr, 15 December 1856, in Spencer, "Old Times in Chapel Hill," 54–56, 54.
35. Laurence R. Veysey, *The Emergence of the American University* (Chicago: University of Chicago Press, 1965); Walter P. Metzger, *Academic Freedom in the Age of the University* (New York: Columbia University Press, 1961), 4–133; Julie A. Reuben, *The Making of the Modern University: Intellectual Transformation and the Marginalization of Morality* (Chicago: University of Chicago Press, 1996).

36. Robert L. Adams, "Conflict over Charges of Heresy in American Protestant Seminaries," *Social Compass* 17 (April 1970): 243–59; Ronald L. Numbers, *Darwinism Comes to America* (Cambridge, MA: Harvard University Press, 1998), 67–73; W. P. Metzger, *Academic Freedom*, 46–92.
37. Andrew Dickson White, *A History of the Warfare of Science with Theology in Christendom* (New York: Appleton, 1896), 1:ix. See also, W. P. Metzger, *Academic Freedom*, 53n26; Ronald L. Numbers, "Science and Religion," *Osiris*, 2nd ser., 1, *Historical Writing on American Science* (1985): 59–80.
38. Mary Engel, "A Chapter in the History of Academic Freedom: The Case of Alexander Winchell," *History of Education Journal* 7 (Summer 1956): 157–64; "Alexander Winchell: An Editorial Tribute," *American Geologist* 9 (February 1892): 71–148, 109–11; Paul K. Conkin, *Gone with the Ivy: A Biography of Vanderbilt University* (Knoxville: University of Tennessee Press, 1985): 60–63; A. D. White, *History of the Warfare*, 313–16.
39. A. D. White, *History of the Warfare*, 316–18; Clement Eaton, "Professor James Woodrow and the Freedom of Teaching in the South," *Journal of Southern History* 28 (February 1962): 3–17.
40. Ronald L. Numbers and Lester D. Stephens, "Darwinism in the American South," in *Disseminating Darwinism: The Role of Place, Race, Religion, and Gender*, ed. Ronald L. Numbers and John Stenhouse (New York: Cambridge University Press, 1999), 123–44.
41. Carol Gruber made a similar point in relation to World War I. Carol S. Gruber, *Mars and Minerva: World War I and the Uses of the Higher Learning in America* (Baton Rouge: Louisiana State University Press, 1975), 174.
42. Kent Sagendorph, *Michigan: The Story of the University* (New York: Dutton, 1948), 93; Henry P. Tappan, "Review by Rev. Dr. H. P. Tappan: Historic Statement of My Connections with the University," in *Proceedings of the Board of Regents* (1837–64), ed. University of Michigan Board of Regents (Ann Arbor: University of Michigan), 1119–66.
43. Eaton, "Professor James Woodrow," 14.
44. Jeffrey P. Bouman, "Nonsectarian, not Secular: Students' Curricular and Co-curricular Experience with Christian Faith at Brown University, the University of Michigan, and Cornell University, 1850–1920" (PhD diss., University of Michigan, 2004), 109–10.
45. Conkin, *Gone with the Ivy*, 59.
46. That there were extreme restrictions based on sex and race is, of course, true. The professoriate was overwhelmingly white, male, and Protestant well into the twentieth century. Patricia Albjerg Graham, "Expansion and Exclusion: A History of Women in American Higher Education," *Signs* 3 (Summer 1978): 759–73; James D. Anderson,

"Race, Meritocracy, and the American Academy during the Immediate Post–World War II Era," *History of Education Quarterly* 33 (Summer 1993): 151–75.
47. R. L. Adams, "Conflict over Charges."
48. W. P. Metzger, *Academic Freedom*, 66.
49. Hugh Hawkins, *Pioneer: The History of the Johns Hopkins University, 1874–1889* (Baltimore, MD: Johns Hopkins University Press, 1984), 69–72, 189.
50. Morris Bishop, *A History of Cornell* (Ithaca, NY: Cornell University Press, 1962), 192–93; Bouman, "Nonsectarian, not Secular"; W. P. Metzger, *Academic Freedom*, 66.
51. Porter to Sumner, 6 December 1879, in Harris E. Starr, *William Graham Sumner* (New York: Holt, 1925), 346–47, 346.
52. William Graham Sumner, "A Private and Personal Communication to the Members of the Corporation and to the Permanent Officers of Yale College," June 1881, in ibid., 357–66, 362.
53. Ibid., 363.
54. Ibid., 357–66; W. P. Metzger, *Academic Freedom*, 61–64. Historical treatments have generally lauded Sumner to the neglect of Porter. For arguments more supportive of Porter, see George Levesque, "Noah Porter Revisited," *Perspectives on the History of Higher Education* 26 (2007): 29–66; George M. Marsden, *Soul of the American University: From Protestant Establishment to Established Nonbelief* (New York: Oxford University Press, 1994), 123–33.
55. Hawkins, *Pioneer*, 175–76, 176.
56. Charles W. Pearson, "Open Inspiration Versus a Closed Canon and Infallible Bible," *Open Court* 16 (March 1902): 175–81, 175.
57. Robert E. Bisbee, "An Echo of the Inquisition," *Arena* 27 (June 1902): 592–603. See also Marsden, *Soul of the American University*, 280.
58. W. P. Metzger, *Academic Freedom*, 93–138; Walter P. Metzger, "The German Contribution to the American Theory of Academic Freedom," *Bulletin of the AAUP* 41 (Summer 1955): 214–30.
59. Charles Franklin Thwing, *The American and the German University: One Hundred Years of History* (New York: Macmillan, 1928), 144.
60. W. P. Metzger, *Academic Freedom*, 93–138; W. P. Metzger, "German Contribution."
61. Ellen W. Schrecker, *No Ivory Tower: McCarthyism and the Universities* (New York: Oxford University Press, 1986), 15; Clyde W. Barrow, *Universities and the Capitalist State: Corporate Liberalism and the Reconstruction of American Higher Education, 1894–1928* (Madison: University of Wisconsin Press, 1990), 187; W. P. Metzger, *Academic Freedom*.
62. Andrew F. West, "What Is Academic Freedom?" *North American Review* 140 (May 1885): 432–44. See also Henry W. Farnam, "Academic Freedom in Germany," *New Englander and Yale Review*

46 (January 1887): 67–71; N. S. Shaler, "The Problem of Discipline in Higher Education," *Atlantic Monthly* 64 (July 1889): 24–37, 30; Albion Small, "Academic Freedom," *Arena* 22 (October 1899): 463–72; Walter P. Metzger, "Essay II," in *Freedom and Order in the University*, ed. Samuel Gorovitz (Cleveland, OH: Press of Western Reserve University, 1967), 59–71, 63; W. P. Metzger, *Academic Freedom*, 123–24.
63. Small, "Academic Freedom," 463 (emphasis in original).
64. Schrecker, *No Ivory Tower*, 15; Mary O. Furner, *Advocacy and Objectivity: A Crisis in the Professionalization of the Social Sciences* (Lexington: University Press of Kentucky, 1975), 127.
65. Furner, *Advocacy and Objectivity*, 127–42; A. W. Coats, "Henry Carter Adams: A Case Study in the Emergence of the Social Sciences in the United States, 1850–1900," *Journal of American Studies* 2 (October 1968): 177–97; Nancy Cohen, *The Reconstruction of American Liberalism, 1865–1914* (Chapel Hill: University of North Carolina Press, 2002), 171–73; "Sibley College Lectures—XI," *Scientific American Supplement* 555 (August 21, 1886): 8861–63; "Sibley College Lectures—XI," *Scientific American Supplement* 556 (August 28, 1886): 8877–80.
66. H. C. Adams to J. B. Angell, 15 March 1887, as cited by Joseph Dorfman in "Introductory Essay: Henry Carter Adams, the Harmonizer of Liberty and Reform," in Henry Carter Adams, *Relation of the State to Industrial Action and Economics and Jurisprudence: Two Essays*, ed. Joseph Dorfman (New York: Columbia University Press, 1954), 1–55, 38.
67. J. B. Angell to H. C. Adams, 26 March 1887, Box 2, Henry Carter Adams Papers, Bentley Historical Library, University of Michigan.
68. H. C. Adams to J. B. Angell, 15 March 1887, Box 3, James Burrill Angell Papers, Bentley Historical Library, University of Michigan.
69. Furner, *Advocacy and Objectivity*, 140–41.
70. Theron F. Schlabach, "An Aristocrat on Trial: The Case of Richard T. Ely," *Wisconsin Magazine of History* 47 (Winter 1963–64): 140–59.
71. Furner, *Advocacy and Objectivity*, 205–22; Elizabeth Donnan, "A Nineteenth-Century Academic Cause Célèbre," *New England Quarterly* 25 (March 1952): 23–46.
72. Arthur G. Beach, *A Pioneer College: The Story of Marietta* (Chicago: Privately printed, 1935), 226–27; Furner, *Advocacy and Objectivity*, 222–28; W. P. Metzger, *Academic Freedom*, 149–51; Beauregard, *History of Academic Freedom*, 36–40.
73. W. P. Metzger, *Academic Freedom*, 162–71; Furner, *Advocacy and Objectivity*, 229–57. See also Howard Bromberg, "Revising History," *Stanford Magazine* (March–April 1996): 116; Warren J. Samuels, "The Firing of E. A. Ross from Stanford University: Injustice Compounded by Deception?" *Journal of Economic Education* 22 (Spring 1991): 183–90.

74. Terry Lee Matthews, "The Emergence of a Prophet: Andrew Sledd and the 'Sledd Affair' of 1902" (PhD diss., Duke University, 1990), 84–121, 181–84.
75. Andrew Sledd, "The Negro: Another View," *Atlantic Monthly* 90 (July 1902): 65–73, 66.
76. Ralph E. Reed Jr., "Emory College and the Sledd Affair of 1902: A Case Study in Southern Honor and Racial Attitudes," *Georgia Historical Quarterly* 72 (Fall 1988): 463–92, 471. On Felton, see John Erwin Talmadge, *Rebecca Latimer Felton* (Athens: University of Georgia Press, 1960).
77. Mrs. W. H. [Rebecca Latimer] Felton, "The Negro, as Discussed by Mr. Andrew Sledd," *Atlanta Constitution*, August 3, 1902; Matthews, "Emergence of a Prophet," 165.
78. Reed, "Emory College"; Henry Y. Warnock, "Andrew Sledd, Southern Methodists, and the Negro: A Case Study," *Journal of Southern History* 31 (August 1965): 251–71; Terry L. Matthews, "The Voice of a Prophet: Andrew Sledd Revisited," *Journal of Southern Religion* 6 (December 2003): 1–13; Matthews, "Emergence of a Prophet," 162–79.
79. Reed, "Emory College," 481–84; Matthews, "Emergence of a Prophet," 195–225.
80. J. C. Kilgo to W. A Candler, 14 August 1902, in Earl W. Porter, *Trinity and Duke, 1892–1924* (Durham, NC: Duke University Press, 1964), 100–101, 100.
81. [John Spencer Bassett], "Stirring Up the Fires of Race Antipathy," *South Atlantic Quarterly* 2 (October 1903): 297–305, 299.
82. Porter, *Trinity and Duke*, 96–139; W. P. Metzger, *Academic Freedom*, 172–77. See also Earl W. Porter, "The Bassett Affair: Something to Remember," *South Atlantic Quarterly* 72 (Autumn 1973): 451–60.
83. Joseph L. Morrison, "Josephus Daniels and the Bassett Academic Freedom Case," *Journalism Quarterly* 39 (Spring 1962): 187–95; Porter, *Trinity and Duke*, 79–84, 104–5, 131–32, 135.
84. Bruce Clayton, *The Savage Ideal: Intolerance and Intellectual Leadership in the South, 1890–1914* (Baltimore, MD: Johns Hopkins University Press, 1972): 127–28. On Kilgo, see Joseph M. Stetar, "In Search of a Direction: Southern Higher Education after the Civil War," *History of Education Quarterly* 25 (Autumn 1985): 341–67.
85. Porter, *Trinity and Duke*, 122–31; Clayton, *Savage Ideal*, 84–99; Fred Arthur Bailey, *William Edward Dodd: The South's Yeoman Scholar* (Charlottesville: University Press of Virginia, 1997), 38–39.
86. William Garrett Brown was visiting his friend William Preston Few, a faculty member, dean, and future Trinity and Duke president. Porter, *Trinity and Duke*, 131; Memorial from the Faculty to the Trustees, in "Trinity College and Academic Liberty," *South Atlantic Quarterly* 3 (January 1904): 62–72, 65–66.
87. Edwin Mims to Walter H. Page, 4 December 1904, Walter Hines Page Papers, Houghton Library, Harvard University, as cited in Porter, *Trinity and Duke*, 132–33.

88. Porter, *Trinity and Duke*, 131–34; W. P. Metzger, *Academic Freedom*, 172–77.
89. The Statement of the Trustees in "Trinity College and Academic Liberty," *South Atlantic Quarterly* 3 (January 1904): 62–72, 63.
90. Porter, *Trinity and Duke*, 133–137.
91. Theodore Roosevelt, "At Durham, N. C., October 19, 1905," in *Presidential Addresses and State Papers of Theodore Roosevelt* 4 (New York: Collier & Sons, [1905]), 478–81, 479.
92. John Spencer Bassett to William K. Boyd, 2 January 1912, Bassett Papers, as cited in Clayton, *Savage Ideal*, 101.
93. William E. Dodd, "Some Difficulties of the History Teacher in the South," *South Atlantic Quarterly* 3 (April 1904): 117–22. Bassett, a close friend, offered his support for Dodd in an editorial, arguing that critics inherently challenge conservatism and threaten those who benefit from the status quo but that they should be praised for generating conversation and prompting change. John Spencer Bassett, "The Task of the Critic," *South Atlantic Quarterly* 3 (October 1904): 297–301.
94. William E. Dodd, "Freedom of Speech in the South," *Nation* 84 (April 25, 1907): 383–84, 383.
95. Bailey, *William Edward Dodd*, 34–42.
96. Enoch Marvin Banks, "A Semi-Centennial View of Secession," *Independent* 70 (February 9, 1911): 299–303. Sledd used his settlement money from Emory to complete his doctorate at Yale University and then taught for a year at Southern University in Greensboro, Alabama, prior to his appointment at Florida. In 1909, he was removed as part of a larger political struggle that also included concerns over his efforts to raise academic standards. Sledd then served as president of Southern before Candler, in his role as chancellor, brought him back to Emory. On Sledd at Florida, see Carl Van Ness, "Florida's Sledd Affair: Andrew Sledd and the Fight for Higher Education in Florida," *Florida Historical Quarterly* 87 (Winter 2009): 319–51.
97. Banks, "Semi-Centennial View," 302.
98. Ibid., 299.
99. Fred Arthur Bailey, "Free Speech at the University of Florida: The Enoch Marvin Banks Case," *Florida Historical Quarterly* 71 (July 1992): 1–17. See also Seth Weitz, "Defending the Old South: The Myth of the Lost Cause and Political Immorality in Florida, 1865–1968," *Historian* 71 (Spring 2009): 79–92.
100. Andrew Sledd, "The Dismissal of Professor Banks," *Independent* 70 (May 25, 1911): 1113.
101. Eric Anderson and Alfred Moss, *Dangerous Donations: Northern Philanthropy and Southern Black Education, 1902–1930* (Columbia: University of Missouri Press, 1999), 44–45.
102. Warren A. Candler, *Dangerous Donations and Degrading Doles, or A Vast Scheme for Capturing and Controlling the Colleges and Universities of the Country* ([Atlanta?]: Author, 1909), 12.

103. Ibid., 22.
104. The landmark work in the field is James D. Anderson, *Education of Blacks in the South, 1860–1935* (Chapel Hill: University of North Carolina Press, 1988). E. Anderson and Moss, in *Dangerous Donations*, have viewed the philanthropists in a more favorable light. See also Marybeth Gasman, "Education in Black and White: New Perspectives on the History of Historically Black Colleges and Universities," *Teachers College Record*, Date Published: January 25, 2006, http://www.tcrecord.org ID Number: 12302.
105. Anderson, "Race, Meritocracy."
106. Elmer Ellsworth Brown, "Academic Freedom," *Educational Review* 19 (March 1900): 209–31; Thomas Elmer Will, "A Menace to Freedom: The College Trust," *Arena* 26 (September 1901): 244–57, reprinted in *The American Concept of Academic Freedom in Formation: A Collection of Essays and Reports*, ed. Walter P. Metzger (New York: Arno Press, 1977).
107. John Dewey, "Academic Freedom," *Educational Review* 23 (January 1902): 1–14.
108. Charles F. Thwing, *College Administration* (New York: Century, 1900), 92.
109. Charles W. Eliot, "Academic Freedom," *Science* n.s. 36 (July 5, 1907): 1–12, 6; Nicholas Murray Butler, "Academic Freedom," *Educational Review* 47 (March 1914): 291–94, 291.
110. Andrew F. West, "The Changing Conception of 'The Faculty' in American Universities," *Association of American Universities, Proceedings of the Annual Conference* 7 (1906): 65–73, 66.
111. Veysey, *Emergence of the American University*, 416.
112. Ibid.; Karen Christine Nelson, "Historical Origins of the Linkage of Academic Freedom and Faculty Tenure" (PhD diss., University of Denver, 1984), 40; Edward T. Silva and Sheila A. Slaughter, *Serving Power: The Making of the Academic Social Science Expert* (Westport, CT: Greenwood Press, 1984), 276.
113. His were the anonymous cases referred to in Upton Sinclair's *Goosestep: A Study of American Education* (Pasadena, CA: Author, 1923), 422–23.
114. William E. Bohn to the Board of Regents, 5 January 1910, Box 1, Harry B. Hutchins Papers, Bentley Historical Library, University of Michigan (hereafter cited as Hutchins Papers).
115. For example, see Charles K. Latham to Harry B. Hutchins, 3 December 1909; Hinton E. Spaulding to Hutchins, 13 December 1909, Box 1, Hutchins Papers.
116. Cooley to Hutchins, 14 December 1909; Hutchins to Cooley, 15 December 1909, Box 1, Hutchins Papers.
117. Walter H. Sawyer to H. B. Hutchins, 9 April 1910; H. B. Hutchins to W. H. Sawyer, 11 April 1910, Box 1, Hutchins Papers.

2 Associating and Academic Freedom

1. Andrew Sledd, "The Dismissal of Professor Banks," *Independent* 70 (May 25, 1911): 1113.
2. Walter P. Metzger, *Academic Freedom in the Age of the University* (New York: Columbia University Press, 1961), 194–202; Karen Christine Nelson, "Historical Origins of the Linkage of Academic Freedom and Faculty Tenure" (PhD diss., University of Denver, 1984), 50–61.
3. John Dewey, "American Association of University Professors Introductory Address," *Science* 41 (January 29, 1915): 147–51, 148.
4. K. C. Nelson, "Historical Origins," 40; Daniel H. Pollitt and Jordan E. Kurland, "Entering the Academic Freedom Arena Running: The AAUP's First Year," *Academe* 84 (July–August 1998): 45–52, 46; Loya F. Metzger, "Professors in Trouble: A Quantitative Analysis of Academic Freedom and Tenure Cases" (PhD diss., Columbia University, 1978), 43.
5. Laurence R. Veysey, *The Emergence of the American University* (Chicago: University of Chicago Press, 1965), 393–94.
6. Thorstein Veblen, *The Higher Learning in America: A Memorandum on the Conduct of Universities by Business Men* (New York: Huebsch, 1918). Reprinted with Introduction by Louis M. Hacker (New York: Sagamore Press, 1957), 69.
7. Ibid., 57.
8. Timothy Reese Cain, "The First Attempts to Unionize the Faculty," *Teachers College Record* 112 (March 2010): 875–913, 880–81.
9. George Cram Cook, "The Third American Sex," *Forum* 50 (October 1913): 445–63, 461.
10. F. B. R. Hellems, "The Professorial Quintain," *Forum* 51 (March 1914): 321–32, 331.
11. James McKeen Cattell, *University Control* (New York: Science Press, 1913), 31, 36.
12. Ibid., 38–44, 61.
13. Mark Beach, "Professional versus Professorial Control of Higher Education," *Educational Record* 49 (Summer 1968): 263–73.
14. Pollitt and Kurland, "Entering," 49–50; K. C. Nelson, "Historical Origins," 63–64.
15. George M. Marsden, "The Ambiguities of Academic Freedom," *Church History* 62 (June 1993): 221–36.
16. Howard Crosby Warren, "Academic Freedom," *Atlantic Monthly* 114 (November 1914): 689–99, 695.
17. John M. Mecklin, *My Quest for Freedom* (New York: Charles Scribner's Sons, 1945), 160; Marsden, "Ambiguities of Academic Freedom"; K. C. Nelson, "Historical Origins," 68–71; Robert P. Ludlum, "Academic Freedom and Tenure: A History," *Antioch Review* 10 (Spring 1950): 3–34, 11–13; A. O. Lovejoy and Associates, "The Case

of Professor Mecklin: Report of the Committee of Inquiry of the American Philosophical Association and the American Psychological Association," *Journal of Philosophy, Psychology and Scientific Methods* 11 (January 29, 1914): 67–81.
18. "Minutes of the Business Meeting at Minneapolis," *American Economic Review* 4, Supplement (March 1914): 196–200, 196–97.
19. Edwin R. A. Seligman, "The Committee on Academic Freedom of the American Association of University Professors," *Educational Review* 50 (September 1915): 184–89, 185; Edwin R. A. Seligman and Associates, "Preliminary Report of the Joint Committee on Academic Freedom and Academic Tenure," *American Economic Review* 5, Supplement (March 1915): 316–23. On extramural speech, see Matthew W. Finkin and Robert C. Post, *For the Common Good: Principles of American Academic Freedom* (New Haven, CT: Yale University Press, 2009), 127–48.
20. Cattell to Lovejoy, 20 May 1913, Box 4, AAUP Records, Series Historical Files, George Washington University Special Collections (hereafter cited as AAUP Historical Files).
21. Quoted in "A National Association of University Professors," *Science* n.s. 39 (March 27, 1914): 458–59, 458.
22. The institutions represented were Clark, Columbia, Cornell, Harvard, Princeton, Johns Hopkins, and Yale Universities, and the University of Wisconsin. The other two institutions invited were likely the Universities of Michigan and Pennsylvania. Lloyd to Dewey, 11 November 1913, Box 4, AAUP Historical Files; K. C. Nelson, "Historical Origins," 66; "National Association of University Professors," 459.
23. Dewey and Lovejoy to the Members of the Committee on the Organization of an Association of University Professors, n.d., Box 1, William H. Hobbs Papers, Bentley Historical Library, University of Michigan (hereafter cited as Hobbs Papers). Those in attendance were Dewey, Edward Capps, William H. Hobbs, Cassius Jackson Keyser, M. Learned, Lovejoy, and Frank Thilly.
24. A. O. Lovejoy, "A. U. P.: Minutes of Meeting of Committee on Organization," 14 November 1914, Box 1, Hobbs Papers. Those in attendance were Dewey, R. G. Harrison, Morris Jastrow, Alvin S. Johnson, Lovejoy, W. B. Munro, Henry Taber, and John S. P. Tatlock.
25. K. C. Nelson, "Historical Origins," 86–93.
26. "The American Association of University Professors," *School and Society* 1 (January 2, 1915): 17.
27. Warren, "Academic Freedom," 697.
28. Ibid., 698.
29. Dewey, "American Association of University Professors," 150.
30. Seligman, "Committee on Academic Freedom," 186–87.
31. Walter P. Metzger, "The First Investigation," *AAUP Bulletin* 47 (Autumn 1961): 206–10, 207.

32. Dewey personally paid the expenses. W. P. Metzger, "First Investigation," 206–7.
33. "Conditions at the University of Utah," *Science* n.s. 41 (April 30, 1915): 637.
34. "Preliminary Summary of Findings of the Committee of Inquiry of the American Association of University Professors on Conditions at the University of Utah," *School and Society* 1 (June 12, 1915): 861–64; W. P. Metzger, "First Investigation," 206–10; Pollitt and Kurland, "Entering," 46–48.
35. Pollitt and Kurland, "Entering," 48–49.
36. Ibid., 50–52.
37. Ibid., 49–50; "Summary Report of the Committee on Academic Freedom and Academic Tenure on the Case of Professor Willard C. Fisher of Wesleyan University," *Bulletin of the AAUP* 2 (April 1916, part 2): 73–76.
38. K. C. Nelson, "Historical Origins," 103–8.
39. John Dewey, "Address of the President," *Bulletin of the AAUP* 1 (December 1915, part 1): 7–13, 11–12.
40. "General Report of the Committee on Academic Freedom and Academic Tenure," *Bulletin of the AAUP* 1 (December 1915, part 1): 15–43, 20.
41. Ibid., 32.
42. Ibid., 37.
43. Ibid., 40–42.
44. *Report of Proceedings, Meeting of the American Association of University Professors*, December 31, 1915–January 1, 1916, 74, Box 2, AAUP Historical Files.
45. *Report of Proceedings*, 74–115.
46. John H. Wigmore, "President's Report for 1916," Bulletin of the AAUP 2 (November 1916): 9–52, 15–16.
47. *Report of Proceedings*, 74–115.
48. "General Announcements," *Bulletin of the AAUP* 2 (April 1916): 3–4, 3; "General Announcements," *Bulletin of the AAUP* 2 (May 1916): 3–5, 4.
49. William L. Chenery, "From a Union Professor," *Chicago Herald*, July 17, 1916.
50. "Professors' Union."
51. Hugh Hawkins, *Banding Together: The Rise of National Associations in American Higher Education, 1887–1950* (Baltimore, MD: Johns Hopkins University Press, 1992), 16.
52. Stephen B. L. Penrose, "The Relation of the College Association to Existing Associations," *AAC Bulletin* 1 (1915): 54–59.
53. R. Watson Cooper, signed section (pp. 43–47) of "The Place and Function of the Proposed Association," *AAC Bulletin* 1 (1915): 39–54.

54. Robert L. Kelly, signed section (pp. 39–43, 42) of ibid.
55. Herbert Welch, "Academic Freedom and Tenure of Office," *AAC Bulletin* 2 (April 1916): 157–71, 162–63.
56. Ibid., 158.
57. Ibid., 165.
58. Ulysses G. Weatherly, "Discussion," *AAC Bulletin* 2 (April 1916): 171–79, 173–74.
59. Ibid., 171–79.
60. Alexander Meiklejohn, "Discussion," *AAC Bulletin* 2 (April 1916): 179–87, 180.
61. Ibid., 181.
62. Ibid., 186.
63. "Academic Freedom and Tenure of Office: Report of Committee," *AAC Bulletin* 3 (April 1917): 48–56.
64. On the concern, see U. G. Weatherly to J. Dewey, 7 December 1914; A. S. Warthin to A. O. Lovejoy, 17 December 1914; J. E. Creighton to J. Dewey, 31 December 1914; "Chamberlin of Chicago" to J. Dewey, 3 December 1914; Box 4, AAUP Historical Files.
65. K. C. Nelson, "Historical Origins," 68.
66. Ludlum, "Academic Freedom and Tenure," 16.
67. Despite these misgivings, Ziwet would become a member of the organization after its founding. Alexander Ziwet to William H. Hobbs, 25 May 1914, Box 1, Hobbs Papers.
68. Dewey, "American Association of University Professors," 150.
69. Frank Thilly, "Address of the President to the Members of the Association," *Bulletin of the AAUP* 3 (February 1917): 7–10, 10.
70. See, for example, Frank Thilly, "Report of the President," *Bulletin of the AAUP* 3 (November 1917): 11–24, 15; "General Announcements," *Bulletin of the AAUP* 3 (March 1917): 3–5.
71. J. M. Coulter, "To the Members of the Association," *Bulletin of the AAUP* 4 (January 1918): 3.
72. In its first year, Lovejoy investigated four of the five cases, since no one else was willing to help. Seligman sought relief from the chairmanship and was replaced by A. A. Young in 1916.
73. "Report of Committee A on Academic Freedom and Academic Tenure," *Bulletin of the AAUP* 4 (February–March 1918): 16–28, 16.
74. L. Metzger, "Professors in Trouble," 50–51.
75. "Report of the Third Annual Meeting," *Bulletin of the AAUP* 3 (February 1917): 11–22, 12.
76. Ibid., 12–13.
77. "Report of Committee A"; Cattell, *University Control*, 38–44.
78. Only Frank Heywood Hodder disagreed with this emphasis, arguing that Committee A should be a protective organization that pursued redress to every violation of academic freedom. "Report of Committee A," 28.

79. Wayne J. Urban, *Why Teachers Organized* (Detroit, MI: Wayne State University Press, 1982), 134–40; Marjorie Murphy, *Blackboard Unions: The AFT and the NEA, 1900–1980* (Ithaca, NY: Cornell University Press, 1990), 83–87; Timothy Reese Cain, "The First Attempts."
80. M. Murphy, *Blackboard Unions*, 84–90; Urban, *Why Teachers Organized*, 136–37.
81. Walter Dyson, *Howard University: The Capstone of Negro Education* (Washington, DC: Howard University, 1941), 88, 96.
82. "The Present Crisis," *Federation Bulletin* 2, no. 1 (1915): 1, Box 68, American Federation of Teachers Inventory, Part I, Series 1, President's Department Collection, Archives of Labor and Urban Affairs, Wayne State University.
83. "Resolution Adopted by the American Federation of Teachers Convention Assembled, Chicago, December 30, 1916," Box 1, American Federation of Teachers Inventory, Part II, Series 13, AFT Annual Conventions, Archives of Labor and Urban Affairs, Wayne State University (hereafter cited as AFT Conventions Collection).
84. "Platform of the American Federation of Teachers," 29–30 December 1916, Box 1, Folder: Election Material, December 1916, AFT Conventions Collection.

3 Treason and the "Farce" of Academic Freedom

1. Carol S. Gruber, *Mars and Minerva: World War I and the Uses of the Higher Learning in America* (Baton Rouge: Louisiana State University Press, 1975); David O. Levine, *The American College and the Culture of Aspiration, 1915–1940* (Ithaca, NY: Cornell University Press, 1986), 23–44.
2. "General Report," 20.
3. "Scores Academic Freedom; Dr. Hibben Defines Service of College to State," *New York Tribune*, October 20, 1917.
4. Walter P. Metzger, "The German Contribution to the American Theory of Academic Freedom," *Bulletin of the AAUP* 41 (Summer 1955): 214–30.
5. Charles Franklin Thwing, *The American and the German University: One Hundred Years of History* (New York: Macmillan, 1928), 40–105; Jurgen Herbst, *The German Historical School in American Scholarship: A Study in the Transfer of Culture* (Ithaca, NY: Cornell University Press, 1965), 1–22.
6. For the full text of the manifesto, see Samuel Harden Church, *The American Verdict on the War: A Reply to the Appeal to the Civilized World of 93 German Professors* (Baltimore, MD: Norman, Remington, 1915), 26–32.

7. See, for example, Rudolf Eucken and Ernst Haeckel's efforts to develop the German University League to unite American scholars educated in Germany behind Germany's cause. Rudolf Eucken and Ernst Haeckel, "A German Declaration," *New York Times*, September 10, 1914; Frank Jewett Mather Jr., letter to the editor, *New York Times*, September 12, 1914; Gruber, *Mars and Minerva*, 20.
8. John Jay Chapman, *Deutschland über Alles; or, Germany Speaks* (New York: Putnam's Sons), 16, 43.
9. William Roscoe Thayer, *Germany vs. Civilization: Notes on the Atrocious War* (Boston: Houghton Mifflin, 1916), 159–60.
10. "German Scholars and the 'Truth about Germany,'" *Nation* 99 (September 24, 1914): 376.
11. Gruber, *Mars and Minerva*, 67–68.
12. "Pro-German Admits Failure in America," *New York Times*, February 25, 1915.
13. Gruber, *Mars and Minerva*, 54; Merle Eugene Curti and Vernon Rosco Carstensen, *The University of Wisconsin: A History, 1848–1925* (Madison: University of Wisconsin Press, 1949), 56.
14. Morris Bishop, *A History of Cornell* (Ithaca, NY: Cornell University Press, 1962), 426.
15. Timothy Reese Cain, "'Silence and Cowardice' at the University of Michigan: World War I and the Pursuit of Un-American Faculty," *History of Education Quarterly* 51, no. 3 (2011): 297–329.
16. "Incensed Students Burn LaFollette in Effigy," *Daily Illini*, March 7, 1917; "What They Think of LaFollette," *Daily Illini*, March 8, 1917.
17. "9 Girls' Colleges Express Loyalty," *Washington Post*, March 31, 1917.
18. See, for example, William Elmer Nicholas III, "Academic Dissent in World War I, 1917–1918" (PhD diss., Tulane University, 1970), 18–19; David Starr Jordan, *The Days of Man: Being Memories of a Naturalist, Teacher, and Minor Prophet of Democracy* (Yonkers-on-Hudson, NY: World Book, 1922), 2:722.
19. "Dr. Jordan Hissed by Princeton Men," *New York Times*, March 27, 1917.
20. Jordan later denied newspaper reports of a negative reception at Harvard. Jordan, *Days of Man*, 715–24.
21. George Wilson Pierson, *Yale: College and University, 1871–1937*, vol. 1, *Yale College: An Educational History, 1871–1921* (New Haven, CT: Yale University Press, 1952), 465–66.
22. "Rout Big Pacifist Meeting, Hush David Starr Jordan," *Spokesman-Review* (Spokane, WA), April 2, 1917; see also "Pacifists Riot and Are Rioted Against in East," *Chicago Daily Tribune*, April 2, 1917; "Pacifists' Meeting Ends in Riot; Mob Breaks In; Police Use Clubs; Prominent Men Are Badly Beaten," *Sun* (Baltimore), April 2, 1917.
23. Phyllis Keller, *States of Belonging: German-American Intellectuals and the First World War* (Cambridge, MA: Harvard University Press, 1979),

76–118; Henry Aaron Yeomans, *Abbott Lawrence Lowell, 1856–1943* (Cambridge, MA: Harvard University Press, 1948), 315–16; "Suggest that Harvard Oust Muensterberg," *New York Times*, October 22, 1916.
24. A. Lawrence Lowell, "President's Report," in *Reports of the President and the Treasurer of Harvard College, 1916–17* (Cambridge, MA: Harvard University, 1918), 5–27, 25.
25. "Harvard Barred Meyer," *New York Times*, April 28, 1915; "Prof. Meyer Told Harvard Will Not Curb Free Speech," *St. Louis Dispatch*, April 29, 1914.
26. P. Keller, *States of Belonging*. See also Margaret Münsterberg, *Hugo Münsterberg: His Life and Work* (New York: Appleton, 1922), 256–329.
27. P. Keller, *States of Belonging*, 284.
28. Timothy Reese Cain and Steven E. Gump, "John Ervin Kirkpatrick and the Rulers of American Colleges," *AAUP Journal of Academic Freedom* 2 (2011): 1–43; available at http://www.academicfreedomjournal.org/VolumeTwo/CainGump.pdf.
29. "The Demobilized Professor," *Atlantic Monthly* 123 (April 1919): 537–45, 540.
30. Gruber, *Mars and Minerva*; Cain, "'Silence and Cowardice.'"
31. Peter J. Wedel, *The Story of Bethel College*, ed. Edmund G. Kaufman (North Newton, KS: Bethel College, 1954), 235–40; Gerlof D. Homan, *American Mennonites and the Great War, 1914–1918* (Scottdale, PA: Herald Press, 1994), 64.
32. Nicholas, "Academic Dissent," 79–81.
33. David C. Smith, *The First Century: A History of the University of Maine, 1865–1965* (Orono: University of Maine at Orono Press, 1979), 104–13; "The University of Maine and Dean Walz," *School and Society* 7 (March 16, 1918): 313–14, 314.
34. On the continuing controversy, see "Would Restore Dean Walz of University of Maine," *Boston Globe*, February 8, 1920; "Alumni Came Hundreds of Miles to Secure Justice for Dean of U. of M. College of Law," *Lewiston (ME) Evening Journal*, August 12, 1920; "Claim Trustees of the University of Maine Violated Agreement," *Lewiston (ME) Evening Journal*, December 27, 1920; "'No Agreement' Says Chairman Gould of University Trustees," *Lewiston (ME) Evening Journal*, December 27, 1920.
35. Gruber, *Mars and Minerva*, 187–206; Carol Signer Gruber, "Academic Freedom at Columbia University, 1917–1918," *AAUP Bulletin* 63 (September 1972), 297–305; Walter P. Metzger, *Academic Freedom in the Age of the University* (New York: Columbia University Press, 1961), 224–28; William Summerscales, *Affirmation and Dissent: Columbia's Response to the Crisis of World War I* (New York: Teachers College Press, 1970), 72–102.
36. Gruber, *Mars and Minerva*, 187–206.

37. "War View Opposed, Quits," *Reading (PA) Eagle*, January 30, 1918; "Woman Clears Scheidt," *New York Times*, March 5, 1918; W. Bruce Leslie, *Gentlemen and Scholars: College and Community in the "Age of the University," 1865–1917* (University Park: Pennsylvania State University Press, 1992), 163.
38. Curti and Carstensen, *University of Wisconsin*, 114.
39. "Professors of Northland Tarred and Feathered," *Ashland (WI) Daily Press*, April 1, 1918; "Schimmler [sic] Is Released," *Ashland (WI) Daily Press*, April 2, 1918; "Knights of Liberty Talk Thro [sic] Press," *Ashland (WI) Daily Press*, April 6, 1918; "Did Not Teach Disloyalty at Northland," *Ashland (WI) Daily Press*, April 6, 1918.
40. Bruce Tap, "Suppression of Dissent: Academic Freedom at the University of Illinois during the World War I Era," *Illinois Historical Journal* 85 (Spring 1992): 2–22.
41. Nicholas, "Academic Dissent," 152–67.
42. Oswald Garrison Villard, "The Allen Eaton Case," *Nation* 105 (November 15, 1917): 537–78; Sharon Lee Smith, "Allen Henderson Eaton, the Early Years: Winning Back the Pleasure of Life" (master's thesis, University of Oregon, 1997), 69–111.
43. "State University to Oust Disloyal," *Los Angeles Times*, April 24, 1918; "Berkeley Ousts Two Professors on Navy Charge," *Chicago Tribune*, April 3, 1918; "Berkeley Professor Ousted as Pro-Hun," *Los Angeles Times*, May 2, 1918.
44. Cain, "'Silence and Cowardice'"; Nicholas, "Academic Dissent."
45. Ibid.
46. Harry W. Laidler, "Academic Freedom," in *The American Labor Year Book, 1919–1920*, ed. Alexander Trachtenberg (New York: Rand School of Social Science, 1920), 86–89.
47. Gruber, *Mars and Minerva*, 241.
48. "Memorandum for the Information of the Committee on Academic Freedom," n.d., Box 3, AAUP Records, Series Historical Files, George Washington University Special Collections (hereafter cited as AAUP Historical Files).
49. A. O. Lovejoy to the Editor, *Nation* 106 (April 4, 1918): 401–2. See Box 24, Arthur O. Lovejoy Papers, Ms. 38, Special Collections, Milton S. Eisenhower Library, Johns Hopkins University (hereafter cited as Lovejoy Papers).
50. A. O. Lovejoy to A. A. Young, 9 October 1917; Young to Lovejoy, 15 October 1917, Box 24, Lovejoy Papers.
51. William H. Hobbs to A. A. Young, 17 October 1917; George Lefevre to Young, 26 October 1917; Richard T. Ely to Young, 1 November 1917, Box 24, Lovejoy Papers.
52. It appears that only one potential member, C. E. Bennett of Cornell, was rejected for being too extreme in his patriotism. Young urged Lovejoy to chair the committee, as Lovejoy had been "consistently

anti-German" and his "patriotic attitude is thoroughly well known." Young to Lovejoy, 27 October 1917, Box 24, Lovejoy Papers.
53. "Report of Committee on Academic Freedom in Wartime," *Bulletin of the AAUP* 4 (February–March 1918): 29–47, 34.
54. Ibid., 34–40.
55. Ibid., 41.
56. "Notes on the German-Teacher Problem," Box 24, Lovejoy Papers. This unsigned document was likely written by Young. See A. A. Young to A. O. Lovejoy, 17 December 1917, Box 3, Folder: Committee A—Wartime Report, 1917, AAUP Historical Files.
57. F. H. Hodder to A. O. Lovejoy, 29 January 1918, Box 24, Lovejoy Papers.
58. "Annual Meeting, 1917, Stenographic Report," 40–51, Box 2; H. W. Tyler to A. O. Lovejoy, 31 December 1917, Box 3, AAUP Historical Files.
59. "The Professors in Battle Array," *Nation* 106 (March 7, 1918): 255.
60. A. O. Lovejoy to the Editor.
61. Gruber, *Mars and Minerva*, 115–16; "Suggestions from the Committee on Patriotic Service," *Bulletin of the AAUP* 4 (April 1918): 6–7, 6.
62. Gruber, *Mars and Minerva*, 134–35.
63. Cain, "'Silence and Cowardice.'"
64. Ulysses G. Weatherly to A. A. Young, 17 November 1917, Box 3, AAUP Historical Files.
65. Samuel Walker, *In Defense of American Liberties: A History of the ACLU* (New York: Oxford University Press, 1990), 16–20.
66. Paul L. Murphy, *World War I and the Origins of Civil Liberties in the United States* (New York: Norton, 1979), 159–60.
67. *Proceedings of the Ninth Annual Meeting of the American Association of University Professors*, 4, Box 1, AAUP Historical Files.
68. Edward S. Allen to National Civil Liberties Bureau, 31 July 1919, *American Civil Liberties Union Archives: The Roger Baldwin Years, 1917–1950* (Washington, DC: Scholarly Resources, 1996), microform 109 (hereafter *ACLU Archives*; terminal numbers indicate microform volume).
69. Ibid.
70. Albert DeSilver to Edward S. Allen, 5 August 1919, *ACLU Archives* 109.
71. Walter Nelles to L. Hollingsworth Wood, 29 January 1918, *ACLU Archives* 109.
72. Peter H. Irons, "'Fighting Fair': Zechariah Chafee, Jr., the Department of Justice, and the 'Trial at the Harvard Club,'" *Harvard Law Review* 94 (April 1981): 1205–36.
73. See files in *ACLU Archives* 40 and *ACLU Archives* 109.
74. "Teachers Resent Pledge," *New York Times*, April 27, 1917; "Balk at Loyalty Pledge," *New York Times*, April 29, 1917; Linville to C. Stuart Gager, 23 June 1918, Box 2, AFT Personal Collections, Henry

R. Linville Papers, Archives of Labor and Urban Affairs, Wayne State University (hereafter cited as Linville Papers).

75. "Charges Out in Case of Ousted Teachers," *New York Times*, November 20, 1917; "Disloyal Teachers Must Go, Says Wade," *New York Times*, November 21, 1917.
76. Linville's papers do not reveal the size of the debt, although reference is made to it in several letters. When Teachers Union first considered pursuing legal redress, Linville received advice not to do so as it would cost $2,500, and that defeat would set back the cause. John Martin to Linville, 14 November 1917, Box 3, Folder: 1917, Linville Papers; "Teachers Uphold Demands of Union," *New York Times*, April 13, 1919.
77. Linville to the Editor of the *Evening Post*, n.d., Box 2, Folder: Undated, from Linville, Linville Papers.
78. Linville to Frederick H. Paine, 15 June 1918; Linville to C. Stuart Gager, 23 June 1918; Linville to Miss Joslyn, 3 May 1918, Box 2; Tildsley to Linville, 10 May 1918, Box 3, Linville Papers.
79. Linville to William L. Ettinger, 27 January 1919; Linville to Arthur S. Somers, 16 April 1919, Box 2, Linville Papers.
80. Roe was active in the Free Speech League and the American Union Against Militarism. P. L. Murphy, *World War I*, 162; Walker, *In Defense of American Liberties*, 22; "Quiz Teacher on Trotsky," *New York Times*, January 19, 1919; Linville to Johnson, 9 February 1919 and 10 March 1919, Box 2, Linville Papers.
81. "Begin Teachers Trial," *New York Times*, March 29, 1919; "On Trial as a Bolshevist," *New York Times*, April 5, 1919; "Pupils Defend Glassberg," *New York Times*, May 3, 1919; "Trial of Teacher Ends," *New York Times*, May 10, 1927; "Teacher Is Found Guilty," *New York Times*, May 27, 1919; "Glassberg Is Dismissed," *New York Times*, May 19, 1919; "Principal Accused in Glassberg Case," *New York Times*, November 7, 1924; Linville to Miss Holden, 27 May 1919, Box 2, Linville Papers.
82. Wayne J. Urban, *Why Teachers Organized* (Detroit, MI: Wayne State University Press, 1982), 107.
83. "Disloyal Teacher Problem," *New York Times*, November 25, 1917.
84. See, for example, the discussion of the "Report of the Committee on the Official Organ," *Proceedings of the Fourth Convention*, Box 1, American Federation of Teachers Inventory, Part II, Series 13, AFT Annual Conventions, Archives of Labor and Urban Affairs, Wayne State University (hereafter cited as AFT Conventions Collection).
85. Ibid.
86. Urban, *Why Teachers Organized*, 142–47; Marjorie Murphy, *Blackboard Unions: The AFT and the NEA, 1900–1980* (Ithaca, NY: Cornell University Press, 1990),104–10.
87. "Resolutions Adopted by the American Federation of Teachers in Convention Assembled at Pittsburgh, Pa., July 5, 6, 1918," 1, Box 1, AFT Conventions Collection.

88. Ibid., 3.
89. Ibid.

4   Competition and Collaboration

1. "The Issue of Free Speech," *Review* 1 (December 6, 1919): 634–35.
2. Loya Metzger, "Professors in Trouble: A Quantitative Analysis of Academic Freedom and Tenure Cases" (PhD diss., Columbia University, 1978), 231–43, 316–18.
3. Arthur O. Lovejoy, "Annual Message of the President," *Bulletin of the AAUP* 5 (November–December 1919): 10–40, 19.
4. "Announcements from the Committees: Committee A—Academic Freedom and Academic Tenure," *Bulletin of the AAUP* 5 (October 1919): 8.
5. Lovejoy, "Annual Message," 20.
6. Walter Dyson, *Howard University: The Capstone of Negro Education* (Washington, DC: Howard University, 1941), 86; Timothy Reese Cain, "The First Attempts to Unionize the Faculty," *Teachers College Record* 112 (March 2010): 875–913.
7. "Illinois University Teachers' Union," *Christian Science Monitor*, March 28, 1919; Timothy Reese Cain, "'Learning and Labor': Faculty Unionization at the University of Illinois, 1919–1923," *Labor History* 51 (November 2010): 543–69.
8. Cain, "First Attempts."
9. Ibid, 898–99; Lovejoy, "Annual Message," 22–28; Eliot R. Clark et al. to the Editor, *Bulletin of the AAUP* 6 (April 1920): 14–18; A. O. Lovejoy to W. C. Curtis, 29 March 1920, Box 4, AAUP Records, Series Historical Files, George Washington University Special Collections (hereafter cited as AAUP Historical Files). The debate continued in Winterton C. Curtis, "Unionization from the Standpoint of the University Teacher," *Educational Review* 60 (September 1920): 91–105; and Arthur O. Lovejoy, "Teachers and Trade Unions," *Educational Review* 60 (September 1920): 106–19.
10. *Proceedings of the Fourth Convention*, 1, Box 1, American Federation of Teachers Inventory, Part II, Series 13, AFT Annual Conventions, Archives of Labor and Urban Affairs, Wayne State University (hereafter cited as AFT Conventions Collection).
11. "Untitled," 10–11, Box 1, Folder: Resolutions 1919, AFT Conventions Collection; "Resolutions Adopted by the 5th Annual Convention of the American Federation of Teachers Held in St. Paul, December 28th to 31st, 1920," Box 1, AFT Conventions Collection.
12. Jeannette A. Lester, "The American Federation of Teachers in Higher Education: A History of Union Organization of Faculty Members in Colleges and Universities, 1916–1966" (EdD diss., University of Toledo, 1968), 78.
13. Cain, "First Attempts"; Cain, "'Learning and Labor.'"

14. A draft of Linville and Mufson's manuscript, "American Scholarship in Bondage: A Study of the Control of Education in the Nation," is available in Box 38, Sinclair Mss., 1890–1968, Lilly Library, University of Indiana, Bloomington.
15. Samuel Walker, *In Defense of American Liberties: A History of the ACLU* (New York: Oxford University Press, 1990), 66–70.
16. Paul L. Murphy, *World War I and the Origins of Civil Liberties in the United States* (New York: Norton, 1979), 162.
17. "A Statement Defining the Position of the American Civil Liberties Union on the Issues in the United States Today," *The Fight for Free Speech* (New York: ACLU, 1921), 17–18.
18. Leon Whipple, *The Story of Civil Liberty in the United States* (New York: Vanguard Press for the American Civil Liberties Union, 1927).
19. See "Academic Freedom Correspondence—1921," *American Civil Liberties Union Archives: The Roger Baldwin Years, 1917–1950* (Washington, DC: Scholarly Resources, 1996), microform 164 (hereafter *ACLU Archives*; terminal numbers indicate microform volume).; "Report on Civil Liberties for the Week Ending June 9, 1923," *ACLU Archives* 228A. The AAUP also noted the concerns at Clark by reprinting participants' statements. "Local and Chapter Notes," *Bulletin of the AAUP* 8 (May 1922): 34–45, 34–40.
20. See, for example, ACLU Clippings Files (1922), *ACLU Archives* 199; ACLU Clippings Files (1922–23), *ACLU Archives* 230.
21. Matthew W. Finkin and Robert C. Post, *For the Common Good: Principles of American Academic Freedom* (New Haven, CT: Yale University Press, 2009), 114–19.
22. J. A. Leighton, "Report of Committee T on Place and Function of Faculties in University Government and Administration," *Bulletin of the AAUP* 6 (March 1920): 17–47, 19.
23. Timothy Reese Cain and Steven E. Gump, "John Ervin Kirkpatrick and the Rulers of American Colleges," *AAUP Journal of Academic Freedom* 2 (2011): 1–43; available at http://www.academicfreedomjournal.org/VolumeTwo/CainGump.pdf.
24. Ibid.
25. *Proceedings of the Eleventh Annual Meeting of the American Association of University Professors*, 15, Box 1, AAUP Historical Files.
26. H. M. Bates to H. W. Tyler, 23 December 1922, Box 3; *Proceedings of the Eleventh Annual Meeting*, 30, Box 1; H. W. Tyler to Frank Fetter, 14 February 1927, Box 3, AAUP Historical Files; H. R. Fairclough, "Academic Freedom and Tenure," *Bulletin of the AAUP* 15 (February 1929): 99–101.
27. L. F. Metzger, "Professors in Trouble," 22.
28. *Proceedings of the Eleventh Annual Meeting*, 15, 17.
29. "Report on the University of Tennessee," *Bulletin of the AAUP* 10 (April 1924): 31–68.

30. "A Professorial Fiasco," *New Republic* 39 (May 24, 1924): 6.
31. "Summary of Council Letter #6," [1924], Box 31, AAUP Records, Series Conferences, George Washington University Special Collections (hereafter cited as AAUP Conferences).
32. "University of Tennessee," *Bulletin of the AAUP* 10 (October 1924): 11–18.
33. *Proceedings of the Eleventh Annual Meeting*, 25, Box 1, AAUP Historical Files. Cattell found an earlier report on Middlebury College to be even more troublesome and called for the AAUP to reconsider that report as well. See pages 25, 74–77.
34. "Annual Meeting," *Bulletin of the AAUP* 11 (February 1925): 69–83, 70.
35. H. F. Goodrich to H. W. Tyler, 4 January 1924; Tyler to W. W. Cook, 5 March 1926, Box 3, AAUP Historical Files; O. K. McMurray, "Committee A, Academic Freedom and Tenure," *Bulletin of the AAUP* 12 (February–March 1926): 69–70.
36. "Annual Meeting" (1925), 69; *Proceedings of the Eleventh Annual Meeting*, 32–34; A. O. Leuschner to H. M. Evans, 13 February 1925, Box 5; see extensive correspondence in Box 3, Folder: Committee—A Rules of Procedure, 1916–1927, AAUP Historical Files; Walter P. Metzger, "The 1940 Statement of Principles on Academic Freedom and Tenure," *Law & Contemporary Problems* 53 (Summer 1990): 3–77, 55.
37. H. W. Tyler to H. F. Goodrich, 4 December 1923, Box 3, AAUP Historical Files; Henry M. Bates, "Committee A, Academic Freedom and Tenure," *Bulletin of the AAUP* 9 (February 1923): 12; *Proceedings of the Tenth Annual Meeting of the American Association of University Professors*, 21–24, Box 1, AAUP Historical Files; Joseph V. Denney, "President's Address," *Bulletin of the AAUP* 10 (February 1924): 18–28, 24–25; Tyler to Goodrich, circular letter, 22 January 1925, Box 3, AAUP Historical Files.
38. Lovejoy to Tyler, 14 June 1925, Box 3, AAUP Historical Files.
39. H. W. Tyler, "Memorandum in Regard to Mediation"; Tyler to Roscoe Pound, 10 May 1926; Tyler to Frank A. Fetter, 14 February 1927, Box 3; "Academic Freedom and Tenure Memorandum," 14 February 1928, Box 5, AAUP Historical Files.
40. J. M. Maguire to H. W. Tyler, 9 April 1930, Box 4, AAUP Historical Files.
41. See for example, *Proceedings of the Eleventh Annual Meeting*, 32, 41, 302–4, Box 1; H. W. Tyler to W. W. Cook, 5 March 1926, Box 3, AAUP Historical Files.
42. Roy C. Flickinger, in "Report of the Commission of the Council of Church Boards of Education on Academic Freedom and Tenure of Office," *AAC Bulletin* 7 (April 1921): 81–87.
43. Charles N. Cole, "Report of the Commission on Academic Freedom and Academic Tenure," *AAC Bulletin* 8 (March 1922): 94–104, 96.

44. Ibid., 102; H. W. Tyler, "Academic Freedom," *Educational Review* 60 (December 1920): 386–93.
45. Charles N. Cole, "Report of the Commission on Academic Freedom," *AAC Bulletin* 9 (March 1923): 117–30, 120.
46. Ibid., 128–30.
47. W. P. Metzger, "1940 Statement," 24–25.
48. R. N. Baldwin to Allyn A. Young, 16 April 1924, *ACLU Archives* 248.
49. Harry F. Ward and Henry R. Linville, "Freedom of Speech in Schools and Colleges: A Statement by the American Civil Liberties Union, June 1924," *ACLU Archives* 248.
50. Ibid.
51. R. N. Baldwin to C. R. Skinner, 13 October 1924; V. Scudder to John Haynes Holmes, 28 August 1924; J. B. Peixotto to Holmes, 19 September 1924; Roger Baldwin to E. Freund, 28 August 1924; Holmes to Scudder, 28 August 1924; Holmes to Peixotto, 25 September 1924, *ACLU Archives* 248.
52. R. N. Baldwin to A. A. Young, 29 August 1924, *ACLU Archives* 248.
53. A. A. Young to R. N. Baldwin, 21 October 1924, *ACLU Archives* 248.
54. H. W. Tyler to R. N. Baldwin, 25 October 1924; H. F. Goodrich to Baldwin, 27 October 1924, *ACLU Archives* 248.
55. Harry F. Ward, "Memorandum on Academic Freedom," 1; Harry R. Linville, "American Civil Liberties Union: Tentative Statement of a Plan for Initiating Work on Free-Speech Cases in Schools and Colleges," 7, *ACLU Archives* 248.
56. Ward and Linville, "Freedom of Speech"; "Free Speech in Colleges Tackled by New Group: Civil Liberties Union Forms Committee to Act in Cases of Interference with Students and Teachers," *ACLU Archives* 248.
57. L. B. Milner to H. L. Keenleyside, 26 May 1925; Keenleyside to Milner, 28 May 1925; Forrest Bailey to Harry Elmer Barnes, 16 June 1925; Barnes to Bailey, 18 June 1925; Bailey to Keenleyside, 26 June 1925; Bailey to H. W. Tyler, 23 July 1925; Bailey to Harry Lee, 19 August 1925; Charles H. Richardson to Tyler, 28 September 1925; Bailey to W. E. Pierce, 16 October 1925, *ACLU Archives* 273.
58. Benjamin Glassberg, "The Chronology of a Case," *ACLU Archives* 273.
59. Ibid.; "The Case of Mr. Glassberg," *School and Society* 20 (December 13, 1924): 746.
60. Quoted in Howard K. Beale, *Are American Teachers Free? An Analysis of Restraints upon the Freedom of Teaching in American Schools* (New York: Charles Scribner's Sons, 1936), 127.
61. Henry R. Linville, "A Protest Meeting," 1924, *ACLU Archives* 248; Linville to L. B. Miner, 25 August 1925; F. Bailey to B. Glassberg, 1

September 1925; Bailey to Glassberg, 4 September 1925; Linville to Bailey, 12 September 1925, *ACLU Archives* 273.
62. W. P. Metzger, "1940 Statement," 23; F. S. Deibler to H. W. Tyler, 8 December 1925; Tyler to Deibler, 12 December 1925, Box 6, AAUP Historical Files.
63. "Annual Meeting, 1921," 29–32, Box 1, AAUP Historical Files.
64. K. D. MacMillan, "Report of the Commission on Academic Freedom and Academic Tenure," *AAC Bulletin* 10 (March 1924): 133–34; H. F. Goodrich to H. W. Tyler, 2 January 1924, Box 6, AAUP Historical Files.
65. MacMillan, "Report of the Commission."
66. H. F. Goodrich to H. W. Tyler, 24 September 1924; Tyler to Goodrich, 25 September 1924, Box 6, AAUP Historical Files.
67. C. R. Mann, "Minutes of Conference on Academic Freedom and Tenure," 2 January 1924, Box 6, AAUP Historical Files.
68. These issues were never legitimately considered at the conference. W. P. Metzger, "1940 Statement," 26.
69. Mann, "Minutes of Conference"; John R. Effinger, "Report of the Commission on Academic Freedom and Academic Tenure," *AAC Bulletin* 11 (May 1925): 179–82.
70. Cole, "Report of the Commission on Academic Freedom" (1923); Effinger, "Report of the Commission" (1925).
71. Ibid.
72. Effinger, "Report of the Commission" (1925).
73. John R. Effinger, "Report of the Commission on Academic Freedom and Tenure of Office," *AAC Bulletin* 12 (April 1926): 36–38; Frederick S. Deibler to H. W. Tyler, 8 December 1925, Box 3, AAUP Historical Files.
74. W. P. Metzger, "1940 Statement," 27.
75. John Dewey to A. O. Lovejoy, 1 April 1925; Lovejoy to Dewey, 13 April 1925, Box 6, AAUP Historical Files; W. P. Metzger, "1940 Statement," 29.
76. H. W. Tyler to A. O. Leuschner, 6 May 1925; Leuschner to Tyler, 20 May 1925, Box 6, AAUP Historical Files.
77. H. W. Tyler to John R. Effinger, 6 January 1926, Box 6, AAUP Historical Files. The letter is quoted in Effinger, "Report of the Commission" (1926), 36. H. W. Tyler to W. T. Semple, 16 February 1926, Box 5, AAUP Historical Files.
78. W. P. Metzger, "1940 Statement," 26.
79. "Principles and Procedures Governing Academic Freedom and Tenure," *Bulletin of the AAUP* 18 (May 1932): 329–32, 331, 332.
80. H. W. Tyler to W. T. Semple, 16 February 1926, Box 5, AAUP Historical Files; W. W. Boyd, "Report of the Commission on Academic Freedom and Academic Tenure," *AAC Bulletin* 13 (February 1927): 21–22; W. W. Boyd, "Report of the Commission on Academic Freedom

and Academic Tenure," *AAC Bulletin* 14 (March 1928): 92–94; W. W. Boyd, "Report of the Commission on Academic Freedom and Academic Tenure," *AAC Bulletin* 15 (March 1929): 111–14; "Minutes of the 15th Annual Meeting of the Association of American Colleges," *AAC Bulletin* 15 (March 1929): 181–93.

81. Frederick S. Deibler, "Committee A, Academic Freedom and Tenure" *Bulletin of the AAUP* 8 (February 1922): 36–57, 51.
82. Edwin R. A. Seligman, "Our Association—Its Aims and Its Accomplishments," *Bulletin of the AAUP* 8 (February 1922): 19–22.

5 Freedom of Teaching in Science

1. "A Close Call," *St. Louis Dispatch*, March 13, 1922.
2. "Darwin Wins by One Vote," *Washington Post*, March 13, 1922.
3. Joseph V. Denney, "President's Address," *Bulletin of the AAUP* 10 (February 1924): 18–28, 27.
4. Ibid., 26.
5. William B. Riley, "The Great Divide, or Christ and the Present Crisis," in *God Hath Spoken: Twenty-Five Addresses Delivered at the World Conference on Christian Fundamentals, May 25–June 1, 1919* (New York: Garland, 1988), 27–45, 27. (Reprint; orig. published in 1919 by the Bible Conference Committee.)
6. Charles A. Blanchard, "Report of Committee on Correlation of Colleges, Seminaries and Academies," in ibid., 19–20, 19–20.
7. G. W. McPherson, *The Crisis in Church and College*, rev. and enlarged ed. (Yonkers, NY: Author, [1918] 1919), 193.
8. Jon H. Roberts, "Conservative Evangelicals and Science Education in American Colleges and Universities, 1890–1940," *Journal of the Historical Society* 3 (Fall 2005): 297–329.
9. George M. Marsden, *Fundamentalism and American Culture: The Shaping of Twentieth Century Evangelicalism, 1870–1925* (New York: Oxford University Press, 1980), 118–64, 149; Ronald L. Numbers, "Creation, Evolution, and Holy Ghost Religion: Holiness and Pentecostal Responses to Darwinism," *Religion and American Culture: A Journal of Interpretation* 2 (Summer 1992): 127–58, 130.
10. Adam Laats, *Fundamentalism and Education in the Scopes Era: God, Darwin, and the Roots of America's Culture Wars* (New York: Palgrave Macmillan, 2010), 29–31.
11. George M. Marsden, *Soul of the American University: From Protestant Establishment to Established Nonbelief* (New York: Oxford University Press, 1994); Laats, *Fundamentalism and Education*.
12. William G. McLoughlin Jr., *Billy Sunday Was His Real Name* (Chicago: University of Chicago Press, 1955), 138.
13. James H. Leuba, *The Belief in God and Immortality: A Psychological, Anthropological and Statistical Study* (Boston: Sherman, French, 1916), 203, 213.

14. Michael Leinesch, *In the Beginning: Fundamentalism, the Scopes Trial, and the Making of the Anti-Evolution Movement* (Chapel Hill: University of North Carolina Press, 2007).
15. William B. Riley, *The Menace of Modernism* (New York: Christian Alliance, 1917), 72.
16. Leinesch, *In the Beginning*, 71; Williams Jennings Bryan, *In His Image* (New York: Revell, 1922), 46.
17. Lienesch, *In the Beginning*, 59–82.
18. Billy Sunday, "Back to Old-Time Religion," *Collier's* (July 10, 1926): 8, 34.
19. Willard B. Gatewood Jr., *Preachers, Pedagogues & Politicians: The Evolution Controversy in North Carolina, 1920–1927* (Chapel Hill: University of North Carolina Press, 1966); Marsden, *Soul of the American University*, 321–24; Suzanne Cameron Linder, "William Poteat and the Evolution Controversy," *North Carolina Historical Review* 40 (April 1963): 135–57; Willard B. Gatewood Jr., "Embattled Scholar: Howard W. Odum and the Fundamentalists, 1925–1927," *Journal of Southern History* 31 (November 1965): 375–92.
20. Patsy Ledbetter, "Defense of the Faith: J. Frank Norris and Texas Fundamentalism, 1920–1929," *Arizona and the West* 15 (Spring 1973): 45–62; Laats, *Fundamentalism and Education*, 57–59; Peter W. Agnew, "C. C. Selecman and SMU: The 'Perils' of Methodist Higher Education, 1923–1938," *Legacies: A History Journal for Dallas and North Central Texas* 17 (Fall 2005): 12–24; C. Allyn Russell, "J. Frank Norris: Violent Fundamentalist," *Southwestern Historical Quarterly* 75 (January 1972): 271–302, 276; Lienesch, *In the Beginning*, 79–81; Lynn Ray Musslewhite, "Texas in the 1920's: A History of Social Change" (PhD diss., Texas Tech University, 1975), 298–308.
21. Ledbetter, "Defense of the Faith"; Laats, *Fundamentalism and Education*, 57–59; Lienesch, *In the Beginning*, 79–81; Musslewhite, "Texas in the 1920's," 305–8.
22. "Dixie Baptist College Fires 'Evolution Prof,'" *New York Times*, October 12, 1924; see also "Dismissal of Dr. Henry Fox from the Faculty of Mercer University," *Science*, n.s. 61 (February 13, 1925): 176–78.
23. "Evolutionist Loses Post as College Head," *New York Times*, July 15, 1925.
24. Massachusetts had a similar law in place since the 1820s. ACLU, *The Gag on Teaching* (New York: ACLU, 1931), 8.
25. Richard David Wilhelm, "A Chronology and Analysis of Regulatory Actions Relating to the Teaching of Evolution in Public Schools" (PhD diss, University of Texas at Austin, 1978), 314.
26. Ibid., 323; "Proposed Legislation Against the Teaching of Evolution," *Science*, n.s., 55 (March 24, 1922): 318–20.
27. Alonzo W. Fortune, "The Kentucky Campaign Against the Teaching of Evolution," *Journal of Religion* 2 (May 1922): 224–35; Eric A. Moyen,

Frank L. McVey and the University of Kentucky: A Progressive President and the Modernization of a Southern University (Lexington: University Press of Kentucky, 2011), 107–10.
28. Fortune, "Kentucky Campaign," 228.
29. Ibid., 229.
30. Moyen, *Frank L. McVey*, 112–13; "Democracy and Evolution," *New York Times*, February 6, 1922.
31. "Darwinian Theory Stirs Up Kentucky," *New York Times*, February 2, 1922.
32. "Attacks Evolution Bill," *New York Times*, February 2, 1922.
33. Moyen, *Frank L. McVey*, 118–19; Frank L. McVey, "A University in Jeopardy," in *Controversy in the Twenties: Fundamentalism, Modernism, and Evolution*, ed. Willard B. Gatewood Jr. (Nashville, TN: Vanderbilt University Press, 1969), 276–79.
34. Fortune, "Kentucky Campaign," 235.
35. Clark McAdams, "Just a Minute...," *St. Louis Post-Dispatch*, March 10, 1922.
36. Demaree was already planning on leaving for a position in California at the end of the year. "Evolution Exponent Refuses to Retract," *New York Times*, April 10, 1923; "College Reinstates Evolution Exponent," *New York Times*, April 11, 1923. In all, five professors were suspended from the institution in the era. Roy Ginger, *Six Days or Forever?: Tennessee vs. John Thomas Scopes* (London: Oxford University Press, 1958).
37. R. Halliburton Jr. "The Nation's First Anti-Darwin Law: Passage and Repeal," *Southwestern Social Science Quarterly* 41 (1960–61): 123–35, 126.
38. "From Drouth to Deluge," *St. Louis Post-Dispatch*, February 15, 1922.
39. "Quits Goucher's Board After Evolution Clash," *Washington Post*, May 30, 1923.
40. A. Wakefield Slaten, "Academic Freedom, Fundamentalism and the Dotted Line," *Educational Review* 65 (February 1923): 74–77.
41. "General Report of the Committee on Academic Freedom and Academic Tenure," *Bulletin of the AAUP* 1 (December 1915, part 1): 15–43, 22; Committee A on Academic Freedom and Academic Tenure, "Report of Enquiry into Conditions at Bethany College," *Bulletin of the AAUP* 5 (May 1919): 26–61.
42. "The Dartmouth Chapter," *Bulletin of the AAUP* 8 (May 1922): 40–41.
43. Marsden, *Fundamentalism and American Culture*, 171–74.
44. J. V. Denney to Henry M. Bates, 15 June 1922, Box 3, AAUP Records, Series Historical Files, George Washington University Special Collections (hereafter cited as AAUP Historical Files).
45. *Proceedings of the Tenth Annual Meeting of the AAUP*, 138–42, Box 1, AAUP Historical Files.
46. Ibid., 140.

47. S. J. Holmes, "Report of Committee M," *Bulletin of the AAUP* 11 (February 1925): 93–95, 94.
48. As cited by L. Sprague de Camp, *The Great Monkey Trial* (Garden City, NY: Doubleday, 1968), 2.
49. Edward J. Larson, *Summer for the Gods: The Scopes Trial and America's Continuing Debate Over Science and Religion* (New York: Basic Books, 1997), 57–59, 88–92.
50. Roger N. Baldwin, "Dayton's First Issue," in *D-Days at Dayton: Reflections on the Scopes Trial*, ed. Jerry R. Tompkins (Baton Rouge: Louisiana State University Press, 1965), 55–56.
51. Larson, *Summer for the Gods*, 87–92, 99. Sue Hicks was named for his mother, who died in childbirth.
52. Ibid., 96–103.
53. Ibid., 212–21.
54. Forrest Bailey to Charles H. Strong, 17 August 1925, *American Civil Liberties Union Archives: The Roger Baldwin Years, 1917–1950* (Washington, DC: Scholarly Resources, 1996), microform 274 (hereafter *ACLU Archives*; terminal numbers indicate microform volume).
55. "Scientists Pledge Support to Tennessee Professor Arrested for Teaching Evolution," *Daily Science News Bulletin*, May 18, 1925, *ACLU Archives* 273.
56. "Tennessee," *Bulletin of the AAUP* 7 (October 1925): 309–10.
57. Shailer Mathews, "Committee M, Freedom of Teaching in Science," *Bulletin of the AAUP* 12 (February–March 1926): 74–75.
58. Larson, *Summer for the Gods*, 73.
59. Untitled resolution, Box 1, American Federation of Teachers Inventory, Part II, Series 13, AFT Annual Conventions, Archives of Labor and Urban Affairs, Wayne State University.
60. Freeland G. Stecker, "Freedom in Teaching," 17 May 1925, Box 6, American Federation of Teachers Inventory, Part II, Series 11: Memos and Mimeographed Material, Archives of Labor and Urban Affairs, Wayne State University.
61. Larson, *Summer for the Gods*, 122.
62. "States Leagues to Seek Antievolution Laws," *Los Angeles Times*, July 2, 1925; Mary Duncan France, "'A Year of Monkey War': The Anti-Evolution Campaign and the Florida Legislature," *Florida Historical Quarterly* 54 (October 1975): 156–77; Gatewood, *Preachers, Pedagogues & Politicians*; Ferenc M. Szasz, "William B. Riley and the Fight against Teaching of Evolution in Minnesota," *Minnesota History* 41 (Spring 1969): 201–26; Wilhelm, "Chronology and Analysis," 56–71; Cal Ledbetter Jr., "The Antievolution Law: Church and State in Arkansas," *Arkansas Historical Quarterly* 38 (Winter 1979): 299–327, 309–14; Laats, *Fundamentalism and Education*, 99–120.
63. Maynard Shipley, "The Science League of America," *Science*, ns. 62 (September 4, 1925): 221–22; Maynard Shipley, *The War on Modern Science* (New York: Knopf, 1927).

64. "Report of the Washington Office at the Convention," *American Teacher* 11 (September 1926): 6.
65. *Proceedings of the Thirteenth Annual Meeting*, 24, 27, Box 1, AAUP Historical Files.
66. "Anti-Evolution Legislation," *Bulletin of the AAUP* 13 (February 1927): 75.
67. H. W. Tyler, "Secretary's Report," *Bulletin of the AAUP* 14 (February 1928): 120–21; S. J. Holmes, "Proposed Laws against the Teaching of Evolution," *Bulletin of the AAUP* 13 (December 1927): 549–54; "Freedom of Teaching in Science," *Bulletin of the AAUP* 15 (February 1929): 96–97.
68. Robert S. Keebler to Forrest Bailey, 5 January 1929, *ACLU Archives* 357.
69. Extensive correspondence among the ACLU, these men, and other interested parties appears under "Arkansas," *ACLU Archives* 337, 357.
70. Arthur O. Lovejoy to Frank Thone, 16 October 1929, *ACLU Archives* 357.
71. Arthur O. Lovejoy, "Anti-Evolution Laws and the Principle of Religious Neutrality," *School & Society* 29 (February 2, 1929): 133–38.
72. Ibid.
73. See for example, ACLU, "The Work Ahead and In Hand," in *The Fight for Civil Liberty, 1927–28* (New York: ACLU, [1928]), 39; ACLU, "The Program Ahead," in *The Fight for Civil Liberty: 1928–29* (New York: ACLU, 1929), 30.
74. ACLU, "Executive Committee Minutes," *ACLU Archives* 444.
75. Epperson v. Arkansas, 393 U.S. 97 (1968).
76. Marsden, *Soul of the American University*, 317.
77. Richard Hofstadter, *Anti-intellectualism in American Life* (New York: Vintage, 1966), 126, 129–30.

6 Education, Protests, and Blacklists

1. See, for example, "Academic Freedom and History Textbooks," *American Teacher* 11 (February 1927): 12.
2. "Convention Notes," *American Teacher* 11 (October 1926): 8–11.
3. "Attacks on Tenure and Academic Freedom," *American Teacher* 11 (November 1926): 16–17; "Our Locals," *American Teacher* 11 (January 1927): 23; R. W. Everett, "Report of the Committee on Academic Freedom and Tenure," *American Teacher* 11 (March 1927): 3–5, 11.
4. Everett, "Report of the Committee," 3.
5. "The Report of the Committee on Academic Freedom and Tenure," in AFT, *Report of the Proceedings of the Twelfth Annual Convention of the American Federation of Teachers* (Chicago: AFT, 1928), 70–73, 70; Henry R. Linville, "Preliminary Report on the Problem of Freedom of

Teaching: Analysis and Development of the Problem," in AFT, *Report of the Proceedings of the Twelfth*, 157–58; "Report of the Committee on Academic Freedom," in AFT, *Report of the Proceedings of the Thirteenth Annual Convention of the American Federation of Teachers* (Chicago: AFT, 1929), 59–67; Paul Douglas, "Freedom of Discussion through Organization," in AFT, *Report of the Proceedings of the Thirteenth*, 67–84.

6. Henry R. Linville, "Report on the Organization of a Committee on Academic Freedom," in AFT, *Report of the Proceedings of the Fourteenth Annual Convention of the American Federation of Teachers* (Chicago: AFT, 1930); 63–64; "On the Report of the Committee on Academic Freedom," in AFT, *Report of the Proceedings of the Fourteenth*, 116; "Executive Council Proceedings, 29, 30 June, 3 July 1930," Box 21, American Federation of Teachers Inventory, Part I, Series 3: Executive Council, Archives of Labor and Urban Affairs, Wayne State University; "Academic Freedom," in AFT, *Report of the Proceedings of the Fifteenth Annual Convention of the American Federation of Teachers* (Chicago: AFT, 1931), 90–94, 91; Timothy Reese Cain, "For Education and Employment: The American Federation of Teachers and Academic Freedom, 1926–1941," *Perspectives on the History of Higher Education* 26 (2007): 67–102, 73–74.

7. "High Lights of the Memphis Convention," *American Teacher* 15 (September 1930): 1–2; "Teachers, Propaganda, and Liberty," *American Teacher* 14 (January 1930): 8.

8. "Academic Freedom," (1931), 91. See also Henry R. Linville, "Freedom in Teaching," 19 February 1932, Box 1, AFT Personal Collections, Henry R. Linville Papers, Archives of Labor and Urban Affairs, Wayne State University.

9. See the annual "Report of the Legislative Committee" from any of the reports of the *Proceedings of the American Federation of Teachers* from the late 1920s through mid-1930s; Florence C. Hanson, "Report of the Secretary-Treasurer (Abridged) to the Seventeenth Convention," *American Teacher* 18 (September 1933): 12; "Loyalty Pledges for Teachers," *American Teacher* 17 (January 1933): 17; Cain, "For Education and Employment," 74–75.

10. A. M. Kidd, "Academic Freedom and Tenure," *Bulletin of the AAUP* 14 (February 1928): 102–6; AAUP, *Proceedings of the Fourteenth Annual Meeting of the American Association of University Professors*, [1927], 135–36, Box 1; Edward S. Allen, "Security of Freedom for the Younger Members," Box 4; Allen to H. W. Tyler, 28 November 1928, Box 4; Tyler to Allen, 7 December 1928, Box 4; H. R. Fairclough to Tyler, 1 December 1928, Box 3, AAUP Records, Series Historical Files, George Washington University Special Collections (hereafter cited as AAUP Historical Files); Fairclough, "Academic Freedom and Tenure"; Loya F. Metzger, "Professors in Trouble: A Quantitative Analysis

of Academic Freedom and Tenure Cases" (PhD diss., Columbia University, 1978), 132.
11. Lovejoy, "Annual Message," 19–20.
12. John H. Wigmore, "President's Report for 1916," Bulletin of the AAUP 2 (November 1916): 9–52, 14.
13. Timothy Reese Cain and Steven E. Gump, "John Ervin Kirkpatrick and the Rulers of American Colleges," *AAUP Journal of Academic Freedom* 2 (2011): 1–43, 17–18; available at http://www.academic freedomjournal.org/VolumeTwo/CainGump.pdf.
14. AAUP, *Proceedings of the Eleventh Annual Meeting of the American Association of University Professors*, [1924], 16–17, 299–302, Box 1, AAUP Historical Files.
15. "Academic Freedom at the University of Missouri: Report on the Dismissal of Professor DeGraff and the Suspension of Professor Meyer," *Bulletin of the AAUP* 16 (February 1930): 143–76.
16. L. L. Thurstone to H. W. Tyler, 21 November 1929, in "Thurstone-Girard [sic] Proposals," 2–3, Box 4, AAUP Historical Files.
17. "The Thurstone Proposals," in "Thurstone-Girard [sic] Proposals," 2, Box 4, AAUP Historical Files.
18. H. W. Tyler to L. L. Thurstone, 29 November 1929, in "Thurstone-Girard [sic] Proposals," Box 4, AAUP Historical Files.
19. R. W. Gerard to A. J. Carlson, 29 November 1929, "Memorandum by President and Secretary on Gerard Proposal," in "Thurstone-Girard [sic] Proposals," 5, 7, Box 4, AAUP Historical Files.
20. "Thurstone-Girard [sic] Proposals," 9–13; E. Bernbaum to H. Crew and H. W. Tyler, 16 December 1929, Box 4; L. L. Thurstone to Tyler, 31 March 1930, Box 3; AAUP, *Proceedings of the Sixteenth Annual Meeting of the American Association of University Professors*, [1929], 12, 16, Box 1, AAUP Historical Files. On the negative response to the proposals by campus chapters, see "Summary of Replies to Chapter Letter No. 2," Box 4, AAUP Historical Files.
21. L. L. Thurstone, "Academic Freedom," *Journal of Higher Education* 1 (March 1930): 136–40; H. W. Tyler to A. J. Carlson, 9 April 1930, Box 3, AAUP Historical Files; Jonathan Knight, "The AAUP's Censure List," *Academe* 89 (January–February 2003): 44–59, 48.
22. H. W. Tyler, "Academic Freedom," *New Republic* 65 (December 31, 1930): 194; "Bouncer Bilbo," *Time* (December 29, 1930): 16–17; "University of Mississippi, Tenure Conditions," *Bulletin of the AAUP* 16 (November 1930): 551–53; "University of Mississippi, Tenure Conditions," *Bulletin of the AAUP* 16 (December 1930): 614–15.
23. H. W. Tyler, "Report of the General Secretary," *Bulletin of the AAUP* 17 (February 1931): 164–67; "Academic Freedom and Tenure," *Bulletin of the AAUP* 17 (February 1931): 136–39.
24. "Eligibility of Institutions," *Bulletin of the AAUP* 17 (February 1931): 140; "Mississippi State Institutions," *Bulletin of the AAUP* 17

(February 1931): 141; Chapter Letter No. 1, 12 January 1931, Box 4, AAUP Records, Series General Files, George Washington University Special Collections.
25. "Extracts from Council Record of April 25, 1931"; "Circular Letter to Specialist re Cooperation," Box 6, AAUP Historical Files; Knight, "AAUP's Censure List."
26. David Edison Bunting, *Liberty and Learning: The Activities of the American Civil Liberties Union in Behalf of Freedom of Education* (Washington, DC: American Council on Public Affairs, 1942), 76–82.
27. Ibid., 79–82; "Academic Freedom and Tenure at The Ohio State University: Report on the Dismissal of Professor Herbert A. Miller," *Bulletin of the AAUP* 17 (October 1931): 443–73; Kimberly Ann Marinucci, "Probing the Nation: Americanism, Public Universities, and the Politics of Academic Freedom, 1918–1946" (PhD diss., State University of New York at Stony Brook, 2001), 109–44.
28. Bunting, *Liberty and Learning*, 80–82.
29. "Academic Freedom" (1931), 93.
30. Bunting, *Liberty and Learning*, 82.
31. "Academic Freedom and Tenure at The Ohio State University," 459.
32. Marinucci, "Probing the Nation," 134.
33. "Academic Freedom and Tenure," *Bulletin of the AAUP* 18 (January 1932): 29–31, 30.
34. Henry R. Linville, "Academic Freedom," *Report of the Proceedings of the Fifteenth Annual Convention of the American Federation of Teachers* (Chicago: American Federation of Teachers, 1931), 93; Bunting, *Liberty and Learning*, 82.
35. John Earle Uhler, *Cane Juice: A Story of Southern Louisiana* (New York: Century, 1931). On suggestions that a previous controversy involving the expulsion of a pro-Long student may have also been implicated, see Richard D. White Jr., *Kingfish: The Reign of Huey P. Long* (New York: Random House, 2006), 147–48.
36. "Cane Juice," *Time* (October 26, 1931): 28.
37. Bunting, *Liberty and Learning*, 76.
38. Press Release, October 9, 1931, *American Civil Liberties Union Archives: The Roger Baldwin Years, 1917–1950* (Washington, DC: Scholarly Resources, 1996), microform 336 (hereafter *ACLU Archives*; terminal numbers indicate microform volume).
39. Bunting, *Liberty and Learning*, 76–79.
40. F. Bailey to J. E. Uhler, 22 October 1931; Press Release, November 17, 1931, *ACLU Archives* 446.
41. "Ousted Professor Gets His Salary," *American Teacher* 16 (February 1932): 10.
42. H. W. Tyler to S. A. Mitchell, 17 November 1931, Box 4, AAUP Historical Files.

43. J. E. Uhler to Forrest Bailey and Roger Baldwin, 15 April 1932, *ACLU Archives* 520.
44. Forrest Bailey to William H. Kilpatrick, 22 January 1931, *ACLU Archives* 446.
45. ACLU, *The Gag on Teaching* (New York: ACLU, 1931), 30; ACLU, *Civil Liberties Quarterly* 1 (July 1931): 4.
46. ACLU, *Gag on Teaching* (1931), 16–17, 31.
47. S. P. Breckenridge to Roger N. Baldwin, 27 June 1931; Forrest Bailey to Breckenridge, 3 July 1931; Breckenridge to Bailey, 6 July 1931, *ACLU Archives* 448.
48. See, for example, Roger N. Baldwin to John Lapp, 8 July 1932; F. P. Graham to Roger N. Baldwin, 4 October 1932; Lucille B. Milner to H. Thompson, 18 October 1932; Baldwin to A. O. Lovejoy, 19 October 1932, *ACLU Archives* 519.
49. S. A. Mitchell, "Academic Freedom and Tenure, Report of Committee A," *Bulletin of the AAUP* 19 (February 1933): 92–97; S. A. Mitchell to Lucille B. Milner, 4 June 1934, *ACLU Archives* 689.
50. Bunting, *Liberty and Learning*, 20–22. For intermediary drafts and related correspondence, see *ACLU Archives* 448, 519, 596, 689.
51. ACLU Committee on Academic Freedom, *The Principles of Academic Freedom* (New York: ACLU, 1934).
52. Ibid., 1–2.
53. Bunting, *Liberty and Learning*, 86–89. On Harris, see Robert Cohen, *When the Old Left Was Young: Student Radicals and America's First Mass Student Movement, 1929–1941* (New York: Oxford University Press, 1993), 55–68.
54. ACLU, *School Buildings as Public Forums* (New York: ACLU, 1934).
55. David O. Oshinsky, Richard P. McCormick, and Daniel Horn, *The Case of the Nazi Professor* (New Brunswick, NJ: Rutgers University Press, 1989); Michael Greenberg and Seymour Zenchelsky, "The Confrontation with Nazism at Rutgers: Academic Bureaucracy and Moral Failure," *History of Education Quarterly* 30 (Autumn 1990): 325–49.
56. ACLU, "Report of Investigators for the American Civil Liberties Union on Trustee's Investigation into Dismissal of Lienhard Bergel from the German Department at the New Jersey College for Women," August 1935; Reinhold Niebuhr et al. to the Board of Trustees of Rutgers University, 11 September 1935, Box 1, Progressive Education Association Records, 1924–61, Record Series 10/6/20, University of Illinois Archives.
57. Greenberg and Zenchelsky, "Confrontation with Nazism," 325–26.
58. ACLU, *Liberty Under the New Deal: The Record for 1933–34* (New York: ACLU, 1934), 25–26.
59. S. A. Mitchell, "Academic Freedom and Tenure," *Bulletin of the AAUP* 18 (January 1932): 29–31.

60. Mitchell, "Academic Freedom and Tenure, Report of Committee A" (1933). Committee A did not handle cases merely involving justified dismissals for financial cause, although the Committee Z tracked the troubles and proposed appropriate procedures for institutions' financial crises, and Committee Y studied the effects of the Depression. See Malcolm M. Willey for Committee Y of the American Association of University Professors, *Depression, Recovery and Higher Education: A Report of Committee Y of the American Association of University Professors* (New York: McGraw-Hill, 1937).
61. S. A. Mitchell, "Academic Freedom and Tenure, Report of Committee A," *Bulletin of the AAUP* (1934): 99–101; Carl Wittke, "Academic Freedom and Tenure, Report of Committee A," *Bulletin of the AAUP* 21 (February 1935): 148–53.
62. Mitchell, "Academic Freedom and Tenure" (1932); Mitchell, "Academic Freedom and Tenure, Report of Committee A," (1933); Mitchell, "Academic Freedom and Tenure, Report of Committee A" (1934); AAUP, *Twentieth Annual Meeting Proceedings*, [1933], Box 2, AAUP Historical Files; Wittke, "Academic Freedom and Tenure."
63. Ibid.
64. Wittke, "Academic Freedom and Tenure," 153.
65. Mitchell, "Academic Freedom and Tenure, Report of Committee A" (1934), 102.
66. Matthew W. Finkin and Robert C. Post, *For the Common Good: Principles of American Academic Freedom* (New Haven, CT: Yale University Press, 2009), 122–23.
67. Arthur O. Lovejoy and Austin S. Edwards, "Academic Freedom and Tenure, Rollins College Report," *Bulletin of the AAUP* 19 (November 1933): 416–39.
68. AAUP, *Twentieth Annual Meeting Proceedings*, 134–35, 138. For a critique that specifically references Rollins, see "Professional Security," *Social Frontier* 1 (October 1934): 9–10. In 1935, University of Pittsburgh faculty similarly tried to stop the AAUP from placing their institution on the ineligible list, fearing that it would damage their efforts to improve the security of tenure at the institution. AAUP, *Twenty-Second Annual Meeting Proceedings*, [1935], Box 2, AAUP Historical Files, 101.
69. AAUP, *Twentieth Annual Meeting Proceedings*, 126–30.
70. "Academic Freedom Policy and Procedure," *Bulletin of the AAUP* 21 (April 1935): 315–17.
71. "Eligibility of Institutions," *Bulletin of the AAUP* 21 (January 1935): 132–33; AAUP, *Twenty-Second Annual Meeting Proceedings*, 87, 111–20.
72. S. P. Capen, "Privileges and Immunities," *Bulletin of the AAUP* 23 (March 1937): 190–201; H. W. Tyler, "Comments on the Address by Dr. Capen," *Bulletin of the AAUP* 23 (March 1937): 202–6.

73. AAUP, *Proceedings of the Twenty-Third Annual Meeting*, [1936], 26–31, 30, Box 2, AAUP Historical Files.
74. *Annual Meeting 1938—Steno Notes*, 19, Box 1, AAUP Conferences.

7 Toward a Less "Dangerous Occupation"

1. Philip G. Altbach, *Student Politics in America: A Historical Analysis* (New York: McGraw-Hill Book Company, 1974), 57.
2. Florence Hanson to the Executive Council, 23 January 1935, Box 7, American Federation of Teachers Inventory, Part II, Series 11: Memos and Mimeographed Material, Archives of Labor and Urban Affairs, Wayne State University (hereafter cited as AFT Memos).
3. Ellen W. Schrecker, *No Ivory Tower: McCarthyism and the Universities* (New York: Oxford University Press, 1986), 63–83.
4. William McGuffey Hepburn, "Academic Freedom and Tenure," *Bulletin of the AAUP* (December 1937): 642–53, 646.
5. Robert W. Iversen, *The Communists and the Schools* (New York: Harcourt, Brace, 1959), 181–90; Schrecker, *No Ivory Tower*, 69–70; "Hutchins Sees Check on College Probes," *Boston Globe*, July 4, 1935; Lawrence H. Chamberlain, *Loyalty and Legislative Action: A Survey of Activity by the New York State Legislature, 1919–1949* (Ithaca, NY: Cornell University Press, 1951), 55–63.
6. Schrecker, *No Ivory Tower*, 68–69; Henry R. Linville, *Oaths of Loyalty for Teachers* (Chicago: American Federation of Teachers, [1935]); Malcolm M. Willey for Committee Y of the American Association of University Professors, *Depression, Recovery and Higher Education: A Report of Committee Y of the American Association of University Professors* (New York: McGraw-Hill, 1937), 437–50; Shawn Michael Lynch, "'In Defense of True Americanism': The Civil Liberties Union of Massachusetts and Radical Free Speech, 1915–1945" (PhD diss., Boston College, 2006), 103–65; A. G. Ruthven to W. R. Humphreys, 9 October 1935, Box 15, Alexander Grant Ruthven Papers, Bentley Historical Library, University of Michigan.
7. A. G. Ruthven, "The Commencement Address," *Michigan Alumnus* (Spring 1936): 210–13.
8. A. J. Carlson and A. O. Lovejoy, "Teachers' Oaths of Loyalty, Statement of Committee B," *Bulletin of the AAUP* 23 (January 1937): 26–36, 32; "Annual Meeting," *Bulletin of the AAUP* 22 (February 1936): 98–100; "Notes from the Washington Office," *Bulletin of the AAUP* 22 (March 1936): 201–2.
9. David Edison Bunting, *Liberty and Learning: The Activities of the American Civil Liberties Union in Behalf of Freedom of Education* (Washington, DC: American Council on Public Affairs, 1942), 26–27, 47–60; Samuel Walker, *In Defense of American Liberties: A History of*

the *ACLU* (New York: Oxford University Press, 1990), 124; ACLU, *Still the Fish Committee Nonsense!* (New York: ACLU, 1932).
10. Linville, *Oaths of Loyalty*; Lionel Heap, "The Little Red Rider," *Social Frontier* 2 (May 1936): 254–55; Andrew Hartman, *Education and the Cold War: The Battle for the American School* (New York: Palgrave Macmillan, 2008), 48–49.
11. James L. Hymes, Jr., "The Progressive Education Association," *Childhood Education* 52 (October 1975): 25–30; Patricia Albjerg Graham, *Progressive Education from Arcady to Academe: A History of the Progressive Education Association, 1919–1955* (New York: Teachers College Press, 1967); George S. Counts, *Dare the Schools Build a New Social Order* (New York: Day, 1932).
12. Committee on Social and Economic Problems, *A Call to Teachers of the Nation* (New York: Day, 1933).
13. Howard K. Beale, "Dare Society Deny Its Teachers Freedom?," *Progressive Education* 11 (January–February 1934): 13–25, 21.
14. James M. Shields, *Just Plain Larnin'* (New York: Coward-McCann, 1934); H. Gordon Hullfish, "A Report from the Commission on Educational Freedom," 26 April 1940, Box 4; "Minutes, Meeting on Academic Freedom Called by the Progressive Education Association," November 10, 1934; William H. Kilpatrick to H. L. Smith, 22 August 1934; "A Program for Academic Freedom," [1934]; F. Redefer to Goodwin Watson, 14 August 1934; Karl W. Guenther to Redefer, 15 September 1934; Redefer to Boyd H. Bode, 18 October 1934; Redefer to H. R. Linville, undated telegram; Redefer to Howard K. Beale, 21 November 1934; Redefer to James M. Shields, 21 November 1934, Box 1, Progressive Education Association Records, 1924–61, Record Series 10/6/20, University of Illinois Archives (hereafter cited as PEA Records).
15. "Minutes, Meeting on Academic Freedom Called by the Progressive Education Association," 7, November 10, 1934, Box 1, PEA Records.
16. "Minutes, Second Meeting of National Associations on Academic Freedom," 15 December 1934; "A Proposal for the Establishment of a National Commission on Academic Freedom in Public and Private Elementary and Secondary Schools"; Boyd Bode, "Academic Freedom and Education"; Frank Baker, "A Code of Ethics"; National Advisory Council on Educational Freedom, *Educational Freedom and Democracy*, Box 1, PEA Records; Hullfish, "Report from the Commission."
17. The organization was at times referred to as the National Advisory Council on Educational Freedom. "Report of the Committee on Organization"; "Minutes, Second Meeting of National Associations on Academic Freedom"; "A Proposal for the Establishment"; Frederick Redefer to Eduard C. Lindeman, 19 September 1935, Box 1, PEA Records.

18. F. Redefer to Lindeman, 19 September 1935; Frank E. Baker to Redefer, 17 October 1935; Redefer to Ben Davidson, 20 December 1935; Redefer to All Members of the National Advisory Council, 25 May 1936; "Minutes of the Fourth Meeting of National Associations on Academic Freedom," 24 November 1935, Box 1, PEA Records.
19. Redefer to Lindeman, 19 September 1935, Box 1, PEA Records.
20. Emily Tarbell to F. Redefer, 7 April 1937; Redefer to Tarbell, 16 June 1937, Box 1; The Executive Committee of the Commission on Educational Freedom to the Board of Directors, Progressive Education Association, 3 November 1938, Box 4, PEA Records; "Minutes of the Fourth Meeting."
21. Hullifsh, "Report from the Commission"; W. T. Laprade to Ralph E. Himstead, 30 November 1939, Box 3, American Association of University Professors Records, 1934–1953, University Archives, David M. Rubenstein Rare Book and Manuscript Library, Duke University (hereafter cited as AAUP Records, Duke); NACAF, "Summary of an Inquiry Concerning the National Situation as It Pertains to Educational Freedom," Box 1, PEA Records.
22. Timothy Reese Cain, "The NEA's Early Conflict Over Educational Freedom," *American Educational History Journal* 36, no. 2 (2009): 371–85.
23. Quoted in ACLU, *The Gag on Teaching* (New York: ACLU, 1937), 45; Cain, "The NEA's Early Conflict."
24. Cain, "NEA's Early Conflict"; Hullfish, "Report from the Commission," 3; NACAF, "Summary of an Inquiry."
25. Cain, "NEA's Early Conflict."
26. "Resolutions on Academic Freedom," 23 February 1935, Box 1, PEA Records.
27. Redefer to Boyd H. Bode and Frank Baker, 30 September 1935, Box 1, PEA Records.
28. Hullfish, "Report from the Commission."
29. Unsigned letters to Frederick L. Redefer, Box 4, PEA Records.
30. Progressive Education Association Commission on Educational Freedom, *Educational Freedom: A Study Guide for Use by Professional Groups and Educational Institutions* (New York: Progressive Education Association, 1938).
31. Goodwin Watson to Members of the Commission on Educational Freedom, 10 May 1937, Box 4, PEA Records.
32. Philip W. L. Cox to Goodwin Watson, 22 May 1937, Box 4, PEA Records. See also Eugene Smith to Carson Ryan, 20 May 1937; F. C. Borgeson to Watson, 26 May 1937, Box 4, PEA Records.
33. Carleton Washburne to Carson Ryan, 29 June 1937, Box 4, PEA Records.
34. Hullfish, "Report from the Commission," 6.
35. Ibid.

36. Hanson, "Report of the Secretary-Treasurer," 12.
37. M. Murphy, Marjorie Murphy, *Blackboard Unions: The AFT and the NEA, 1900–1980* (Ithaca, NY: Cornell University Press, 1990), 161–64.
38. Timothy Reese Cain, "For Education and Employment: The American Federation of Teachers and Academic Freedom, 1926–1941," *Perspectives on the History of Higher Education* 26 (2007): 67–102, 77–78; "New Executive Council Meeting," August 30–31, 1935; Executive Council Minutes, 16 August 1936, Box 21, American Federation of Teachers Inventory, Part I, Series 3: Executive Council, Archives of Labor and Urban Affairs, Wayne State University (hereafter cited as AFT Executive Council).
39. Cain, "For Education and Employment," 79–84; Arnold Shukotoff, "Yale Corporation vs. Freedom," *American Teacher* 21 (November–December 1936): 5–7; Jerome Davis, *Capitalism and Its Culture* (New York: Farrar & Rinehart, 1935), 335–71; Deborah Sue Elkin, "Labor and the Left: The Limits of Acceptable Dissent at Yale University, 1920s to 1950s" (PhD diss., Yale University, 1995), 358–63; AFT, *The Jerome Davis Case: Final Report of an Investigation Conducted by the American Federation of Teachers into the Proposed Dismissal of Professor Jerome Davis from the Stark Chair of Practical Philosophy at the Yale Divinity School* (Chicago: American Federation of Teachers, 1937); "A Sheaf of Protests," *American Teacher* 21 (November–December 1936): 7–9; "Yale on Trial," *New Republic* 89 (November 18, 1936): 85–92.
40. Ben Davidson to Irvin Kuenzli, 29 November 1936, Box 2, American Federation of Teachers Secretary-Treasurer's Office Collection, Series 3, Irvin R. Kuenzli Files, 1936–1953, Archives of Labor and Urban Affairs, Wayne State University (hereafter cited as AFT Kuenzli Files).
41. Arnold Shukotoff to Maynard C. Krueger, 21 October 1936; Irvin R. Kuenzli to Shukotoff, 3 November 1936; Kuenzli to Shukotoff, 12 March 1937 and 17 March 1937, Box 2, AFT Kuenzli Files.
42. AFT, Jerome Davis Case, 59.
43. Arnold Shukotoff, "Lessons of the Jerome Davis Case," *American Teacher* 22 (September–October 1937): 11; Bella (Visono) Dodd, *School of Darkness* (New York: Kenedy, 1954), 103; "A Year's Victories," *American Teacher* 22 (November–December 1937): 6; Cain, "For Education and Employment," 83.
44. See Folder: Jerome Davis, Box 4, PEA Records; "Report of an Investigation by the National Education Association Tenure Committee: The Jerome Davis Case," June 8, 1937, Jerome Davis Papers, Knight Library, University of Oregon (hereafter cited as Davis Papers, Oregon).
45. "Summary of Memorandum to Committee A (Yale-Davis Report), February 25, 1937," 1–3; A. O. Lovejoy to A. J. Carslon et al., 8

December 1936; Lovejoy to A. N. Holcombe, 3 March 1937; Lovejoy to Himstead, 4 March 1937, Box 5; J. M. Maguire to Ralph E. Himstead, 22 November 1936, Box 6, AAUP Records, Series Historical Files, George Washington University Special Collections (hereafter cited as AAUP Historical Files); "Minutes, Mid-Winter Meeting, Executive Council," December 30–31, 1936, AFT Executive Council.

46. "Academic Freedom and Tenure: Yale University," *Bulletin of the AAUP* 23 (May 1937): 353–82.

47. Elkin, "Labor and the Left," 432–41; R. E. Himstead to G. H. Sabine, 13 September 1937; Himstead to J. L. McConaughy, 10 November 1937, Box 1, AAUP Records, Duke; Cain, "For Education and Employment," 86–87.

48. Cain, "For Education and Employment," 84–86; Arnold Shukotoff, "Report of the National Academic Freedom Committee, September 15, 1937–August 15, 1938," Box 1, PEA Records; AFT, *Report of the Proceedings of the Twenty-First Annual Convention of the American Federation of Teachers* (Chicago: AFT, 1937), 23–24; AFT, *Report of the Proceedings of the Twenty-Second Annual Convention of the American Federation of Teachers* (Chicago: AFT, 1938), 20, 43–44, 56–58; *Academic Freedom* 1 (January 1938), AFT National Defense Fund Collection, Series 2 Defense Fund Office Files, 1937–1964, Archive of Labor and Urban Affairs, Wayne State University (hereafter cited as AFT Defense Fund).

49. AFT, *Report of the Proceedings of the Twenty-Third Annual Convention of the American Federation of Teachers* (Chicago: AFT, 1939), 58, 70–71.

50. Cain, "For Education and Employment," 84–86; "Executive Council Proceedings, August 19–27, 1939," 44, 65, Box 23; "AFT Defense Fund Checks Issued to Date," June 30, 1954, Box 7, AFT Executive Council; Irvin R. Kuenzli to Arnold Shukotoff, 3 December 1938, Box 14, AFT Defense Fund; Irvin R. Kuenzli to Alice Hanson, 22 October 1940; Shukotoff to Kuenzli, 4 November 1937; Kuenzli to Shukotoff, 24 November 1937; Shukotoff to Venal Wagoner, 17 January 1938, Box 14, AFT Defense Fund; Shukotoff to Jerome Davis, 19 September 1938, Box 2, Davis Papers, Oregon.

51. Walter P. Metzger, "Academic Tenure in America: A Historical Essay," in *Faculty Tenure: A Report and Recommendations*, ed. Commission on Academic Tenure in Higher Education (San Francisco: Jossey-Bass, 1973), 93, 151–52; Loya F. Metzger, "Professors in Trouble: A Quantitative Analysis of Academic Freedom and Tenure Cases" (PhD diss., Columbia University, 1978), 64–65; Paul C. Reinert, *Faculty Tenure in Colleges and Universities from 1900 to 1940* (St. Louis, MO: St. Louis University Press, 1946).

52. Walter Wheeler Cook, "Study of Tenure of University and College Teachers," *Bulletin of the AAUP* 18 (April 1932): 255–59.

53. Caitlin Rosenthal, "Fundamental Freedom or Fringe Benefit: Rice University and the Administrative History of Tenure, 1935–1963," *AAUP Journal of Academic Freedom* 2 (2011); available: www.academicfreedomjournal.org/VolumeTwo/Rosenthal.pdf.
54. Ibid.; *Harvard's Liberalism: Myth or Reality; A Statement on the Dismissal of J. Raymond Walsh and Alan R. Sweezy* (Cambridge, MA: Cambridge Union of University Teachers, 1937); Special Committee Appointed by the President of Harvard University, *Report on the Terminating Appointments of Dr. J. R. Walsh and Dr. A. R. Sweezy* (Cambridge, MA: Harvard University, [1938]); Morton Keller and Phyllis Keller, *Making Harvard Modern: The Rise of America's University* (New York: Oxford University Press, 2001), 65–68; Richard Norton Smith, *The Harvard Century: The Making of a University to a Nation* (New York: Simon and Schuster, 1986), 133–36.
55. Special Committee Appointed by the President of Harvard University, *Report on Some Problems of Personnel in the Faculty of Arts and Sciences* (Cambridge, MA: Harvard University, [1939]); M. Keller and P. Keller, *Making Harvard Modern*, 68–70; R. N. Smith, *Harvard Century*, 136–38.
56. Arthur O. Lovejoy, "Harvard University and Drs. Walsh and Sweezy: A Review of the Faculty Committee's Report," *Bulletin of the AAUP* 24 (December 1938): 598–608; "Academic Freedom and Tenure: Yale University."
57. Walter P. Metzger, "The 1940 Statement of Principles on Academic Freedom and Tenure," *Law & Contemporary Problems* 53 (Summer 1990): 3–77, 72–73.
58. Timothy Reese Cain, "'Only Organized Effort Will Find the Way Out!': Faculty Unionization at Howard University, 1918–1950," *Perspectives on the History of Higher Education* 29 (Forthcoming 2012).
59. Arnold Shukotoff, "Annual Report of the National Academic Freedom Committee, 1939–1940," Box 16, AFT Defense Fund.
60. Hepburn, "Academic Freedom and Tenure."
61. W. T. Laprade, "Academic Freedom and Tenure: Report of Committee A," *Bulletin of the AAUP* 27 (February 1941), 29–39.
62. L. F. Metzger, "Professors in Trouble," 59, 73–76, 340–44.
63. Ralph E. Himstead, "Concerning the Bulletin," *Bulletin of the AAUP* 24 (October 1938): 550–52.
64. L. F. Metzger, "Professors in Trouble," 338.
65. See the following issues of the *Bulletin of the AAUP*: University of Pittsburgh, 21 (March 1935): 226–66; Rensselaer Polytechnic Institute 22 (January 1936): 15–24; Washington State College 23 (January 1937): 19–21; Park College, 23 (December 1937): 631–41; Montana State University, 24 (April 1938): 321–48; North Dakota Agricultural College, 24 (December 1938): 585–97, 673; West Chester State Teachers College 25 (February 1939): 44–72; University

of Tennessee, 25 (June 1939): 310–39; John B. Stetson University, 25 (October 1939): 377–99; St. Louis University, 25 (December 1939): 514–35; Montana State University, 26 (December 1940): 602–6.

66. See, for example, Himstead to Paul V. West, 7 April 1938; Himstead to Laura A. White, 24 May 1938, Box 3; A. O. Lovejoy to A. J. Carlson et al., n.d., Box 5, AAUP Historical Files; R. E. Himstead to J. L. McConaughy, 10 November 1937; H. W. Tyler to Himstead, 15 February 1937; Laprade to Himstead, 20 April 1938, Box 1; Himstead to Richard Hartshorne, 26 May 1938, Box 2; Himstead to Carlson, 11 March 1938; A. M. Holcombe to W. T. Laprade, 15 March 1938, Box 3, AAUP Records, Duke; Arnold Shukotoff, "Mid-Year Report of the National Academic Freedom Committee, September 15, 1938–December 15, 1938," Box 23, Jerome Davis Papers, Franklin D. Roosevelt Library, Hyde Park, New York; Ralph E. Himstead, "Council Record," *Bulletin of the AAUP* 25 (October 1939): 470–82, 479; Cain, "For Education and Employment."

67. "What the American Association of University Professors Is and What It Is Not," *Bulletin of the AAUP* 24 (March 1938): 230–48, 247; "Annual Meeting 1938–Steno Notes," Box 1, AAUP Records, Series Conferences, George Washington University Special Collections; R. E. Himstead, "From the Annual Report of the General Secretary," *Bulletin of the AAUP* 27 (April 1941): 238–42, 238; H. W. Tyler, "Some Problems of the Association," *Bulletin of the AAUP* 24 (February 1938): 201–4; Arthur O. Lovejoy, "Professional Association or Trade Union?," *Bulletin of the AAUP* 24 (May 1938): 409–17.

68. "The Revival of the Commission on Academic Freedom and Academic Tenure," *Bulletin of the AAC* 20 (March 1934): 138–39.

69. W. P. Metzger, "1940 Statement," 25.

70. James L. McConaughy to Ralph E. Himstead, 16 November 1937; Himstead to McConaughy, 26 November 1935, Box 1, AAUP Records, Duke; "Statement by Dr. W. W. Cook," *Bulletin of the AAC* 21 (March 1935): 183–86, 185.

71. James L. McConaughy, "Interim Report of Commission on Academic Freedom and Academic Tenure," *Bulletin of the AAC* 21 (May 1935): 379–80.

72. James L. McConaughy, "Report of the Commission on Academic Freedom and Academic Tenure for 1936–37," *Bulletin of the AAC* 23 (March 1937): 128–31; W. P. Metzger, "1940 Statement," 48. See also J. M. Maguire to R. E. Himstead, 26 April 1937, Box 1, AAUP Records, Duke.

73. H. W. Tyler to Himstead, 5 April 1937; McConaughy to Himstead, 16 November 1937, Box 1, AAUP Records, Duke; Himstead to Mark H. Ingraham, 13 December 1937, Box 3; R. E. Himstead to J. L. McConaughy, 3 April 1937, Box 5, AAUP Historical Files; W. P. Metzger, "1940 Statement," 49. See also additional letters in Folder O, Box 5, AAUP Historical Files.

74. L. F. Metzger, "Professors in Trouble," 63–64; W. P. Metzger, "1940 Statement," 47–49; Henry M. Wriston, "Academic Freedom and Tenure," *Bulletin of the AAC* 25 (March 1939): 110–23; R. E. Himstead to A. J. Carlson et al., 29 September 1937; H. M. Wriston to Himstead, 10 September 1937; Himstead to Wriston, 11 September 1937; Himstead to J. M. Maguire, 2 December 1937, Box 1, AAUP Records, Duke.
75. W. P. Metzger, "1940 Statement," 54–59; "Minutes of the Conference" October 4, 1937; J. M. Maguire, "Tentative Redraft of Passages Relating to Extra-Mural Utterances"; R. L. Dewey to R. E. Himstead, 28 October 1937, Box 1, AAUP Records, Duke. See, also, extensive correspondence on Maguire's draft in Folder: Association of American Colleges, Box 1, AAUP Records, Duke.
76. J. M. Maguire to R. E. Himstead, 18 November 1937; W. W. Cook to Himstead, 12 September [October] 1937; Dewey to Himstead, 28 October 1937; W. T. Laprade to Mark H. Ingraham, Box 1, AAUP Records, Duke.
77. W. P. Metzger, "1940 Statement," 59.
78. Ibid., 68–73.
79. Wriston, "Academic Freedom and Tenure"; R. E. Himstead to H. M. Wriston, 9 January 1939, Box 1, AAUP Records, Duke.
80. Wriston, "Academic Freedom and Tenure," 120.
81. W. P. Metzger, "1940 *Statement*," 49.
82. Ibid., 60–61; Ralph E. Himstead to A. J. Carlson, 15 December 1938, Box 1, AAUP Records, Duke; "Minutes of the 25th Annual Meeting of the Association of American Colleges," *Bulletin of the AAC* 25 (March 1939): 142–50.
83. Ralph E. Himstead to Henry M. Wriston, 2 February 1940; Himstead to Professors Carlson et al., 5 February 1940; Himstead to Wriston, 4 November 1940, Box 1, AAUP Records, Duke.
84. 1940 *Statement of Principles on Academic Freedom and Tenure*. Available at http://www.aaup.org/AAUP/pubsres/policydocs/contents/1940statement.htm; W. P. Metzger, "1940 *Statement*," 70–76.
85. Wriston, "Academic Freedom and Tenure," 115.
86. 1940 *Statement*.
87. Sheila Slaughter, "The Danger Zone: Academic Freedom and Civil Liberties," *Annals of the American Academy of Political and Social Sciences* 448 (March 1980): 46–61, 56–57.
88. Dan W. Gilbert, "Radicals Exploit Students' Rights," *National Republic* (November 1937): 13–14.
89. "Order Inquiry into Teaching of Communism," [*St. Petersburg*] *Evening Independent*, May 22, 1937; William Gellermann, *Martin Dies* (New York: Day, 1944), 116–37; Jeffrey E. Mirel, "Radicalism and Public Education: The Dies Committee in Detroit, 1938–39," in *Michigan: Explorations in Its Social History*, ed. Francis X. Blouin Jr. and Maris

A. Vinovskis (Ann Arbor: Historical Society of Michigan, 1987), 1–22; Edwin F. Abels, Clarence P. Oakes, and A. F. Cross, "Transmittal Report to the Dies Committee Accompanying Evidence and Board of Regents' Documentation in the Don Henry Case to the Special Committee on Un-American Activities, House of Representatives" (Topeka: Kansas House of Representatives, 1939); John Aubrey Douglass, *The California Idea and American Higher Education: 1850 to the 1960 Master Plan* (Stanford, CA: Stanford University Press, 2000), 207.

90. Carol Smith, "The Dress Rehearsal for McCarthyism," *Academe* 97 (July–August 2011): 48–51; Stephen Leberstein, "Purging the Profs: The Rapp Coudert Committee in New York, 1940–1942," in *New Studies in the Politics and Culture of U.S. Communism*, ed. Michael E. Brown, Randy Martin, Frank Rosengarten, and George Snedeker (New York: Monthly Review, 1993), 91–122; Schrecker, *No Ivory Tower*, 75–83.

91. "53 Educators Form Democracy Group," *New York Times*, March 19, 1939; Waldemar Kaempffert, "Science in the News," *New York Times*, October 8, 1939; "Aliens Defended in 'Race' Dispute," *New York Times*, July 23, 1939; "Tribute to Boas, 81, Led by President," *New York Times*, July 10, 1939; "Schools Rebuked on Racial Errors," *New York Times*, July 17, 1939; New York Committee for Democracy and Intellectual Freedom, "Manifesto of Educators," April 24, 1939, Box 3, Gardner Jackson Papers, Franklin D. Roosevelt Library, Hyde Park, New York (hereafter Jackson Papers); ACDIF, "The Activities of the Dies Committee," Box 3, Jackson Papers.

92. ACDIF, Press Release, 18 March 1939, Box 3, Jackson Papers.

93. "New Group Fights Any Curb to Freedom," *New York Times*, May 15, 1939.

94. M. Murphy, *Blackboard Unions*, 164–74; Iversen, *Communists and the Schools*, 99–118; Schrecker, *No Ivory Tower*, 54–57; Clarence Taylor, *Reds at the Blackboard: Communism, Civil Rights, and the New York City Teachers Union* (New York: Columbia University Press, 2011), 61–74.

95. Cain, "For Education and Employment," 89–91.

96. ACLU, *Eternal Vigilance! The Story of Civil Liberty, 1937–1938* (New York: ACLU, 1938), 58–62; ACLU, *The Bill of Rights, 150 Years After: The Story of Civil Liberty 1938–1939* (New York: ACLU, 1939), 45–47; ACLU, *Liberty's National Emergency: The Story of Civil Liberty in the Crisis Year 1940–1941* (New York: ACLU, 1941), 32–36.

97. Walker, *In Defense of American Liberties*, 121–26, 130–33; Bunting, *Liberty and Learning*, 56–59.

Conclusion

1. Cary Nelson and Stephen Watt, "Academic Freedom," in *Academic Keywords: A Devil's Dictionary for Higher Education* (New York:

Routledge, 1999), 22; Catherine Stimpson, "Dirty Minds, Dirty Bodies, Clean Speech," in *Unfettered Expression*, ed. Peggie J. Hollingsworth (Ann Arbor: University of Michigan Press, 2000), 51; William G. Tierney, "Academic Freedom and Tenure: Between Fiction and Reality," *Journal of Higher Education* 75 (March–April 2004): 161–77, 166; Dennis J. Pavlich, "Academic Freedom and Inclusivity: A Perspective," in *Academic Freedom in the Inclusive University*, ed. Dennis J. Pavlich and Sharon E. Kahn (Vancouver: University of British Columbia Press, 2000), viii.
2. Sweezy v. New Hampshire, 354 U.S. 250 (1957).
3. Robert L. Kelly, "The Sphere and Possibilities of the Association," *AAC Bulletin* 2 (April 1916): 21–29.
4. Alexander Meiklejohn, "Discussion," *AAC Bulletin* 2 (April 1916): 179–87.
5. Sheila Slaughter, "The Danger Zone: Academic Freedom and Civil Liberties," *Annals of the American Academy of Political and Social Sciences* 448 (March 1980): 46–61.
6. J. M. M[aguire] to R. E. H[imstead], 15 February 1939, Box 1, American Association of University Professors Records, 1934–1953, University Archives, David M. Rubenstein Rare Book and Manuscript Library, Duke University.
7. Roger Baldwin to David Edison Bunting, 24 May 1941. Quoted in David Edison Bunting, *Liberty and Learning: The Activities of the American Civil Liberties Union in Behalf of Freedom of Education* (Washington, DC: American Council on Public Affairs, 1942),, 105.
8. On these and other modern challenges, see Robert M. O'Neil, *Academic Freedom in the Wired World: Political Extremism, Corporate Power, and the University* (Cambridge, MA: Harvard University Press, 2009); Garcetti v. Ceballos, 547 U.S. 410 (2006).
9. 1940 *Statement of Principles on Academic Freedom and Tenure.* Available at http://www.aaup.org/AAUP/pubsres/policydocs/contents/1940statement.htm.
10. Walter P. Metzger, "The 1940 Statement of Principles on Academic Freedom and Tenure," *Law & Contemporary Problems* 53 (Summer 1990): 3–77, 69, 71.

INDEX

Note: Cases involving academic freedom and tenure are listed under the names of key participants and institutions.

1915 *Declaration of Principles*, xii, 38–44, 49, 63–4, 88, 90, 110–12, 158, 174–5, 179

1925 *Conference Statement on Academic Freedom and Tenure*, xvii, 77, 93–8, 99, 121, 138, 142, 158, 165, 167

1940 *Statement of Principles on Academic Freedom and Tenure*, xi–xii, 142, 160, 163–9, 174–5, 177, 179–80, 182

Adams, Charles Kendall, 14
Adams, Henry Carter, 14–15
Adams, Herbert Baxter, 11–12
Adams, Horace, 118
Adams, Robert L., 10
Adler, Felix, 10–11
Alexander, William J., 10
Aley, Robert J., 58–9
Allen, Edward, 62, 67–8, 124–5
American Academy of Arts and Sciences, 144
American Association for the Advancement of Science (AAAS), 102, 115
American Association of University Professors (AAUP)
and AAC, xi, 41–4, 93–8, 163–9
and ACLU, 90–2, 132–4, 135
and AFT, xiv, 48, 76, 77–8, 123–4, 142, 154–6, 162–3, 166–7, 173–5

censure, 124–8, 132, 136–8
Committee A, 35, 36, 45–7, 62–6, 82–6, 98, 130–1, 135–8, 154–6; criticism of, 81–4, 90–2, 123, 136–7, 139–40, 178; difficulties, 46, 76, 81, 82, 135, 142, 161; judiciousness, 36–8, 82–6, 98–9, 136–8; mediation, 85–6, 135–6, 161; reorganization of, 84–6; and tenure, 155, 161, 178
Committee B on Freedom of Speech, 144
Committee M on Freedom of Teaching in Science, *see* American Association of University Professors:evolution
Committee on Academic Freedom in Wartime, 63–6
Committee on Patriotic Service, 66
Committee T on Place and Function of Faculty in University Government and Administration, 80–1
Committee W on the Conditions of Tenure, 158
Committee Y on Effect of Depression and Recovery, 217n16
evolution, 101–2, 110–12, 115, 117–18

American Association—*Continued*
    founding, xiii, 30–5
    and junior faculty, 35, 44, 124–7, 138, 160, 166–7
    and the National Advisory Council on Academic Freedom, 146–8
    and professionalization v. unionization, xiii, xiv–xv, 34–5, 44–7, 76–8, 98, 124–8, 136, 162–3, 173–4, 178
    and proprietary institutions, 32, 39
    and World War I, 52, 62–6, 72
    see also individual cases and statements
American Association of University Women (AAUW), 94–6, 146–8
American Bar Association (ABA), xiv–xv, 34, 45
American Bible League, *see* Bible League of North America
American Civil Liberties Union (ACLU)
    and AAUP, 90–2, 132–4, 135
    and AFT, 76, 79, 123–4, 178–9
    Committee on Academic Freedom, 80, 90–3, 99, 122, 129–5, 139, 172–3
    and Communism, xvii, 67, 80, 144–5, 170, 180
    and evolution, xvii, 102–3, 113–19
    founding, xiii, 76
    and NACAF, 146–8
    see also American Union Against Militarism; *Gag on Teaching*; National Civil Liberties Bureau
American Committee for Democracy and Intellectual Freedom (ACDIF), 170–1
American Council on Education, 77, 93–6, 127–8, 136, 144
American Defense Society, 70

American Economic Association (AEA), 16, 17, 30, 32–3, 35, 37
American Federation of Labor (AFL), xiv, 47, 122
American Federation of Teachers (AFT), xv, 77–9, 115, 129–31, 139–40, 144–5, 151–8
    and AAUP, xiv, 48, 76, 77–8, 123–4, 142, 154–6, 162–3, 166–7, 173–5
    academic freedom policies, 123–4, 151–8
    and ACLU, 76, 79, 123–4, 178–9
    college faculty, 48, 69, 76, 81
    Communism, 78, 142, 152, 158, 180
    founding, xiii–xiv, 47–9
    local activity, 69–71
    militancy, 123–4, 152–4
    National Defense Fund, 153–7, 174
    see also individual cases and locals
American Legion, 93, 124, 129, 141, 143
American Medical Association (AMA), xiv–xv, 34, 45
American Philosophical Association, 32
American Psychological Association, 31
American Political Science Association (APSA), 30, 32–3, 35
American Rights League, 56
American Society of Civil Engineers, 127
American Sociological Society (ASS; now American Sociological Association), 30, 32–3
American Union Against Militarism (AUAM), 52, 55, 66–7
Amherst College, 80

Index

Andrews, Elisha Benjamin, 16, 20, 75
Angell, James Burrill, 14–15
Angell, James Rowland, 153–6
anti–Communism, *see* Communism
Anti–Evolution League, 102
anti–Semitism, 70, 93
Arkansas Agricultural and Mechanical College (now University of Arkansas at Pine Bluff), 103, 118
Associated Teachers Union of New York (AFT Local 71), 79
Association of American Colleges (AAC; now Association of American Colleges and Universities)
  and AAUP, xi, 41–4, 93–8, 163–9
  Commission on Academic Freedom and Academic Tenure, 86–9
  Committee on Academic Freedom and Tenure of Office, 44
  founding, xiii, 41–2
  limitations on academic freedom, 42–4, 88, 110
  membership, 89, 94
  tenure, 89
Association of American Universities (AAU), 26, 93, 110, 127
Association of Governing Boards of State Universities (AGBSU; now Association of Governing Boards of Colleges and Universities), 94–6
Association of Land Grant Colleges (ALGC; now Association of Public and Land-grant Universities), 94–6
Association of Urban Universities, 94–6

Bailey, Forrest, 114, 131
Baker, Frank E., 146–7, 171
Baldwin, Roger, 66–7, 79, 90–1, 113–14, 118, 180
Banks, Enoch Marvin, xvi–xvii, 23–4, 26, 29
Bassett, John Spencer, xvi–xvii, 19–4, 26, 125
Bates, Henry M., 82
Battle Creek College, 137
Beale, Howard K., 145–7
Beard, Charles A., 60, 69, 125
Beecroft, Eric A., 160
Bemis, Edward W., 15–16
Bergel, Lienhard, 134–5
Bethany College, 110
Bethel College, 58
Bible League of North America, 103
Bilbo, Theodore G., 127–8
Blanchard, Charles A., 102
Boas, Franz, 170–1
Bode, Boyd H., 146–7
Bohn, William, 26–7
Bowdoin College, 4
boycotting, 123–8
  see also American Association of University Professors
Boyd, William W., 97–8
Bradbury, Ora C., 106
Brady, Anna Mae, 78
Brewster, James, 36–7
Brooklyn College, 152
Brown, Elmer E., 25
Brown, William Garrett, 21, 75
Brown University, 16
Bryan, William Jennings, 16, 103, 104, 108–9, 111, 114–15
Bryn Mawr College, 130
Butler, John W., 112–13
Butler, Nicholas Murray, 25–6, 47, 59–60, 75, 108–9

Cabot, Robert C., 56
Calhoun, Andrew, 26

Index

Callis, Arthur, 160
Cambridge Union of University Teachers (AFT Local 431), 159
Candler, Warren Akin, 18–19, 24, 191n96
Capen, Samuel, 93–5, 138
Capps, Edward, 64–5
Carlson, Anton J., 126–7, 138, 144, 165, 171
Cattell, James McKeen, 31–2, 45, 47, 59–60, 63, 75, 84, 125, 205n33
Cedar Crest College, 148
Chafee, Zechariah, 68, 144
Chapman, John Jay, 31, 53
Chase, Harry W., 116
Chicago Federation of Men Teachers, 47–8
City College of New York, 148, 170, 172
Clap, Thomas, 2
Claxton, Philander P., 108
Clodd, Edward, 11–12
Clothier, Robert C., 134–5
Coffman, Lotus D., 116
Cole, Arthur C., 77
Cole, Charles N., 86, 88, 94
College of South Carolina (now University of South Carolina), 3, 9, 10
Columbia Theological Seminary, 8–9
Columbia University, 31, 55, 59–60, 63, 75, 125, 134
Commission on Academic Freedom and Tenure of Office, *see* Association of American Colleges
Committee A, *see* American Association of University Professors
Committee for Cultural Freedom (CCF), 171
Committee on Academic Freedom in Wartime, *see* "Report on Academic Freedom in Wartime"
Communism, xvii, 61–2, 65–6, 67, 78–9, 129, 140, 141–5, 158–60, 169–73
see also individual cases and organizations
Conant, James B., 144, 159–60, 168
Cook, George Cram, 31
Cook, Walter Wheeler, 138, 164–6
Cooley, Charles H., 27
Cooley, Mortimer, 62
Cooper, Richard Watson, 41
Cooper, Thomas, 3–4
Cornell University, 10–11, 14–15, 54, 61, 143
Corwin, Margaret, 134–5
Coulter, John Merle, 45
Council of Church Boards of Education (CCBE), 41, 86
Counts, George S., 145, 171–2
Cox, Philip W. L., 150–1
Creighton, J. E., 31
Crew, Henry, 127
Croly, Herbert, 35
Croyle, H. I., 110
Curtis, Winterton C., 77–8, 83, 115

Dana, Henry Wadsworth Longfellow, 59–60
Daniels, Josephus, 19–22
Danish Lutheran Seminary, 107
Darrow, Clarence, 114
Dartmouth College, 4, 110
Daughters of the American Revolution, 124, 141, 143
Davenport, Frances Isabel, 68
Davidson, Ben, 152–3, 156
Davis, Jerome, 152–6, 160, 162–3, 166, 167, 171, 174, 179
Deibler, Frederick S., 94
Demaree, Ralph, 109, 210n36
Denney, Joseph Villiers, 85, 101, 111–12

INDEX 233

Dennis, William Cullen, 167–8
DeSilver, Albert, 67–8
Dewey, John, 25, 30, 34–5, 36, 38, 40, 45, 59–60, 69, 77, 96–7, 145, 171, 177
Dewey, Ralph L., 166
DeWitt Clinton High School, 69–70
Dickey, James E., 18–19
Dies, Martin, 170
Dilbert, Frank, 93
Dilling, Elizabeth, 141, 143, 169
Dodd, Bella, 172
Dodd, William E., 20, 22–3, 24, 26
Douglas, Paul H., 123, 171
Dow, Grove Samuel, 106
due process, 38–42, 63, 66, 87–9, 132, 155–7, 168
 see also individual cases and statements
Duke University, *see* Trinity College
Dunster, Henry, 2
DuShane, Donald, 149–50

Eastman, Crystal Catherine, 66–7
Eaton, Allen H., 61
Eaton, Clemont, 4–5
Edgemont School, 150–1
Effinger, John R., 94–7
Eliot, Charles W., 25, 145
Ely, Richard T., 15, 33, 63–4, 66
Emergency Peace Foundation, 55
Emory College (now Emory University), 17–19, 22
extramural speech, 5–7, 12–17, 26–7, 37–8, 54–6, 59–60, 64–5, 129–30
 see also individual cases, organizations, and statements
Everett, R. W., 122–3
evolution, xvii, 7–10, 101–20

Federation of Teachers of the University of Illinois (AFT Local 41), 77, 79

Fellows, George A., xiii
Felton, Rebecca Latimer, 18–19
Fetter, Frank A., 33
Few, William Preston, 21, 105–6
Finkin, Matthew W., xvi
Fish, Hamilton, Jr., 143–4
Fisher, Willard C., 28, 32, 33, 37–8
Flickinger, Roy C., 86
Florida Education Association, 116
Florida Purity League, 116
Florida State College for Women (now Florida State University), 26, 169–70
Fortune, Alonzo W., 109
Fox, Amy, 123
Fox, Austen, 68
Fox, Henry, 107
Francke, Kuno, 57
Frank, Glenn, 143
Franklin and Marshall College, 60
Franklin College, 4
Freund, Ernst, 90–1
Fuchs, Ralph F., 2
Furner, Mary O., 17
fundamentalism, *see* evolution

Gag on Teaching, 131–3, 173
General Education Board (GEB), 24
Gerard, Ralph Waldo, 126–7
Germany, 7, 12–15, 103–4, 134, 170–1
 see also World War I
Gilbert, Dan W., 169–70
Girardeau, John L., 9
Glassberg, Benjamin, 70, 92–3
Goodrich, Herbert F., 85, 91, 94
Goucher College, 110
Graham, Frank P., 133, 171
Graves, Frank, 92–3
Groves, Harold, 171
Gruber, Carol S., xvi, 60, 62
Guth, William Westley, 110

Haggard, Wallace, 113
Haley, Margaret, 47–8
Hanson, Alice, 172
Hanson, Florence, 141, 152–3
harmony, *see* intramural speech
Harper, William Rainey, 15–16
Harris, Reed, 134
Harrisse, Henry, 6
Harris Teachers College, 137
Hauptman, Friedrich J., 134–5
Harvard University, 2, 4, 55–7, 68, 144, 158–60
Haverford College, 61
Hawaii College, 61
Hawkins, W. E., 106
Hays, Arthur Garfield, 114
hearings, *see* due process
Hearst press, 141, 152, 169
Hebrew University, 61
Hedrick, Benjamin Sherwood, 5–7
Hedrick, Mary Ellen, 6
Hellems, Fred Burton Rennie, 31
Henry, Don, 170
Hepburn, William McGuffey, 142, 161
Hibben, John Grier, 52
Hicks, Glanville, 161–2
Hicks, Herbert, 113
Hicks, Sue, 113
Himstead, Ralph E., 155, 160–3
Hobbs, William Henry, 54, 61–2, 63, 66, 67
Hodder, Frank Heywood, 65, 196n78
Hofstadter, Richard, xv–xvi, 2, 119
Hojbjerg, Carl P., 107
Holden, William W., 5
Holmes, John Haynes, 90–1, 171
Holmes, Samuel J., 112, 117
Holt, Hamilton, 116, 136–7
Hook, Sidney, 133, 173
Howard Teachers Union (AFT Local 440), 160
Howard University, 48, 77, 79

Howard University Teachers Union (AFT Local 33), 77, 79
Hullfish, H. Gordon, 151
Hutchins, Harry Burns, 27, 54, 62
Hutchins, Robert Maynard, 143
Huxley, Thomas, 10

Indiana University, 61, 66
intramural speech, 37, 64, 75, 80–2, 129–30, 136–7
   see also individual cases, organizations, and statements

Jastrow, Joseph, 31
Jefferson, Thomas, 2–3
John B. Stetson University (now Stetson University), 162
Johns Hopkins University, 10, 11–12, 14, 30, 31, 33, 55
Jones, Virgil, 118
Jordan, David Starr, 17, 55
Judd, Charles H., 108
Judson, Frederick N., 35

Kansas State Agricultural College (now Kansas State University), 16
Keeney, Philip O., 157–8, 172
Keenleyside, Hugh L., 92
Kellogg, Paul U., 66–7
Kelly, Robert L., 41–2, 44, 163–4, 177
Kentucky Wesleyan College, 109
Kerr, W. C., 6
Kilgo, John C., 19–21, 24
Kilpatrick, William H., 133, 171
King, D. F., 105
Kingsbury, J. T., 36
Kirkpatrick, John Ervin, 81–2, 125–6
Kliewer, John W., 58
Knights of Labor, 14
Knights of Liberty, 60–1
Krueger, Maynard, 154
Ku Klux Klan, 107, 129

Index

Lafayette College, 28, 32
La Follette, Robert M., 54, 92
Laprade, William T., 166
LeFevre, George, 63
Lefkowitz, Abraham, 69
Lehrfreiheit, 12–13, 15
Leighton, Joseph A., 80–1
Lernfreiheit, 12–13
Leuba, James H., 104
Leuschner, Armin O., 82, 84, 94
Lillie, Frank, 76
Linville, Henry R., 69–71, 72, 79, 90–3, 115, 122–4, 129–30, 139–40, 144–5, 157
Lock Haven State Teachers College (now Lock Haven University), 148–50
Long, Huey P., 130, 215n35
Looney, William H., 58–9
Loring, Edward Greely, 4
Louisiana State University, 130–1, 139
Lovejoy, Arthur O.
   and 1915 *Declaration*, 38–9
   and 1925 *Conference Statement*, 94–7
   and AAUP founding, xiii, 30, 32
   and AAUP investigations, 36–7, 81–2, 84, 126, 137, 155, 196n72, 200n52
   and ACLU, 133
   and Committee B, 144
   and Committee on Cultural Freedom, 171
   and evolution, 117, 118, 119
   and mediation, 85–6
   at Stanford 17, 30, 125
   and tenure, 160
   and unionization, 76, 77–8, 162
   in wartime, 53, 63–6
Lowell, A. Lawrence, 55–7, 68, 167
Loyalty League, 58
loyalty oaths, 61, 69–70, 107, 122, 132, 133, 141, 143–5, 148, 152, 157

Madison State Normal School, 78
Maguire, John M., 85–6, 135, 166
Malone, Dudley Field, 114
Manly, Charles, 5–6
Marckwardt, Otto, 62
Marietta College, 16, 61
Marsden, George M., 103, 105–6
Martin, Thomas Theodore, 102, 104, 105, 116
Martin Luther College, 61
Mathews, Shailer, 108, 115
McAdams, Clark, 109
McNaboe, John J., 143
McPherson, George Wilson, 102, 104
McTyeire, Holland Nimmons, 8
McVey, Frank L., 108–10, 116, 119
Mecklin, John Moffat, 28, 32
Meiklejohn, Alexander, 43–4, 80, 179
Mercer College (now Mercer University), 107
Merrill, Elmer Truesdell, 65
Metz, Charles F., 162
Metzger, Walter P., xv–xvi, 89, 96, 164, 182
Meyer, Kuno, 56
Middlebury College, 205n33
Miller, Herbert, 129–30, 139
Milner, Lucille B., 92
Mississippi Agricultural and Mechanical College (now Mississippi State University), 127–8
Mississippi State College for Women (now Mississippi University for Women), 127–8, 169–70
Missouri University Teachers Union (AFT Local 126), 77–8
Mitchell, Samuel A., 131, 135–6, 171
modernism and higher education, 103–5

Montana State University, 157–8, 162, 172
Mufson, Thomas A., 69–70, 79–80
Munroe, James P., 31
Münsterberg, Hugo, 55–7
Murphree, Albert A., 23

National Advisory Council on Academic Freedom (NACAF), xvii, 145–9
National Association for the Advancement of Colored People (NAACP), 129
National Association of State Universities (NASU; now Association of Public and Land-grant Universities), 94–6
National Civil Liberties Bureau (NCLB), xiii, 51–2, 66–8, 73, 76
  see also American Civil Liberties Union
National Congress of Parents and Teachers (now National PTA), 146–8
National Council of Religion in Higher Education (NCRHE; now Society for Values in Higher Education), 146–8
National Education Association (NEA), xvii, 41, 47, 78, 115, 122, 123, 146–50, 154
National Security League (NSL), 52, 54, 62, 66
Neal, John R., 114
Nearing, Scott, 28, 37, 80
Nelson, Karen Christine, 26
New Jersey College for Women (now Rutgers, the State University of New Jersey), 134–5
New York College Teachers Union (AFT Local 537), 171–2
New York Federation of Teachers, 172

New York Teachers Union (Teachers Union of the City of New York; AFT Local 5), 69–71, 76, 79, 92–3, 122, 152, 170, 171–2, 202n76
New York Training School for Teachers, 68
Niebuhr, Reinhold, 173
Norris, J. Frank, 103, 106
North Dakota Agricultural College (now North Dakota State University), 162
Northern Arizona Normal School (now Northern Arizona University), 61
Northland College, 60–1
Northwestern University, 12

Oberlin College, 61
Odum, Howard W., 105–6
Ogden, Robert, 24
Ohio State University, 61, 121, 129–30, 139
Olivet College, 57, 82

Pace, Lula, 106
Park College, 162
Parsons, Frank, 16
Patton, Stewart, 31
Pearson, Charles W., 12
Peay, Austin, 113
Peixotto, Jessica, 90–1
Pennsylvania State Education Association (PSEA), 149
Penrose, Stephen B. L., 41
People's Council of Democracy and Peace, 61
Phi Delta Kappa, 147–8
Philadelphia Teachers Union (AFT Local 192), 171–2
Phillips, Charles, 6
Porter, J. W., 108
Porter, Noah, 11
Post, Robert C., xvi

Index

Poteat, William Louis, 105–6, 110, 119
Pound, Roscoe, 33
Powers, Harry Huntington, 17
"Preliminary Report of the Joint Committee on Academic Freedom and Academic Tenure," 33
Princeton University, 52
Progressive Education Association (PEA), xvii, 142, 145–51, 154, 179

race, 17–25
see also slavery
Randolph–Macon College, 22–3, 26
Rappleyea, George Washington, 113
Redefer, Frederick, 145–8
regionalism, 4–9, 17–25
Remsen, Ira, 32
"Report on Academic Freedom in Wartime," 52, 64–6, 67, 88
research, freedom of, 1, 7, 25, 39, 43, 47, 76, 87, 89, 98, 111, 134, 168, 170, 178
see also individual cases, organizations, and statements
Rice, John A., 106, 136–7
Rice Institute(now Rice University), 62, 158
Rightmire, George W., 130
Riley, William B., 101–7, 116
Riley, Woodbridge, 117
Rochester Polytechnic Institute, 161–2
Rockefeller, John D., 24
Roe, Gilbert E., 70, 79
Rollins College, 136–7
Ross, Edward A., 16–17, 30, 75, 125
Russell, Bertrand, 170, 172
Russell, C. Allyn, 106
Rutherford, Geddes W., 125–6

Ruthven, Alexander Grant, 144
Ryan, George J., 93
Ryan, W. Carson, 171

Sage, Henry, 14
Schappes, Morris U., 152–4, 170
Scheidt, Richard Conrad, 60
Schimler, E. A., 60–1
Schmalhausen, Samuel D., 69–70
Schneer, A. Henry, 69–70
Schoolmasters Association, 70
Schrecker, Ellen W., xiv, xvi, 141
Science League of America, 102, 116–17
Scopes, John T., 112–15
Scudder, Vida, 90–1
Seligman, Edwin R. A., 16, 33, 35, 37–8, 38–41, 59, 196n72
Shanklin, William, 37
Shields, James M., 146
Shipley, Maynard, 116–17
Shukotoff, Arnold, 153–8, 160, 163, 172
Silva, Edward T., 26
Simmons, Ernest, 160
Simmons, Furnifold M., 21
Slaughter, Sheila A., xvi, 26
slavery, 4–7
Sledd, Andrew, 18–19, 23, 26, 29
Small, Albion, 13
Smith, J. Allen, 16
Smith College, 22
Social Science Research Council, 144
Somers, Arthur, 93
South Carolina College, *see* College of South Carolina
Southern Association of Colleges and Secondary Schools, 127
Southern Methodist University, 106, 136–7
Southwestern University, 106
Spencer, Herbert, 11
Stanford, Jane Lathrop, 17, 30

Stanford University, 16–17, 20, 30, 75
Stecker, Freeland, 78
Steele, Walter S., 169
Stewart, Lyman, 103
Stewart, Milton, 103
Stillman, Charles, 48, 71
St. Louis University, 162
student immaturity, 5, 11, 13, 33, 39, 43, 87–9, 134, 156–7, 170
Sugrue, Michael, 3
Sumner, William Graham, 11
Sunday, Billy, 103–4
Swain, David L., 5–6
Sweezy, Alan, 158–60
Syracuse University, 92

Tappan, Henry, 9–10
Teachers Union of the City of New York, *see* New York Teachers Union
teaching, freedom of, 3, 4, 11, 12–13, 33, 39, 43, 70, 87–9, 126, 134, 156–7, 168, 178
  see also individual cases; evolution; *individual organizations*
tenure, 31, 32–3, 39–40, 44–7, 49, 83, 87–8, 95–6, 98, 122–4, 129–30, 135, 138, 141, 147, 149, 156, 158–69, 174, 177, 178, 181
  see also individual cases and statements
Thayer, William Roscoe, 53, 56
Thilly, Frank, 45
Thomas, Norman, 129
Thompson, Holland, 133
Thurstone, Louis L., 126–8
Thwing, Charles F., 12–13, 25
Tildsley, John L., 70
Townsend, Luther T., 103
Trinity College (now Duke University), 19–22, 23, 26, 105–6, 125

Tulane University, 61
Tyler, Harry Walter, 76, 82, 85–6, 87, 91, 94–7, 117, 125–8

Uhler, John Earle, 130–1
University of Akron 61
University of Arkansas, 116, 118
University of California, 61, 160
University of Chicago, 20, 143
University of Colorado, 36–7, 46, 48
University of Florida, 23, 29
University of Illinois, 54, 61, 77, 79
University of Kansas, 170
University of Maine, 58–9
University of Michigan, 8–10, 14–15, 26–7, 54, 61–2, 67–8, 89, 124–5, 144
University of Minnesota, 61
University of Mississippi, 127–8
University of Missouri, 77–8, 121, 126
University of Montana, 37
University of Nebraska, 61
University of North Carolina, 5–7, 105–6, 115
University of Oregon, 61
University of Pennsylvania, 28, 37, 48, 58
University of Pittsburgh, 134, 162
University of Tennessee, 83–4, 107, 114, 162
University of Texas, 61, 62
University of Utah, 36, 37, 42, 48, 65
University of Vermont, 61
University of Virginia, 2–3, 61, 79
University of Washington, 16
University of Wisconsin, 15, 54, 60, 80, 143

Vanderbilt University, 8, 10, 62
Van Hise, Charles, 54
Van Kleeck, Mary, 94

Index

Veblen, Thorstein, 30–1, 75
Veysey, Laurence R., 7, 26

Wake Forest College (now Wake Forest University), 105–6, 110
Wald, Lillian, 66–7
Walsh, J. Raymond, 158–60
Walsh, Sara, 156
Walz, William E., 58–9
Ward, Harry F., 79, 80, 90–2
Warfield, Ethelbert Dudley, 32
Warne, Colston, 153–4
Warren, Earl, 177
Warren, Howard Crosby, 32, 35
Washington, Booker T., 19
Washington State College (now Washington State University), 162
Washburn, George F., 116
Washburn College (now Washburn University), 81–2, 125–6, 136.
Watson, Goodwin, 150–1
Weigle, Luther, 155
Welch, Herbert, 42–3
Wesleyan University, 28, 32, 37
West, Andrew Fleming, 14, 26
West Chester State Teachers College (now West Chester University), 162
Weatherly, Ulysses G., 33, 43, 66

Wellesley College, 61
Wheeler, Benjamin Ide, 61
Whipple, Leon, 79
White, Andrew Dickson, 8, 10
White, Walter, 113
Wiener, Clarence, 55
Wigmore, John H., 1, 28, 40, 125
Wilberforce University, 129
Will, Thomas Elmer, 16
Wilson, Woodrow, 8, 52, 54, 66
Winchell, Alexander, 8, 9–10
Wishart, Charles F., 111
Wittke, Carl, 136
Womer, Parley P., 81–2
Woodrow, James, 8–10
Wooster College, 111
Workman, Mims Thornburg, 106
World Christian Fundamentals Association (WCFA), xvii, 101–2, 106, 114
World War I, 51–73
Wriston, Harry M., 165–8

Yale College, *see* Yale University
Yale University, 2, 11, 55, 153–6, 160, 166
Young, Allyn Abbot, 46, 63–5, 91, 200n52

Ziwet, Alexander, 45, 196n67

GPSR Compliance

The European Union's (EU) General Product Safety Regulation (GPSR) is a set of rules that requires consumer products to be safe and our obligations to ensure this.

If you have any concerns about our products, you can contact us on

ProductSafety@springernature.com

In case Publisher is established outside the EU, the EU authorized representative is:

Springer Nature Customer Service Center GmbH
Europaplatz 3
69115 Heidelberg, Germany

www.ingramcontent.com/pod-product-compliance
Lightning Source LLC
LaVergne TN
LVHW051913060526
838200LV00004B/128